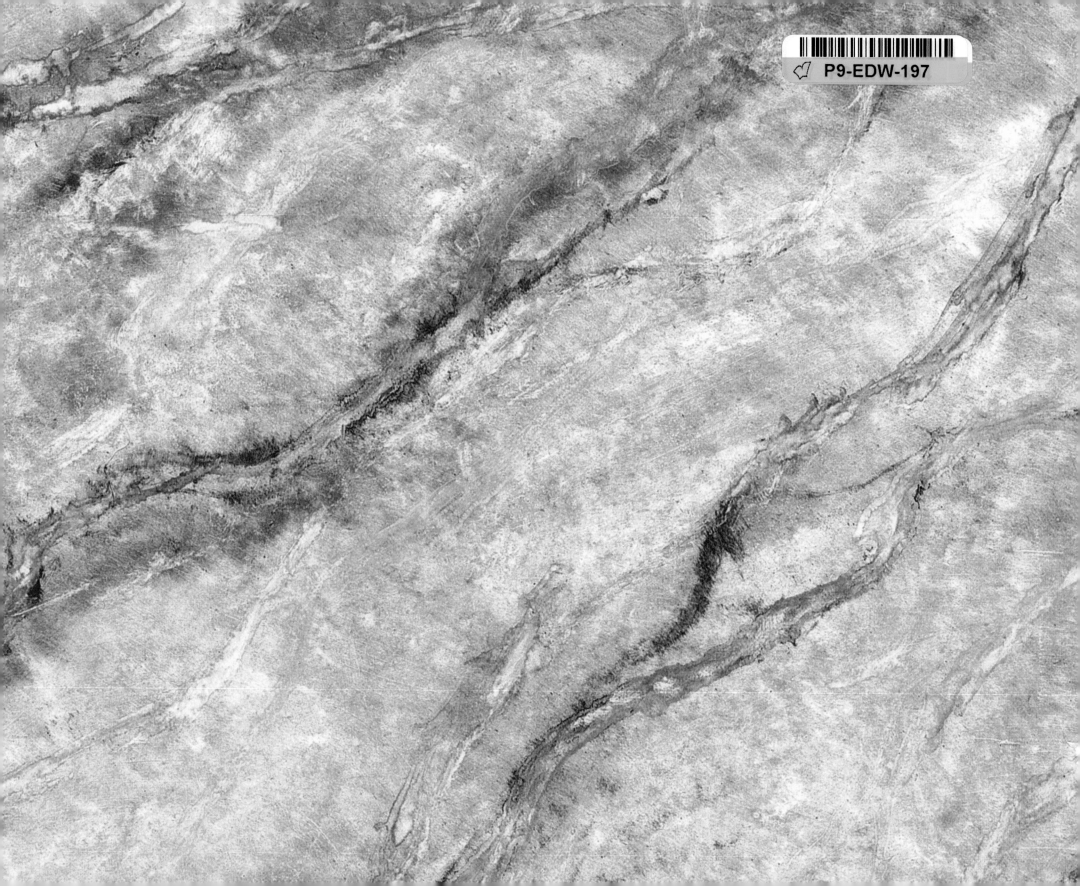

❧ THE IMPOSSIBLE DREAM ❧
RAILWAY TO THE MOON

Writing, design, and page composition: Ken McFarland
Editors: W. Augustus Cheatham, Richard Weismeyer, Waldena Gaede,
Dustin Jones, Heather Reifsnyder, Patricia Thio
Body text 11.5/15 Adobe Caslon Pro
Cover art direction and design: Ed Guthero
Cover illustration: John Williams

DEDICATION

This centennial volume is dedicated to. . .

. . .the founding pioneers of Loma Linda, whose vision, sacrifice, and persistent effort brought an impossible dream to thriving reality. . .

. . .and to the faculty, staff, and students of the University and Medical Center—past and present—each of whom has helped make this a unique place of ministry to a world in need.

CONTENTS

Preface iv

From the President, LLUAHSC vi

From the Board Chair, LLUAHSC vii

Introduction: The Hill Beautiful viii

Foreword and Acknowledgments xi

Chapter 1.   To 1910:   Railway to the Moon 13

Chapter 2.   1911 – 1920:   Crisis and Survival 31

Chapter 3.   1921 – 1930   Reaching for the Sky 47

Chapter 4.   1931 – 1940   To Survive—but More, to Thrive 61

Chapter 5.   1941 – 1950   The Tides of War 77

Chapter 6.   1951 – 1960   One Giant Leap 93

Chapter 7.   1961 – 1970   A New Unity, a New Name, a New Hospital 111

Chapter 8.   1971 – 1980   Longer Ropes—Deeper Stakes 131

Chapter 9.   1981 – 1990   Hyacinths and Headlines 149

Chapter 10.   1991 – 2000   In Full Flight 171

Chapter 11.   2001 – Present   New Century, New Millennium 191

Making Possible "The Impossible Dream" 203

Appendix 215

Index 234

PREFACE

The Impossible Dream—Railway to the Moon is a documentation of God's providential leading to "Fulfill His Vision" for Loma Linda University and Loma Linda University Medical Center.

We preface this publication with remarks by the president and Board chair of Loma Linda University Adventist Health Sciences Center at the Sacred Centennial Concert—featuring pastor and vocalist Wintley Phipps—which took place at the University Church of Seventh-day Adventists on Friday evening, February 11, 2005.

Dr. B. Lyn Behrens, LLUAHSC president/CEO:

You have just witnessed the parade of nations represented in our students, faculty, and staff at this institution. We are blessed to have 118 countries represented among the 16,000 people that daily make this institution come alive.

You are part of that.

It is a privilege to know that as Loma Linda reaches its 100th birthday, people come to us from around the world to learn and to serve—and to serve beyond the borders of this place for those who come to us for care.

It is my privilege to welcome to our campus again our Board chair, Pastor Lowell Cooper, vice president of the General Conference of Seventh-day Adventists.

Thank you for joining us at the beginning of our year of celebration.

Elder Lowell Cooper, vice president, General Conference of Seventh-day Adventists:

Thank you. It is a pleasure to join Dr. Behrens in expressing a word of welcome to you at this inaugural event of Loma Linda's centenary.

Centenaries don't come along that often. And it is, I suppose, a very spe-cial gift that we should be the ones who have the privilege of marking the centenary of Loma Linda and to take this time, to have these moments, to hear again, to remember the great acts of courage, the vision of faith, the energies of people in the past who have placed in our hands this institution and its legacy. It's wonderful that we take a moment like this to gather all the inspiration that it has for us—and to take our place in that long line of those who have faithfully served God and honored His name through this institution.

Welcome.

Dr. Behrens:

I would like you to travel back with me in time tonight to the year 1905.

Southern California was alive with activity. People from the East Coast had traveled west, looking for health and well-being and a new fortune.

The Seventh-day Adventist Church in Southern California was a very small number of people. In 1904, they had purchased Paradise Valley Hospital near San Diego, and in the beginning of 1905, they had purchased Glendale Adventist Hospital—two facilities that serve yet today.

But in the climate of their taking responsibility for those two institutions, a little lady in her seventies in Northern California wrote to people down in this area of the country and said, "Go find another place"—a place that would be for both education and for health care delivery—a place, she said, that would be purchased for much less than its price. So they went looking. She told them to look between Riverside and Redlands.

This valley in 1905 was largely orange groves, sprinkled with just a few homesteads. And there atop Mound Hill was an empty sanitarium. It was elegantly furnished, but its silence spoke to the reality that it was yet another failed business venture.

They went looking—and they found.

By the end of 1905, the Seventh-day Adventist Church would own a third institution in Southern California—the one of which we are stewards today. But what I would ask you in the days that proceed from here—as we reflect on the past—is to remember too that it was God's divine leading that brought us to this place. And it was God's empowerment of a handful of men and women that translated a vision into a reality.

By the end of 1905, the hospital had admitted patients, and the School of Nursing had begun. And Loma Linda was born.

Today, as we look back through the decades, we are very conscious of the way in which God's hand has been evident in Loma Linda's protection and empowerment through the decades. And I would invite you in the weeks and months ahead to remember that we are stewards of His place. We have a divine calling and responsibility to move out from this place as rays of light and love to touch a hurting world.

We celebrate our Father in heaven, and it is with thanksgiving that we meet together.

Thank you for coming.

From Interstate 10 near the Loma Linda exit, this billboard informs passersby of the institution's centenary.

For a century, Loma Linda has remained true to its founding mission— to heal and to teach as Jesus did.

FROM THE PRESIDENT

More than a century ago, developers of a tract of land south of San Bernardino in Southern California called it Loma Linda—Spanish for "Hill Beautiful."

Throughout the past one hundred years, Loma Linda has come to be associated with a thriving university and medical center—as well as the full spectrum of health care education offered here.

Loma Linda University is one of nearly 2,500 colleges and universities—and Loma Linda University Medical Center is one of more than 5,700 hospitals—in the United States. What sets Loma Linda's institutions apart? What keeps them from being "just another" among so many of their kind?

Balak, the Old Testament king of Moab, once hired Balaam to curse God's people on Balak's behalf. But when Balaam tried to deliver the curse, he could only speak God's own words, among them, "What hath God wrought!" Centuries later, these words were the first spoken by Samuel F.B. Morse, when on May 24, 1844, he sent the first message by his new invention—the telegraph.

Today as we mark the centennial of all that is Loma Linda, we can only echo these words. For yes, what God has done in this place is astonishing. Clearly, the divinely ordained dream nurtured in the hearts and minds of Loma Linda's founders has been so dramatically realized that only God's providence can account for it.

Throughout these decades, a beacon of hope to the world has sent its light around the globe—hope for a healthier and happier life now and for an eternal life soon to come. The mission of Loma Linda from the begin-

ning has been to make men and women and children whole—to heal not only the body but the mind and spirit as well.

Yet the growth and progress—indeed, even the survival—of Loma Linda has not always seemed assured. Repeated challenges arose that threatened our very existence. But human sacrifice and total commitment linked with divine and miraculous power to keep Loma Linda alive.

Today, Loma Linda has become a place that glorifies God through service to human beings in need. Here, healing and teaching are equal partners in carrying forward the ministry exemplified by Jesus. But here we seek not just to heal—but to help prevent illness from occurring in the first place and to teach people how to maintain their health through lifestyle changes.

Loma Linda also today has become a place of ongoing research in every medical and academic area. It is an inclusive place that embraces diversity and celebrates the variety and uniqueness of human beings. It is a place that began locally but from the beginning accepted a global mission, so that today, its mission and service encircle the planet.

The legacy of Loma Linda's dedicated pioneers has continued in the service of gifted and passionately committed men and women from 1905 to the present day. All of us mark this great milestone in our history with gratitude for the contributions of all who worked to make Loma Linda what it is today. But most of all, we reserve our greatest gratitude to our true Founder—the greatest of all healers and teachers—our Lord Jesus Christ.

—*B. Lyn Behrens, MBBS, President/CEO*

FROM THE BOARD CHAIR

As a Seventh-day Adventist organization, Loma Linda University Adventist Health Sciences Center—which includes Loma Linda University, Loma Linda University Medical Center, and its affiliated institutions—carries forward a vital and unique mission to its Church, its staff and students, its local area, and the world.

Early in the history of the Adventist Church, Ellen White—one of its cofounders and its guiding voice for seventy years—characterized the Church's medical ministry as "the right arm of the message." The commission of the Church was not alone to win the hearts and minds of people to Christ, but to carry forward His healing and teaching ministry here on earth.

As the primary Seventh-day Adventist center for medical and health-related training in the world, Loma Linda is known not only to Adventists everywhere but to multitudes of others around the world as a place with a focused and driving mission: to make people whole. Wholeness means more than helping people get well. It means ministering to people not just as bodies that need healing or repair but as people with minds and spirits that just as urgently need that same healing. It means looking not just at physical symptoms but at the mental and emotional context of a patient's life. It means taking note of each person's spiritual needs. And it means not just healing disease but preventing it—and teaching people how to maintain health.

Hundreds of other hospitals address the physical symptoms and needs of patients; few, however, approach health care in the same wholistic and comprehensive way that Loma Linda does.

Just as Loma Linda's parent Church considers itself a movement of des-

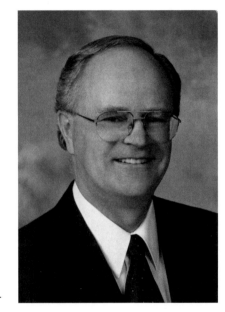

tiny borne of divine providence and commissioned with a divine mission, so too is Loma Linda a place raised up by God to glorify His name and character through a unique ministry of healing and teaching.

As chair of the LLUAHSC Board, it is my privilege to be involved in the vibrant growth and ongoing mission of this great cluster of institutions now a century old. Yes, just as always throughout its hundred-year history, Loma Linda's way is not always smooth. Challenges—even crises—periodically arise that can vex and even dismay. But as Ellen White once said, "We have nothing to fear for the future, except as we shall forget the way the Lord has led us, and His teaching in our past history." When obstacles arise, it is our privilege to seek wisdom and power we do not possess, from a supply that cannot be exhausted.

I am honored to have this chance to offer—on behalf of the Seventh-day Adventist Church—our congratulations, best wishes, and highest hopes to Loma Linda on this occasion of its centennial. Each administrator, teacher, medical professional, student, and staff member at Loma Linda is mindful that this is no ordinary place—that Loma Linda's is no ordinary mission. What we do here, we do not just to heal and teach our fellow human beings, but from gratitude to the God who has done so much for us.

Someday soon, if we do our work well and with daily fidelity, we can begin life in a new place without a single hospital in all the land. Someday, the second century of the founding of Loma Linda will be marked—but I have not a single doubt that when it is, we will all be in that new and better place where there is no more sickness or pain.

—*Lowell C. Cooper, MDiv, MPH, chair, Board of Trustees*

INTRODUCTION

THE HILL BEAUTIFUL

Rising from the valley floor south of San Bernardino, the low hill was of such modest elevation that its late-nineteenth-century developers dubbed it only a "mound." Mound City, they would call the town they intended to build surrounding the hill. New owners would later change the name of this place to the more euphonious "Loma Linda"—Spanish for "Hill Beautiful."

To the south of the Hill Beautiful were nearby hills no one could ever have mistaken as simply mounds. At a distance to the north, looming thousands of feet above the great inland valley, stood the San Bernardino Mountains, high enough to wear the snows of winter for months at a time.

But it would be the Hill Beautiful and not its loftier neighboring prominences from which, early in the twentieth century, a light began to shine that would signal hope and healing. Throughout the next century, this commitment to the restoration—the healing—of humanity would radiate outward from the Hill Beautiful like rings from a pebble dropped into a quiet pond, ultimately reaching the farthest corners of the world. This commitment would include more than treating the body—more than just physical healing—but would focus on the healing of the whole person: body, mind, and spirit.

This book is a centennial history of Loma Linda. And while the dates and facts and names of that century are here, this volume ventures to be more than simply a documented local or regional history. For in these pages unfolds a dramatic story—a story of real and often flawed men and women who nonetheless invested faith and hard work, tears and courage, as they sought and followed evidences of divine providence and overcame daunting obstacles to build around the Hill Beautiful a center for healing and for the training of healers.

On October 12, 1905, the first patient signed in to the newly opened Loma Linda Sanitarium. Slightly more than two months later, the facility had twenty-five patients. From the beginning, however, Loma Linda was more than just a place for health care. Before the year 1905 was out, training for nursing and evangelism began. Today that twin commitment—to health care and to education—continues. Under the umbrella of today's Loma Linda University Adventist Health Sciences Center (LLUAHSC) operate both a world-renowned medical center and an equally respected university.

The philosophy of early Seventh-day Adventist sanitariums envisioned not only healing of the sick but prevention of disease through educating patients to make lifestyle choices that would help keep them well. To restore health was indeed a worthy goal. But unlike most medicine of the day, Loma Linda and its sister sanitariums aimed beyond simply getting people well to keeping them well afterward—as well as to preventing them from getting sick in the first place.

That philosophy of preventive health and health maintenance remains intrinsic to the mission of Loma Linda to this day. It is taught in the various schools of the university even as it is practiced in the medical center.

Long ago, the greatest Healer of all history restored men and women and children ravaged by the results of sin to perfect health of mind and body and spirit. He healed their diseases, but He also showed them a better way to live. Into the darkest corners of human misery and despair, He shined the warm light of hope and healing.

A century ago now, men and women of great faith, vision, and courage followed the leading of the Great Healer and moved forward to pioneer a center for healing and education on the Hill Beautiful and its surrounding land. Marked from the beginning by providences many consider evident miracles, the story of Loma Linda unfolded steadily through successive decades—years during which occasional crises threatening the very existence of Loma Linda alternated with periods of rapid expansion and success.

Today the work of healing and educating that began on the Hill Beautiful moves forward to touch the lives of hundreds of thousands annually, not only in America but in far corners of the planet. But this hill of hope and healing is no common, secular enterprise. Those who minister and teach at Loma Linda share a profound commitment to following in their daily efforts the example of Jesus Christ—who is their own Healer, Savior, and Lord.

God's hand, so clearly evident as Loma Linda began a century ago, is just as markedly present today. The lofty reputation and renown of this special place is a testimony to human effort and commitment, yes. But the true result and mission of Loma Linda brings glory to the God who dreamed of it, opened the way for it, and caused it over the span of a hundred years not just to survive, but to thrive.

God seems fond of hills. He refers to the locale of the New Jerusalem as "My Holy Mountain." He restated His eternal principles of love from Mount Sinai. God the Son described real love in His Sermon on the Mount. Then later, He dramatically demonstrated that same love on another mount called Calvary.

In such company, the little "Hill Beautiful" in Southern California may seem humble by comparison. But God has always enjoyed bringing great things from the small and seemingly inconsequential.

A century ago, God began bringing forth providential blessings for the world from an unremarkable hill in a Southern California valley. One can only wonder, as Loma Linda's second century begins, what mighty things He has yet in store for this place of hope and healing.

Loma Linda (California) Sanitarium, Hospital and Laboratory in foreground.

An early twentieth-century postcard shows the Sanitarium on the "Hill Beautiful," with the first Loma Linda Hospital and Laboratory in the foreground.

Foreword and Acknowledgments

This centennial volume is meant to commemorate the humble beginning and providential growth of a unique ministry of healing and teaching that began a century ago in Southern California. While not intended as an exhaustive historical reference, it is nonetheless based on careful research.

The contributions of some to this book merit special acknowledgment. These include:

Richard Schaefer, upon whose research and writing the author relied often in telling the centennial story.

Sharon Chase, for assistance with design, typography, and page composition.

The Heritage Room staff of Del E. Webb Library, for assistance with photo location and identification:

    Marilyn C. Crane, interim chair, Heritage Room
    Janice Little, library assistant
    James Waworoendeng, library assistant
    Petre Cimpoeru, assistant archivist
    Trish Chapman, library secretary

Alberto Valenzuela, of Mind Over Media, for additional assistance with photo selection.

Carol Berger in University Relations, for assistance with photos and with verifying many facts and details.

RAILWAY TO THE MOON

INSIDE THE LETTER WAS A NOTE SAYING, "I DO NOT KNOW JUST WHAT YOUR IMMEDIATE NEED IS, BUT IF THIS WILL HELP, USE IT"—AND A BANK DEPOSIT FOR $5,000—THE EXACT AMOUNT NEEDED FOUR HOURS LATER ON THAT DEADLINE DAY.

A new morning—and you open a box of Kellogg's cornflakes and shake out a bowlful. You and a few million others, who routinely tote home the cereal pioneered well over a century ago in the labs of a Midwestern surgeon named John Harvey Kellogg, who set about to develop nutritious vegetarian fare for his patients.

Together with his younger brother W.K. Kellogg ("Will"), John formed a company to produce and sell the grain cereals developed in his labs. But the brothers fell to feuding, and Will went his own way to form the cereal business that made Kellogg a household brand name and is today a giant in the food industry.

Ultimately, Will may have become the more famous of the brothers, but John's accomplishments too were notable. In Michigan, he helped found the Battle Creek Sanitarium—a health care facility that soon developed a national reputation.

John was something of a maverick and clashed routinely with the leadership of his still-young church—the Seventh-day Adventists. "The brethren" at headquarters wanted Battle Creek to be owned and operated by the Church. Dr. Kellogg wanted Battle Creek to be an independent institution.

As he saw it, his own brother had more or less "made off" with the cereal he had developed. His Church now seemed intent on taking control of the Sanitarium he had helped found. So perhaps it's no mystery that when John Harvey Kellogg heard of the efforts out west to launch a new health care institution and medical college in Southern California, he felt inclined to pour cold water on the idea. Even as the college graduated its first School of Medicine class in 1914, he wrote in a personal letter to a fellow physician that such an enterprise was "a thing which at this day and age is as impossible as to build a railway to the moon. Even if the thing could be accomplished after a fashion for a short time, its life must necessarily be limited for the profession will not tolerate a medical school with such a strong sectarian coloring as this school must have."[1]

Two years later, Dr. Kellogg vented additional pessimism: "The future of the . . . medical school

Left: An early art rendering of the original Loma Linda Sanitarium.

is absolutely hopeless. The medical profession will not tolerate such a thing as a medical college under sectarian control."[2]

But his own successes should have been evidence enough to Dr. Kellogg that the apparently impossible often proves ultimately possible indeed. The medical school about which the good doctor had such an acute case of sour grapes is today part of a vast medical institution known around the world. And though we never did get to the moon by rail, in 1969 Apollo 11 astronauts did arrive there courtesy of the 363-foot-tall Saturn V moon rocket.

In essence, the story of what has today become Loma Linda University Adventist Health Sciences Center—encompassing

a seven-school university and a renowned medical center—has been an ongoing series of accomplishments no less amazing than building a railway to the moon.

Travel now, not to the moon, but back in time—to the year 1875. South of San Bernardino in Southern California, a group of investors early that year discovered a low hill rising from the valley floor and dreamed of creating a new planned city. With reference to the small hill, they called themselves the Mound City Land Association. The next year, they opened a post office. Low interest rates, a burgeoning citrus industry, and new rail connections fueled optimism for the speculators, who foresaw a possible boomtown in the making.

But not all dreams come true, and plans for Mound City failed. Within a year, the post office closed, and in 1882, a Mr. H.E. Hills bought 267 acres from the Mound City association. Mr. Hills (no irony intended) built his home on the mound itself and turned much of his remaining land into a large farm he called "Mound City Ranch." By late 1886, deteriorating health led Mr. Hills to sell his property to yet another investor group for $30,500. They quickly formed a corporation called the Mound City Land and Water Company.

This new investor group also dreamed of creating a boomtown. Farmers all through the valley were growing rich—not so much from their farming as from buying and selling land. It wasn't a rarity for a parcel of land to double in price and change owners several times in a single day. In early 1887, the two big railways—Southern Pacific and Santa Fe—began a fare war on the Kansas City to Los Angeles route. Ticket rates fell steadily and swiftly from $125 to just $1.

Los Angeles deserved its reputation as a rough-and-tumble frontier town, and even some twenty years after the Civil War, the entire Southern California area remained semi-lawless and sparsely populated. But 1887 brought easy rail access and low fares—and settlers from the East and Midwest flooded into the area, drawn by the prospect of sunshine, land ownership, health, and wealth. The developers of the old Mound City Ranch were convinced their investment would pay off handsomely. An 1888 plat map shows the network of streets they envisioned surrounding the hill. They would retain the name "Mound City"—and intent on luring business to the new development, on the summit of that mound they invested $40,000 to build an ornate, five-story Victorian-style wooden hotel. A local newspaper editor predicted that Mound City was soon to become one of the most popular resorts in Southern California.

But no investment is without risk, and hardly had the Mound City planners finished the hotel, than the building boom collapsed, owing at least in part to the arrival of a prolonged, intermittent drought. Then came the Depression of 1893, forcing Mound City's developers to abandon their plans and put the land on the market.

By the turn of the twentieth century, Mound City and its hotel stood vacant. In time, yet another group—this one composed of eighty physicians and forty businessmen—saw new possibilities as

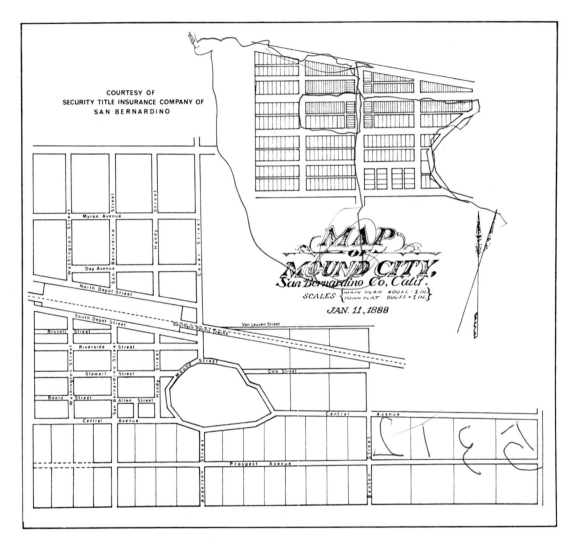

they looked over the parcel of land with a mound in its midst that had aroused the dreams of so many others before them. This consortium of doctors and business investors decided to convert the hotel and its surroundings into a health resort. The 120 investors renamed Mound City as "Loma Linda" (Spanish for "Hill Beauti-

ful"). In September of 1900, the Loma Linda Association filed its Articles of Incorporation, and the next month, they began transactions to purchase the land for $15,000. Once in their possession, the investors poured an additional $155,000 into Loma Linda, intending to bring their new health resort to the front ranks of

The vision of those who developed "Mound City" is reflected in this 1888 plat map. The hill itself occupied the space within the irregular loop at the lower center of the map.

Ellen G. White (right), a cofounder of the Seventh-day Adventist Church, provided the impetus and conviction leading to the purchase of property in Loma Linda for the purpose of health ministry.

the many such developments in Southern California. In addition to its own artesian well, Loma Linda would soon have room for ninety guests, and such leading-edge amenities for that time as private baths, telephones, an on-staff chef and dining room steward, and even riding stables.

Aggressively promoted in a brochure as a resort, Loma Linda was touted as "The Switzerland of California, where health and pleasure are twins."

It seemed as if fortune was finally ready to smile on the mounded tract of land

in the great inland valley. Everything that should be done to ensure its success, Loma Linda's backers did. But again, success slipped from the grasp of yet another group of optimistic owners. Sometimes, the resort had no guests at all. Amazingly, in 1904 the owners reluctantly offered the property for sale for a price that represented a major loss on their investment: $110,000. In April of 1905, the doors of Loma Linda closed. The post office closed again. Area residents called the place "Lonesome Linda."

Might it be that Lonesome Linda, beset by the serially dashed dreams of its successive owners, would even yet realize some special destiny?

As it happened, half a state away to the north near the Napa Valley's little town of St. Helena, the eventual destiny of Loma Linda was stirring in the mind and heart of a woman named Ellen G. White. With her husband, James, and a retired sea captain named Joseph Bates, she had in her youth been a founder of the Seventh-day Adventist Church. Her fellow believers were convinced she possessed the biblical gift of prophecy, and her influence in the Church was profound. Through her lifetime, Ellen White continued building up the Church she had helped to found, writing prolific counsels, speaking extensively, and leading out in establishing firm Church ministries in education, publishing, and health care.

In 1902, Mrs. White had predicted that properties on which buildings already stood, in locations especially suited to sanitarium work, would be "offered to us at much less than their original cost. . . . For months the Lord has given me instruction that He is preparing the way for our people to obtain possession, at little cost, of properties on which there are buildings that can be utilized in our work."[3]

Two years later in 1904, owners of a facility in National City, California (near San Diego), who had invested $25,000, put the property on the market for $12,000. The Southern California Conference of Seventh-day Adventists, with only 1,400 members, eventually purchased it for only $4,000. It became what is today the Paradise Valley Hospital.

Also in 1904, the owners of the $50,000 Glendale Hotel near Los Angeles offered it to the Southern California Conference for $26,000. Later that year, the purchase would be concluded for only $12,000. This property would become what is today the Glendale Adventist Medical Center.

Having now purchased both of these properties, the Southern California Conference, quite frankly, found itself financially strapped. The Adventist world headquarters organization, its General Conference on the East Coast, had not long before

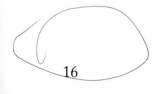

established a no-debt policy for the world Church, which brought high compliance from local conference leaders.

A new incoming president for the Southern California Conference, G. W. Reaser, stepped into the job with the directive to reduce the Conference's debt, which, owing to the two 1904 purchases, was significant.

Despite this new fiscal belt-tightening, Mrs. White—in counsels some considered financially irresponsible if not impossible—advised the purchase of yet a *third* property in Southern California. Why?

Three years earlier in 1901, Ellen White had described a property she had seen in vision on which the Church would build a medical institution on the grounds of which were great shade trees forming a massive, tent-like canopy over patients in wheelchairs enjoying the benefits of fresh outdoor air. Mrs. White knew the property was somewhere to be found—but where?

The Loma Linda property matched that description—but in 1901 was still occupied and not for sale.

Enter now a young Adventist minister named John Allen Burden. Mrs. White had been greatly impressed by this gifted

pastor, who at the age of 29 had managed the St. Helena Sanitarium in Northern California near her home. She described him as a man "of more than ordinary business acumen."

Convinced that a third property in Southern California had yet to be discovered—a property she had previewed in her vision—Mrs. White asked the Church members there to start looking between Riverside, San Bernardino, and Redlands. Pastor Burden was himself now in Southern California, and being a devout believer in Mrs. White's leadership and prophetic gift, he took her request to heart and began actively looking in the area.

In May of 1905, John Burden reported to Mrs. White that he had evaluated a tract of 76 acres a few miles west of Redlands that appeared to match her description. The caretaker of the Loma Linda property told Pastor Burden that though $155,000 had been invested in the land and its buildings (an astonishing $3.1 million in the currency of a century later), it could be purchased for $110,000. This was out of the question for an already debt-laden membership under a strict directive to get itself out of debt. Later, the price came down to $85,000. At this point, Ellen White wrote a letter dated April 12, 1905, to the Church members in Southern California, in which she urged them: "Arouse, and avail yourselves of the opportunities open to you."[4]

Soon afterward, the price dropped again to $45,000. When Pastor Burden relayed this information to Mrs. White, she advised him to stay close to the situation and keep her posted.

Proactive by nature, the young pastor approached the owners again to see if he could determine their rock-bottom price. They quoted him a price of $40,000, firm, with only a few days option to buy at this price.

"What shall we do?" he asked Mrs. White. "We must act at once as the [Loma Linda Association] is anxious to sell, and there are others who want it." Pastor Burden suggested that she confer with Conference leaders.

Based on a confirming vision she had received the night before, she asked her son, W. C. White ("Willie"), to telegram Pastor Burden to immediately secure the option to purchase the Loma Linda property. "I advise Willie to send you a telegram without spending time to ask the advice of the brethren. Secure the property by all means, so that it can be held and then obtain all the money you can and make sufficient payments to hold the place. This is the very property we ought to have. Do not delay; for it is just what is needed. . . . We will do our utmost to help you raise the money."

Pastor John Burden (left) played a leading role in securing the Loma Linda property.

Meanwhile, members of the local conference committee, who were meeting at the time in Washington, D.C., wired Pastor Burden to say, "Developments here warrant advising do not make deposit on sanitarium." John Burden found himself caught squarely in the middle between Mrs. White and "the brethren."

After attempting without success to find a donor or donors to come up with a deposit to hold the property, he ultimately borrowed $1,000 on his own signature, and on May 29, 1905, he put the money down and signed papers. Additional payments were due in July

and in August, with the balance to be secured by a three-year mortgage.

In urging the acquisition of the Loma Linda property, Mrs. White had promised that God would bring funds from "unexpected sources" to complete its purchase.

On July 26, 1905, the due date for the second payment, the Conference committee of the Southern California Conference met in emergency session in Los Angeles. The second installment, $5,000, was due at 2:00 p.m. They didn't have the first dollar of it. Some members again were openly critical of the plan to purchase the property. John Burden later reported that "the intensity of feelings was running high,"

and that they were "in deep perplexity."[5]

Someone suggested that the troubled group wait for the morning mail. Soon they heard the postman walking up the stairs. The mail included a letter from a woman in Atlantic City, New Jersey. The sender was unknown to anyone on the committee and is unknown to this day. The letter had traveled, possibly for weeks, completely across the North American continent. Inside was a note saying, "I do not know just what your immediate need is, but if this will help, use it"—and a bank draft for $5,000, *the exact amount needed four hours later on that deadline day.* Suddenly, there wasn't a dry eye in the place. John Burden later reported, "It was as solemn as the judgment day....We then took new courage, as we felt that our Lord was going before us."[6]

Just as Ellen White had predicted, more money had come from "unexpected sources." One who had been especially critical approached Pastor Burden and acknowledged the providential turn of events. "It seems that the Lord is in this matter," he said.

"Surely He is," he replied, "and He will carry it through to victory."[7]

Carry it through, God did. Through a series of truly remarkable providences, the entire sum was actually paid in full

Even as Pastor John Burden received counsel from Ellen White to purchase the Loma Linda property, he received conflicting direction from his own conference leadership in the telegram at right.

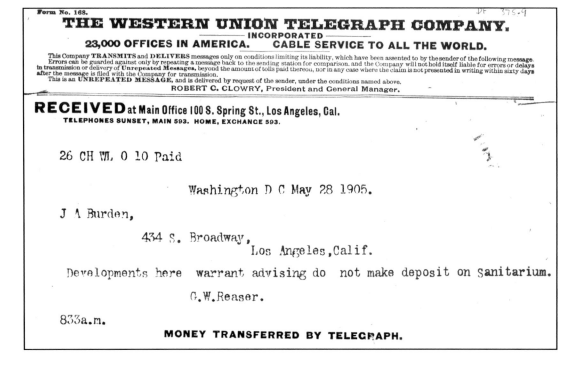

Form No. 168.   DF 375-9

THE WESTERN UNION TELEGRAPH COMPANY.
——— INCORPORATED ———
23,000 OFFICES IN AMERICA.   CABLE SERVICE TO ALL THE WORLD.

This Company TRANSMITS and DELIVERS messages only on conditions limiting its liability, which have been assented to by the sender of the following message. Errors can be guarded against only by repeating a message back to the sending station for comparison, and the Company will not hold itself liable for errors or delays in transmission or delivery of Unrepeated Messages, beyond the amount of tolls paid thereon, nor in any case where the claim is not presented in writing within sixty days after the message is filed with the Company for transmission.
This is an UNREPEATED MESSAGE, and is delivered by request of the sender, under the conditions named above.
ROBERT C. CLOWRY, President and General Manager.

RECEIVED at Main Office 100 S. Spring St., Los Angeles, Cal.
TELEPHONES SUNSET, MAIN 593. HOME, EXCHANGE 593.

26 CH WL O 10 Paid

        Washington D C May 28 1905.

J A Burden,

     434 S. Broadway,

         Los Angeles,Calif.

Developments here warrant advising do not make deposit on sanitarium.

     G.W.Reaser.

833a.m.

MONEY TRANSFERRED BY TELEGRAPH.

within another six months, bringing a discount of $1,100. Thus, for a purchase price of $38,900 (plus $7,000 in interest and taxes), Southern California Adventists now possessed their third property for medical work: seventy-six acres of land, a hotel building, a farmhouse, five spacious cottages, an amusement building, a water plant accompanied by shares of water stock, an artesian well and pumping plant, a water tower and tank, a full set of farm implements, horses, carriages, and cows.

Also, more than $12,000 worth of such furnishings as linens, dishes, and silverware—and orchards of oranges, lemons, olives, apricots, plums, peaches, and pears—were included.

Two weeks after John Burden signed the first papers on Loma Linda, Mrs. White on June 12, 1905, visited the property for the first time. Arriving with her son by express wagon from Redlands, she looked at the main building and said, "Willie, I have been here before."

"No, Mother," Willie responded, "You have never been here."

"Then this is the very place the Lord has shown me, for it is all familiar," she answered. Turning to one of the ministers, she added, "We must have this place. We should reason from cause to effect. The Lord has not given us this property for any common purpose."

On August 22, 1905, Mrs. White wrote in a personal letter that "this is the most delightful situation for a sanitarium I have ever seen. The scenery is magnificent, and everything possible has been done to beautify the premises."[8]

Two days later on August 24, John Burden signed the Articles of Incorporation as the president of the new Loma Linda Sanitarium. He and Mrs. White immediately began an aggressive recruiting effort. The Sanitarium would remain an empty shell until a staff could be assembled and patients admitted. To those who responded, John Burden wrote:

"We are here under God's appointment to start a large institution. We have no funds. We are unable to pay your traveling expenses, and know not when we can begin to pay salaries. The most that we can say to you is that we need help. If your heart is in the work come along and share our poverty with us."

As the remarkable story of the purchase of Loma Linda spread throughout the denomination, potential employees responded and started converging on Loma Linda from across the nation.

The patient register lists two young women on October 12, 1905, as the first patients—one from Chicago and another from Los Angeles. Each was charged $7.50 per week: $1.50 for a private room, $3.00 for board, and $3.00 for routine treatments. Several weeks later a patient was charged

From the Sanitarium rooftop garden, the view northeastward swept over the nearly empty countryside to the snow-dusted San Bernardino Mountains.

$3.00 to board her horse, which was no doubt accommodated in the institution's livery stable. During the first few weeks, the thirty-five Sanitarium employees who had reported for duty by the official Sanitarium opening on November 1, including physicians and nurses, learned that patient revenue ($16 to $25 per week per patient, which included medical care, meals, treatments twice a day, and a room) was not sufficient to meet the payroll. With strong faith to offset their deepening poverty, they cheerfully offered to work for room and board until the patronage increased.

Julia White, MD, arrived in late November to assume leadership of the nursing program, which in December accepted its first students. Elder (the title accorded

Adventist pastors) and Mrs. Stephen N. Haskell also arrived in the fall to teach and sponsor evangelistic activities.

By the end of the year sixty-four guests had registered from as far away as Oregon, Missouri, Illinois, New Jersey, New York, and Massachusetts. By June 30, 1906, Sanitarium accounts were more than $1,000 in the black. Pioneers, both employees and students, considered their involvement in what they believed to be a providentially ordained institution to be a unique privilege.

During the first quarter of 1906, administrators organized "an advanced training school for workers in connection with the Sanitarium." In April, a council consisting of members of the Pacific Union Conference and the Southern California Conference committees met with Mrs. White in Loma Linda to finalize plans for opening the Loma Linda College of Evangelists. They called Professor Warren E. Howell, principal of Healdsburg College, in Northern California, to lead the new venture. John Burden would serve as business manager.

Just two weeks prior to the formal dedication of the Loma Linda Sanitarium, the first class of nurses held their own dedication service on March 29.

Because of the anticipated presence of many various church leaders, institutional administrators scheduled the Sanitarium's dedication to be held on Sunday, April 15, 1906. They sent invitations to members of local churches, businessmen, and leading citizens of the region. Mrs. White delivered the keynote address to an audience of about 500 guests seated on a sloping lawn among a grove of beautiful pepper trees.[9]

During her address, Mrs. White emphasized that Sanitarium physicians and helpers were to cooperate with God in combating disease not only through the use of natural remedies but also by encouraging patients to claim divine strength by obeying God's commandments.[10]

She stated that the institution was to make a major contribution to the work of the denomination by becoming a training center for students who would be qualified to participate in the Church's worldwide outreach.

In a letter to "Brother and Sister Burden," in December, 1905, Mrs. White had first mentioned her desire that Loma Linda not only train nurses, but physicians as well. "In regard to the school, I would say, make it all you possibly can in the education of nurses and physicians."[11]

In 1906 Mrs. White again emphasized that Loma Linda was to be "not only a sanitarium, but also an educational center."

Ellen White herself recruited most of the professional faculty for the proposed medical training institution from around the United States and as far away as Australia. The calendar issued that summer for the new school year offered four courses: Collegiate, Nurses, Gospel Workers, and a three-year Evangelistic-Medical course that included standard medical school classwork plus Bible classes. Ellen White had counseled, "The healing of the sick and the ministry of the Word are to go hand in hand."[12]

At 10:00 a.m., September 20, 1906, something quite amazing happened. A portion of the faculty met for morning devotions and declared the new school open and in session. They made no lesson assignments *because there were no students!* However, by October 4, the remainder of the faculty and approximately thirty-five students had arrived, and instruction finally began.

The fledgling College of Evangelists was soon compelled to confront questions as to its mission and identity. In those early months, it hadn't become clear just what courses should be offered. And what about accreditation?

On October 23 John Burden wrote Mrs. White and asked for her counsel regarding the future curriculum of the College. Should the institution seek legal recognition as a school of medicine? Or should it seek legal recognition for a class of healer, such as the homeopath, the chiropractor, or the osteopath? Or some eclectic blend of what seemed the best in various healing methodologies? Or should it simply provide instruction for "medical

evangelists," even though graduates would have no legal recognition and could not legally practice medicine? For the time being, Mrs. White delayed in answering.

A year later, however, when Pastor Burden again asked whether the School was "simply to qualify nurses" or whether it should "embrace also the qualification for physicians," she replied, "Physicians are to receive their education here."[13]

Despite this lack of clarity and definition, the School grew. On July 10 of 1907, the first class of nurses held their commencement. The student body grew to 112 for the 1907–1908 school year and to 120 the year after that.

Primitive conditions and financial crises persisted during those early years. But somehow, faculty and students moved ahead and found their way. Until the

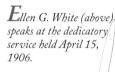

Ellen G. White (above) speaks at the dedicatory service held April 15, 1906.

Members of Loma Linda's first nursing class (right) admire newly arrived Richard Edward Abbott.

Adventist Church's General Conference session convened in June of 1909, the Loma Linda College of Evangelists had not yet been officially included in the family of Adventist colleges.

In the autumn council of that year, however, I. H. Evans, the General Conference treasurer, presented a strong appeal on behalf of the school and gained the agreement of other leaders to support the institution. After the session, John Burden asked Ellen White a question he had asked on earlier occasions: "What shall we do now?"

"Go straight ahead," she replied.

Pastor Burden and the other college leaders did exactly that. On December 9, 1909, they obtained a charter from the State of California to operate under the new name of College of Medical Evangelists (CME)—the name by which the institution would be known for the next half a century until 1961. CME was fully authorized to "establish and maintain, carry on and conduct, literary, scientific, medical, dental, and pharmaceutical, and medical missionary colleges or seminaries of learning." It could grant degrees in liberal arts and sciences, dentistry, and medicine.

It was now clear what CME was authorized to do. It wasn't at all as clear just how to do it. Where would the money come from? Where would the qualified medical faculty come from? Questions also remained as to just what kind of medical training should be offered.

Ellen White's counsel was clear enough on this latter concern. On January 25, 1910, she wrote: "The medical school at Loma Linda is to be of the highest order." The Church's leadership had been duly challenged to aim high.

At an early 1910 meeting, Arthur G. Daniells, the president of the General Conference, responded to the challenge: "We shall now take hold of this enterprise and do the best we can to assist in carrying it forward."

Only five years had passed since the purchase of the Loma Linda property. Both a sanitarium and a training center for medical evangelism were now established. The college was no longer an orphan but a fully adopted child of the Seventh-day Adventist General Conference, to whom it could look for both counsel and support. Increasingly, the institution found its mission and identity coming into clearer focus. In January of 1910, the General Conference and the Church's Pacific Union Conference assumed ownership of CME. They further defined its constituency, named a Board of Trustees, outlined a curriculum, and elected a faculty.

On June 11, 1910, the Board of Trustees elected Wells A. Ruble, MD, medical secretary of the General Conference, as CME president. They also took the important step of forming a new corporation consolidating the sanitarium and the college and their respective boards of trustees.

On firmer ground now, CME set about to build a solid foundation to provide for present needs and future growth. Capital improvements were voted—including a dormitory for female students (later named in honor of Kate Lindsay, MD, who in 1883 had started the first Seventh-day Adventist school of nursing in Battle Creek, Michigan). Curriculum offerings were more fully detailed. Faculty additions brought some very qualified and experienced staff to join in educating the growing roster of students.

Two things, John Harvey Kellogg had said, were equally impossible to build: a railway to the moon—and a successful

The nursing class of 1908 (left).

sectarian medical institution and school in Loma Linda. Give Dr. Kellogg his due. By 1910, not a single track had been laid from earth toward the lunar surface. But the impossible dreams centering on the little mound in the Southern California valley were now there to see and touch and confirm as very real indeed.

Loma Linda seemed poised to grow and thrive and make wonderful contributions to multitudes in need of healing.

But in the unknown years just ahead, challenges loomed that carried the potential to make Dr. Kellogg seem more like a prophet than a pessimist, after all.

NOTES:

1. John Harvey Kellogg, M.D., November 29, 1914, letter to George Thomason, M.D.

2. John Harvey Kellogg, M.D., February 9, 1916, letter to Percy T. Magan, M.D.

3. Ellen G. White Letter 157, October 13, 1902.

4. Ellen G. White, *Special Testimonies*, Series B, No. 3, p. 31.

5. John A. Burden, quoted by D. E. Robinson, "How the Payments Were Met," *The Story of Our Health Message*, p. 358.

6. John A. Burden, "Special Workings of Providence, Loma Linda Seen in Vision," Ellen G. White Document File 9-e, chapter VII, pp. 13, 14.

7. Ibid.

8. Ellen G. White letter to W. J. Stone, August 22, 1905.

9. D. E. Robinson, "An Educational Center," *The Story of Our Health Message*, pp. 365, 366.

10. Ellen G. White, "Dedication of the Loma Linda Sanitarium," *Review and Herald*, June 21, 1906, p. 6.

11. Ellen G. White Letter 325, December 10, 1905.

12. Ellen G. White, "Special Work at Loma Linda," *Testimonies and Experiences Connected With the Loma Linda Sanitarium and College of Medical Evangelists*, p. 23.

13. Ellen G. White, October. 30, 1907. MS 151, 1907.

PHOTO ALBUM

Top row, from left: Ellen G. White, and two views of John H. Kellogg, MD, at different times in his life.

Bottom row, from left: Kellogg's Battle Creek Sanitarium in 1903, John A. Burden as a young man, John and Eleanor Burden, Eleanor Burden.

BELOW: 1910 CALIFORNIA STATE ARTICLES OF INCORPORATION AND CONSOLIDATION FOR THE LOMA LINDA SANITARIUM AND THE COLLEGE OF MEDICAL EVANGELISTS.

RIGHT: PHOTOCOPY OF 1905 LETTER FROM ELLEN G. WHITE TO JOHN BURDEN, URGING PURCHASE OF THE LOMA LINDA PROPERTY.

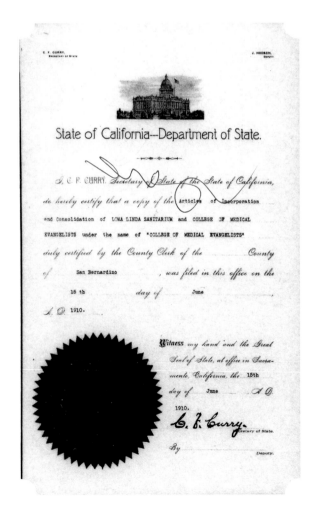

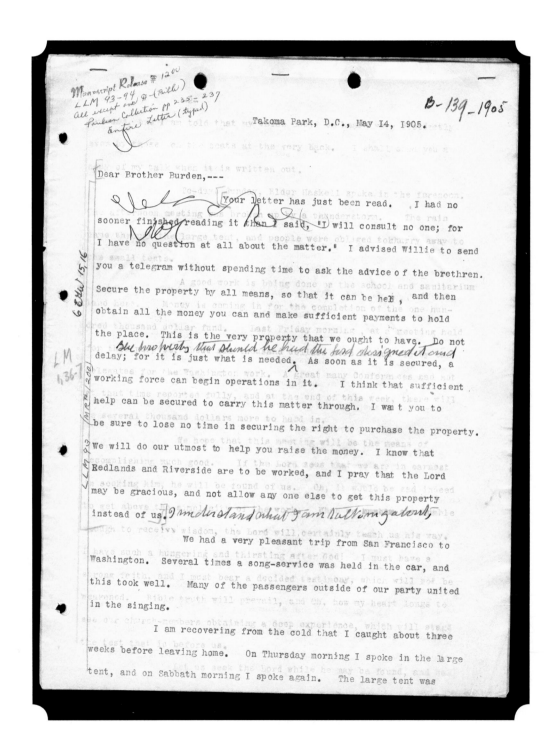

BELOW LEFT: CME's FIRST MEDICAL GRADUATING CLASS, 1914.
BELOW CENTER: A 1908 RECEIPT FOR SUPPLIES FOR THE COOKING SCHOOL.
BELOW RIGHT: ANNOUNCEMENT FOR THE 1909 GRADUATION.

First Medical Graduating Class of CME with
Bible Teacher, Roderick S. Owen - 1914

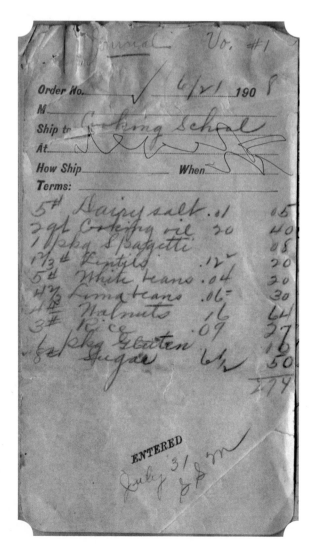

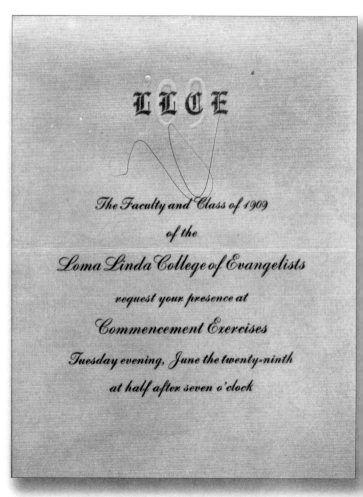

THE IMPOSSIBLE DREAM: RAILWAY TO THE MOON

Nursing class of 1910 (below). Orange groves filled the valley surrounding Loma Linda during its earliest decades (right). An early view of the nurses' library (below right).

Early postcard views of the Loma Linda Sanitarium.

Right: The sun parlor of the old Loma Linda Sanitarium.

Below: A view of the garden-like grounds.

Below right: The exercise area adjacent to the Sanitarium.

SUN PARLOR, LOMA LINDA SANITARIUM,
LOMA LINDA, CALIF.

RIGHT: THE FIRST CHURCH
SCHOOL WAS BUILT IN 1906.

BELOW: LOMA LINDA'S $40,000
PURCHASE PRICE INCLUDED A
HERD OF HEALTHY DAIRY CATTLE.

BELOW RIGHT: GEORGE K.
ABBOTT, MD, TEACHES
A HYDROTHERAPY CLASS
IN OCTOBER OF 1909.

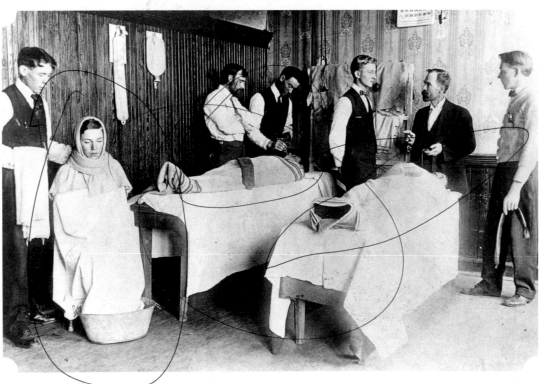

CRISIS AND SURVIVAL

AN OLD, GRAY-HAIRED BROTHER AROSE FROM THE FRONT AND SPOKE IN A QUAVERING VOICE. "YOU KNOW WHO I AM, GEORGE I. BUTLER. I USED TO BE PRESIDENT OF THE GENERAL CONFERENCE..." HE HELD OUT HIS SHAKY ARM AND SAID, "THIS HAND HAS NOT LEARNED HOW TO VOTE TO CLOSE WHAT GOD SAYS SHOULD BE OPEN."

California is home to the world's tallest tree, its largest, and its oldest. The "General Sherman" tree in Sequoia National Park is not only the largest tree in the world—it is among the largest living things on Planet Earth. At its base, this tree is more than one hundred feet in circumference and 30 feet in diameter. Each year it adds enough wood in new growth to make a tree one foot in diameter and more than 100 feet tall.

But the General Sherman—at somewhere between 2,100 and 2,200 years old—is a relative youth in comparison to the oldest known tree—a bristlecone pine named "Methuselah" in the White Mountains of Death Valley that is nearly 4,800 years old.

And at around 275 feet in height, General Sherman yields to the 367-foot-tall "Mendocino Tree" in the northern redwoods.

Surveying these titans of the forest today, one might conclude that from the moment they each burst from their seeds long ages ago, they've enjoyed a steady reach for the sky. But core samples from these massive trees show that to get where they are today, they have endured fire, drought, pests, and the competition of neighboring trees for water, soil, and sunlight. After all, many other seeds split open along with General Sherman, Methuselah, and Mendocino—and never survived.

Surveying the sprawling university/medical complex that is today's Loma Linda University Adventist Health Sciences Center, one might conclude that it too has enjoyed steady, uninterrupted growth and progress over its first century of existence. But the historical record of Loma Linda's early years shows that time and again, challenges and obstacles arose to threaten the young institution's very survival.

As the calendar turned from 1910 to 1911, the previous year had seen a consolidation of Loma Linda's sanitarium and its College of Medical Evangelists. The curriculum was stronger and more focused. New faculty arrived. And in recognition of the centrality of the spiritual on campus, "the Chapel" had been constructed on the western shoulder of the "mound."

In 1911, the new dormitory for female stu-

Left: Staff members tend the gardens adjacent to Loma Linda's first hospital, built in 1913.

dents voted the previous year—later to be named Kate Lindsay Hall—was constructed.

Growth in both college enrollment and the number of sanitarium patients made the need for new construction and expansion an urgent priority. To help raise the original $40,000 purchase price of the old Mound City property, some had suggested selling off some of the valley land for building sites. Ellen White would have none of this idea. In fact, she urged that Loma Linda buy even more adjacent land. During April Board and Constituency meetings, members considered the possibility of purchasing the Kelly tract of about 85 acres adjoining the sanitarium property.

But at the time, they took no action.

Toward the end of April, following further pressing of the matter from Mrs. White, John Burden called a meeting of available workers to discuss what they should do concerning the Kelly tract. Present at the meeting, Mrs. White appealed for the purchase of the land. Pledging $1,000 herself toward the purchase, she said, "This will be one of the greatest blessings to us in the future—one that we do not fully appreciate now, but which we shall appreciate by and by."[1]

A few days later the Loma Linda workers met again. To purchase the land needed Board action to approve it, but the Board had only recently met. Yet in view of Mrs. White's counsel and urging, the workers felt they needed to act. They chose to buy the land themselves, individually, and hold it until it could be purchased by Board approval.

Growing student enrollment taxed Loma Linda's resources. President Ruble asked, "Shall we disappoint them or as a people furnish what is necessary? The call now is for means."[2]

Infrastructure and the need for additional workers were now the continuing focus of Loma Linda's leaders. Spring Board minutes from 1911 show consider-

ation for need of a men's dormitory, a hospital to provide clinical experience, and a laboratory. Administrators reported "almost phenomenal" growth. Sanitarium patronage had increased between 25 percent and 33 percent each year, and patients were even being turned away for lack of space.

The 1911 spring Board voted to begin at once construction of a laboratory to be completed by September 1—and a men's dormitory to be completed a month later. They also voted to postpone for the time being the building of a new hospital, laundry, and central heating plant. Later, they would find it necessary to postpone also the building of the men's dorm.[3]

With rapid growth came severe growing pains, and the needs were everywhere—for buildings, for staff, for equipment, for operating expenses. Loma Linda's administrators and Board met the challenge head-on, proactively and diligently looking for ways to increase revenue. As one such step, the Board voted to invite all sister Seventh-day Adventist sanitariums and treatment rooms across the country to donate a thank offering of 5 percent of their net income to CME. Additonally, the Board voted to ask the General Conference of the Church, various union conferences, and two local conferences to donate a total of $8,000 or more to the building fund during the year 1911. Finally, they voted to employ some-

one to do fundraising for the institution.

Among all the needs calling for attention, one began emerging as the most urgent. The sanitarium served ambulatory patients—largely those in rehabilitation from illness. But a vital need for CME's medical students was for hands-on clinical experience with bedridden patients: those recovering from surgery, who had been seriously injured, or who suffered from acute illness from various diseases. A hospital would provide a place for such clinical training.

In the first move toward a hospital, the 1911 spring Board voted to move surgery from the Sanitarium to the west rooms on the first floor of a large cottage on the hill—this move to be accomplished by November 1.[4]

Meanwhile, leaders launched active efforts to promote CME. They asked Mrs. White to authorize publication of a collection of her testimonies concerning the medical and educational work to be carried forward at Loma Linda. They asked John Burden to write a "brief but comprehensive" history of CME. Plans were set in motion to provide printed promotional material to all the church's ministers and physicians. Dr. Ruble was

Nurses streamed forth from CME in ever-greater numbers. Below is the class of 1912.

As cattle graze contentedly, the School of Medicine building—later to be named North Laboratory (above)—rises between farm and farmhouse.

asked to supply short articles about CME to the union papers. Other leaders were urged to visit camp meetings to promote CME to the church's members.

But despite all this aggressive promotion and fundraising effort, Loma Linda did not presume to meet its burgeoning needs from only the Church beyond its own borders. In order to raise capital for the new laboratory, for example, a group of 125 composed of faculty and local helpers and friends pledged $2,937.50.[5]

For the remainder of the decade leading to 1920, twin challenges would dominate the agenda for Loma Linda—challenges that if met successfully would open the way for continued growth and success, but which if not met could threaten Loma Linda's very survival. To succeed, CME would need official recognition and acceptance from the Council on Medical Education of the American Medical Association (AMA) in the form of advanced ratings. This would give Loma Linda's medical graduates full legitimacy and acceptance by individual state medical boards and licensing agencies.

Loma Linda would also need the full support of the Seventh-day Adventist denomination. This second challenge was eloquently presented by General Conference President George A. Irwin during the spring 1912 CME constituency meeting.

"While this institution," he noted, "is located within the bounds of the Southern California Conference and the Pacific Union Conference it is not in any sense a local enterprise. It is the only school of its kind in the whole denomination, and hence of general interest to all parts of the great field."[6]

To gain the needed ratings from the AMA Council on Medical Education, CME would need to provide its medical students appropriate clinical training and experience. This need was priority one at a November 1912 meeting of the Board.

"Two very essential features of the medical college," the minutes recorded, "are a clinical hospital and a dispensary. The law of the medical association requires that a hospital and dispensary be connected with each college that graduates physicians."[7]

A May 1912 meeting of the Board had already approved construction of a small clinical hospital on the Loma Linda campus. But funds were slow in materializing, and by January of 1913, Dr. Ruble felt it necessary to underscore to the Board just how serious the situation had become. The previous year's survey from the AMA had pronounced CME deficient because of its lack of clinical facilities—a rating that would prevent its graduates from being allowed to sit for state board examinations.

"This means death to our college," Dr. Ruble said in confronting the Board, "unless immediate steps are taken to provide what is necessary for giving a thorough medical course. One year has already passed since this matter was [first] placed before this board, and what we see today was fully prophesied at that time. The question now before us is, Are we to make good in establishing this medical college? If so the Hospital must be built at once."[8]

To emphasize that Loma Linda's administrators were doing all they possibly could with meager resources, Dr. Ruble reported that on October 28, 1912, CME had opened a temporary hospital in a cottage on the east crest of the "hill," with eight rooms accommodating up to ten patients.

T he next day, January 28, 1913, the Constituency meeting responded to the urgent need by approving a new hospital, "at a cost not to exceed $20,000, including furnishings." The Board was directed

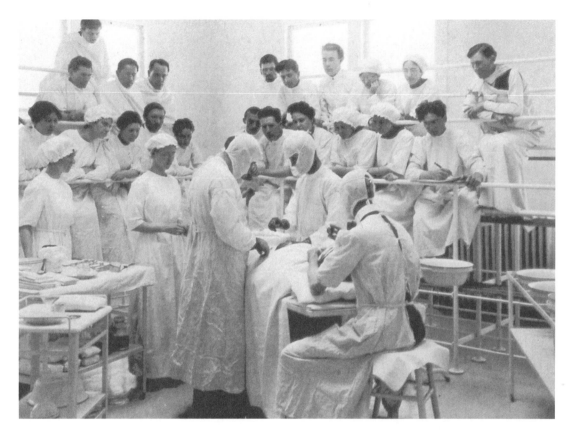

Medical students (left) representing four classes—1914 to 1917—witness an operation performed at Loma Linda Sanitarium by Dr. Thomas Evans at left and Dr. George K. Abbott at right. Dr. A. W. Truman administers the anesthesia.

to arrange for "extensive solicitation for gifts" to finance the new hospital building.

Meanwhile, study had begun focusing on the possibility of locating a dispensary (clinic) in Los Angeles to provide additional clinical experience during the final two years of medical training. Some had reservations about the Los Angeles option, and Mrs. White's counsel was sought. Asked if it would be "right to give the last two years of instruction in Los Angeles or if we should hold all the work

at Loma Linda," she replied through her son Willie in early April of 1912 "that we do in Loma Linda just as much of the work as could be done acceptably there, and carry the remainder to Los Angeles."

The way thus cleared, CME opened its dispensary, the First Street Clinic, at 941 East First Street in the Boyle Heights neighborhood of Los Angeles on September 29, 1913. This would become the first step in creating the clinical division at Los Angeles and what

would in successive stages become the White Memorial Hospital complex.

By the end of the next month, October, the new hospital at Loma Linda, located in the middle of what is today the basic sciences quadrangle, was nearing completion. On November 24, Board members named the new facility "Loma Linda Hospital" and scheduled December 1 as opening day—the day for moving the first patients in. The new hospital was placed under the medical supervision of Dr. Ruble.

Alas, however, in the months following, it became apparent that the Loma Linda Hospital faced a challenge that would lead to its early demise. Financially unable to operate the hospital as a charity institution, and failing also to fill enough beds with paying patients, the seventy-bed facility simply could not provide an adequate number of patients to support a strong clinical education program.

A 1934 CME graduate captured the pain of the hospital's early flameout:

"So the hospital went out, not with a bang, but a whimper. How sad! All that sweat and tears and epinephrine and prayers and cries, and—pffft! All eyes now turned to Los Angeles."[9]

This would not be the end of the line for a hospital at Loma Linda—an obvious fact to anyone visiting Loma Linda today. But the first effort fell short. Students would now spend three and a half years at Loma Linda studying basic sciences, gaining what practical experience they could at the sanitarium—then spend a full year gaining clinical experience in Los Angeles, followed by six months in review and examinations at Loma Linda.

In 1914, CME graduated its first class of physicians. The six included two women and four men: Lavina Baxter (Herzer), Robert Hall, Fred Herzer, Zenobia Nightingale (Bulpitt), John Wier, and Leroy White.

Also in 1914, Dr. Ruble resigned as

president of CME. The story of Loma Linda is a story of events and challenges, of providence and survival. But above all, it is the story of God's working through the lives of dedicated leaders, teachers, and medical personnel. Two gifted men would now come on the scene to move Loma Linda forward. In August, Newton G. Evans, MD, was elected CME's new president. Prior to this, he had served as medical superintendent of the Madison (Tennessee) Sanitarium and professor of pathology at the University of Tennessee.

Shortly after Dr. Evans arrived, Nathan P. Colwell, MD, the secretary of the AMA's Council on Medical Education, inspected CME—including the Los Angeles dispensary. As early as 1911, the AMA had noted the existence of CME, and the following year Dr. Colwell had visited the institution. After that visit, he had politely recommended that CME's promoters abandon their attempt to establish a medical school.

Dr. Evans realized that CME's rating would still likely be too low to ensure full acceptance of its graduates, and to assist him in seeking to attain a higher accreditation rating from the AMA, he remembered one of his educational colleagues from Madison. Evans had years earlier encouraged Percy T. Magan to become a physician. And on January 20, 1915, the CME Board voted to send President Evans, Dr.

By 1918, the primitive First Street Clinic had been superseded by a much-expanded new Dispensary on Boyle Avenue. At first only one story, later this entire level was raised and a new first floor was built under it (left).

Dr. Newton G. Evans (below), CME president from 1914 to 1927, bore the brunt of the struggle for accreditation in its earlier stages.

Magan, and former president Ruble to represent CME to the AMA's Council on Medical Education February meeting in Chicago. Dr. Magan, not yet officially connected with CME, nonetheless formed friendships at this meeting that would become extremely valuable in the future.

On July 16, 1915, at the age of 87, the founding voice and presence that had guided the Church and encouraged the establishment of its first medical institutions fell silent. Ellen White passed away at her home—Elmshaven—in Northern California. But her written counsels

remained to instruct, clarify, and inspire.

The challenge of lifting CME's rating with the AMA seemed daunting indeed. To provide the facilities and staff to offer adequate clinical training would be costly. So much so that when the fall council of the world church met at Loma Linda in 1915, not a few of the delegates attending were prepared seriously to consider closing CME's School of Medicine.

The CME band conducted by T. Gordon Reynolds, MD.

Reaching a painful and almost paralyzing impasse of silence, a subcommittee appointed to study the crisis watched as an old, gray-haired brother arose from the front and spoke in a quavering voice.

"Brethren," he said, "I am bewildered. I can hardly believe my eyes and my ears.

What is this I hear you say? We must close this school? . . . Soon the vote will be taken, but before it is taken, let me say this:

"You know who I am, George I. Butler. I used to be president of the General Conference, and I think I received more testimonies from the servant of the Lord [Mrs.

White] than any of you, and most of them rebuked me. We were at times urged to do what seemed impossible, but when we went forward by faith, the way opened. Brethren, I believe in God and in His prophets! . . .

"Now, Brother Daniells [the president of the General Conference] will soon call for a vote. When he does, here is one old hand that will not go up." Butler then held out his shaky arm and concluded, "This hand has not learned how to vote to close what God says should be open."[10]

Others, unprepared to close the school, nonetheless felt that the curriculum should be reduced to two years of basic sciences, after which students would be encouraged to complete their medical education at established schools of medicine elsewhere. Feelings ran deep.

Heated discussions continued, but a succession of developments began to turn the tide. First, four non-delegate women asked to be heard. The four were: Dr. Florence Keller, a pioneer physician in New Zealand; Josephine Gotzian, a wealthy widow; Mrs. Stephen N. Haskell, a woman of strong faith and belief; and her sister, Mrs. Emma Gray. They urged the delegates to continue the school and suggested that the women of the denomination raise the funds for building a needed clinical teaching hospital in Los Angeles—a hospital they also suggested be named in memory of Ellen G. White. As they spoke, a hush fell over the room.

The next day, General Conference President A.G. Daniells added his voice in support of keeping the school open.

Teachers and students (left) join in a "medical-evangelistic" tour in the Sanitarium truck in 1913.

"My brethren," he said, "I am astounded and I must speak. If I do not say my mind I will be a coward and unworthy of your confidence. Brethren, listen to me. We all profess faith in the spirit of prophecy, but we forget that one of the last things the prophet [Mrs. White] ever wrote was that our young men and women should be given their full training in our own school and should not be forced to go to worldly schools. And here we are, before the prophet is hardly cold in her grave, proposing that our young men and women shall only have half of

their education from us and then shall be turned loose in these worldly schools. Now, I protest against it. That is all that I can do, but I do most earnestly protest it. We can build up this school. We can do anything God wants us to do."[11]

Also present at the meetings by invitation of President Evans was Dr. Percy T. Magan. Near the close of the discussions, Dr. Magan, an acknowledged orator, found that he simply could not contain himself and launched a most eloquent plea for the college to continue as a full four-year school. Of Dr. Magan's

On April 21, 1918, more than 2,500 people gathered (right) for the dedication of the first White Memorial Hospital. Arthur G. Daniells delivered the keynote address, and an earthquake interrupted Percy T. Magan's speech.

speech, a later writer would record that "His words were so pointed and took such a deep hold that men who strongly opposed the continuance of the school were practically unable to answer Magan's arguments, and those who were battling for the school took a new grip."[12]

When the vote came, not a single hand was raised to close the school. The school would teach basic sciences at Loma Linda and provide clinical training in Los Angeles—at the new $61,000 Ellen G. White Memorial Hospital.

That same night, President Evans confronted Dr. Magan. "Now, Percy," he said, "you saved the College tonight, and you've got to come over here and help run it."

Thus Dr. Magan became the dean of the Los Angeles division, with the proviso that he would have to raise his own $23-a-week salary, as there simply wasn't anything in the budget to cover it.

What became known as "the Women's Movement" wasted no time making good on its pledge. Even before the meetings had adjourned, the ladies posed some of the pioneer brethren for photos to be sold for fifty cents each. Mrs. Stephen N. Haskell, the group chair, later reported that "When the aged brethren heard that photographs were to be sold for money, they at first objected, but when they learned that [they] would be used to build the Ellen G. White Memorial Hospital, they were glad to help."[13]

The onset of World War I posed a new threat to CME's medical classes, as only students attending medical schools with the AMA's highest ratings were exempt from being drafted into the army. But in November of 1917, the AMA awarded CME its second-highest rating—a "B"—just in time to prevent CME's classes from being emptied of their young men.

Before the decade ended, the new Ellen G. White Memorial Hospital in Los Angeles was completed. On April 21, 1918, a crowd of more than 2,000

gathered for the dedication ceremony. As Dr. Magan spoke, an earthquake struck, though it caused no serious local damage.

Quick on his feet, Dr. Magan quipped, "It takes a good-sized man to make a speech that will start an earthquake."

During Loma Linda's earliest years—years of crisis and struggle born of growth and success—God brought to the task of founding, to His glory, a medical and educational center around the Hill Beautiful many "good-sized" men and women of stature and commitment.

From California soil had long centuries earlier grown trees of "good size" and height and age. From California soil now grew a center that would steadily grow to bless countless lives the world around with knowledge and healing.

NOTES:

1. Arthur L. White, "A Year of Concentrated Book Preparation, Buy Land, Loma Linda, Buy Land," *Ellen G. White, Vol. 6, The Elmshaven Years, 1905-1915* (Washington, D.C.: Review and Herald Publishing Association, 1982), p. 345.

2. Wells A. Ruble, MD, *The Medical Evangelist*, vol. 2, no. 3, p. 2.

3. CME Board of Trustees *Minutes,* March 30-April 6, 1911, p. 129.

4. Ibid., April 18, p. 139.

5. Ibid., November 17, 1911, p. 161.

6. CME Constituency *Minutes,* March 27-April 2, 1912, pp. 174, 175.

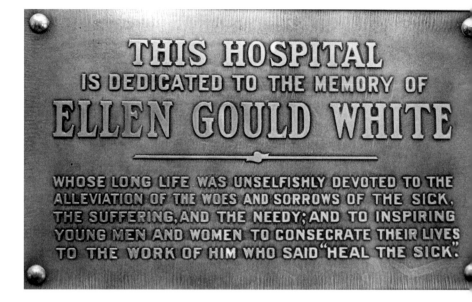

7. CME Board of Trustees *Minutes,* November 9, 1912, pp. 55, 56.

8. CME Board of Trustees *Minutes,* January 27, 1913, p. 147.

9. Carrol S. Small, M.D., *Diamond Memories* (Alumni Association, School of Medicine of Loma Linda University, 1984), p. 29.

10. A.V. Olsen, *Through Crisis to Victory: 1888–1901* (Washington, D.C.: Review and Herald Publishing Association, 1966 [Rev. 1981]), pp. 90, 91.

11. *The Medical Evangelist,* February 15, 1940, p. 4.

12. Merlin L. Neff, "An 'Inspirator' for CME," *For God and CME* (Mountain View, California: Pacific Press Publishing Association, 1964), p. 176.

13. Mrs. S.N. Haskell, "The Veterans' Aid to the Hospital Fund," *Review and Herald,* April 27, 1916, p. 20.

A plaque (above) honors the memory of the remarkable woman for whom the White Memorial Hospital is named.

PHOTO ALBUM

Nurses streamed forth from Loma Linda in ever-greater numbers as CME grew. Below left: Graduation for the class of 1912. Below: The class of 1913.

RUTH J. TEMPLE, MD (RIGHT), WAS THE FIRST AFRICAN-AMERICAN FEMALE GRADUATE FROM CME, IN 1918. DR. TEMPLE AND HER HUSBAND, OTIS BANKS, BOUGHT A HOUSE IN EAST LOS ANGELES AND BEGAN A FREE HEALTH CLINIC, LATER NAMING IT THE TEMPLE HEALTH INSTITUTE. OVERCOMING THE PREJUDICES OF HER TIME, DR. TEMPLE JOINED THE TEACHING STAFF OF WHITE MEMORIAL HOSPITAL, EDUCATING CAUCASIAN MEDICAL STUDENTS. LATER, SHE HELD A NUMBER OF POSITIONS WITH THE LOS ANGELES PUBLIC HEALTH DEPARTMENT. IN 1983, THE EAST LOS ANGELES HEALTH CENTER WAS RENAMED DR. RUTH TEMPLE HEALTH CENTER. DR. TEMPLE DIED IN 1984 AT THE AGE OF 91. BELOW: NURSES (CIRCA 1911) ENJOY A GAME OF "BLIND MAN'S BLUFF" AT A SOCIAL EVENT.

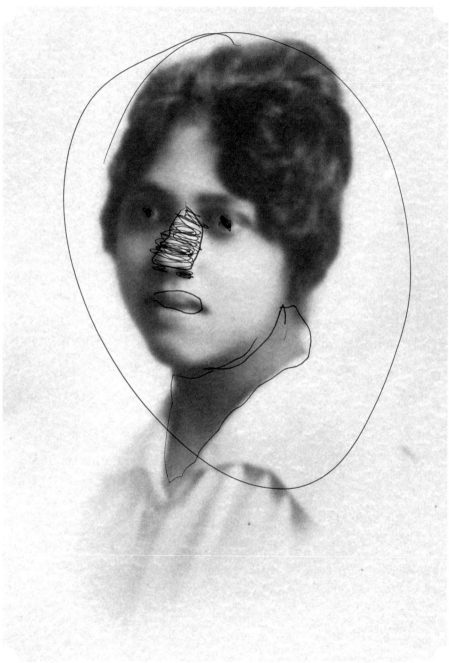

RIGHT: THE LOMA LINDA VOLUNTEER FIRE DEPARTMENT, CIRCA 1915.

BELOW RIGHT: PARTICIPANTS AT THE GROUNDBREAKING FOR THE ORIGINAL WOMEN'S DORMITORY, KATE LINDSAY HALL, WHICH WAS FIRST OCCUPIED IN THE FALL OF 1911.

THE IMPOSSIBLE DREAM: RAILWAY TO THE MOON

Below: CME students (circa 1915) enjoy a countryside picnic.

Below right: Nurses (circa 1919) help Sanitarium patients enjoy the benefits of Southern California sunshine. Notice the early wheelchair design—large wheels in the front, small ones in the back.

REACHING FOR THE SKY

ON NOVEMBER 16, 1922, DR. MAGAN RECEIVED A LETTER WITH THE NEWS CME HAD WAITED YEARS TO HEAR: "IT IS MY MOST PLEASING DUTY TO INFORM YOU THAT AT ITS BUSINESS MEETING ON NOVEMBER 14, THE COUNCIL ON MEDICAL EDUCATION AND HOSPITALS VOTED THAT THE COLLEGE OF MEDICAL EVANGELISTS BE GRANTED A 'CLASS A' RATING."

Three peas lived happily in a pod. Came the day, however, when the pod opened slightly to reveal the rich brown soil below. One pea shrank back in alarm. "The soil is dirty," said Pea No. 1. "We're safe here in our pod. We're green—and should stay as far away from the brown soil as possible."

The second pea had other ideas. Feeling restricted by the pod and odd being green while surrounded by so much brown, No. 2 quickly wriggled free of the pod and rolled around in the soil to get as brown as possible—as quickly as possible.

Pea No. 3 surveyed the soil and said, "You know, we're all green. The soil is brown. Green is just the color the soil needs to see more of."

And with that, Pea No. 3 rolled onto the soil and shared its "green-ness" with the brown earth.

Christians sometimes struggle in relating to the world around them. Some separate themselves as far as possible from "the world" so it can't soil them. Others don't like to be so different—as different as green is from brown—and they plunge into the world so they won't stand out. Finally, some Christians step boldly into the world to share their true colors and make the brown world a greener place.

Like an island of green, the College of Medical Evangelists, too, faced early on the issue of just how to relate to the brown world around it.

On January 30, 1921, CME president Newton Evans, MD, reported to a meeting of the constituency that students from the University of Southern California were on the CME campus taking classes. The previous spring, Percy T. Magan, MD, had presented to the Board a special request. USC was closing its medical department at the end of the 1919-1920 school year, and a number of its medical students had applied for the privilege of completing their education at CME. The majority of the students were ready to enter their senior year. The Board had voted to accept "as many of these applicants as shall be thought advisable by the executive officers of the school, with the understanding that on the completion of their medical course, the school from which they come will issue the degrees."[1]

Now President Evans updated the

Left: The Loma Linda Sanitarium and Hospital, built in 1924, would serve patients until 1966.

The first known photograph of Loma Linda from the air (right), taken in 1920, shows the Sanitarium just left of center—and the College buildings to the lower right. Acres of fertile farmlands and orange groves surrounded the Sanitarium and College.

Constituency concerning this special accommodation for USC students:

"Some time last Spring the Board of Trustees of the University of Southern California suddenly announced that the medical department at that school would be discontinued at the end of the school year 1919–1920. This left a large number of their students in a very difficult situation for various reasons and as a result of this situation members of their students as well as the teachers in the Medical School, earnestly begged us to make plans to accommodate at least their senior and junior classes. A great deal of time and study were given to this problem by our Board and faculty and it was finally decided to accept all of such senior and junior students as it seemed necessary to take on account of the difficulty of their finding other schools in which to finish their work. There were about twenty such senior students and fifteen juniors. It was arranged that for the most part their class work and clinics should be conducted in separate classes from our own medical students and practically all of the old medical teachers in the University of Southern California consented to help in the task of carrying these two classes through until the time of graduation. These plans have been carried out and the work seems to be going along smoothly and satisfactorily. Classrooms for these students are provided in the Los Angeles County Hospital."[2]

In 1921, CME graduated thirty-three medical students from the University of Southern California. A year later in the 1922 spring constituency meeting, Dr. Magan reported further on the progress of the USC "experiment." In doing so, he acknowledged the fears some peas in the CME pod had entertained about the risks of educating nonbelievers:

"You will all remember with what misgivings we took hold of the matter of trying to train and help the students of the University of Southern California Medical College. There was considerable feeling that they might lead us astray and be a detriment to the school. Of course you realize most of their work was carried on at the Los Angeles County Hospital.

When the University of Southern California closed its medical school in 1920, CME agreed to accept the "stranded" junior and senior classes so they could complete their training. The Los Angeles County General Hospital (left) provided classrooms for these students.

One of those classes passed on and was graduated by the University last spring. Sixteen of their students remain with us in what came to us in a Junior class and will finish this year. We have all noticed, and noticed with a great deal of happiness and joy, the influence which our teachers and school has had over them.

"I think Doctor Coyne and Doctor Keller will bear me out that they do not make us a bit of trouble, and they mingle among us much the same as our own folks, eat at our cafeteria, and generally behave themselves in a most quiet and Christian manner.

"Two things of special interest have occurred. One of those students became converted, was baptized and joined our church, and I would like the privilege of reading a few lines which I received from this student, Dr. Judith Ahlem. She is taking an internship in the Alameda County Hospital."[3]

Dr. Magan then read the letter and commented that it had touched him "very much."

"I have missed you people of the White Memorial so much. Although I never seem to be able to live up to the principles of our church, yet I am glad that I can try—and I am glad that the dear Lord has answered so many of my prayers, because it makes me feel that my life may not be in vain after all. It has been my joyful privilege to speak a few words of the precious Truth to a few of my patients here. I wish you could have seen the smile of happiness that passed over the face of a repentant criminal (a mere lad of 18 years) when he was told that his sins could be forgiven—(at first he didn't really think it possible.) He asked to be told more of the word of God, said

he had learned a hard lesson, and that he would begin life anew. That was all a week ago. He has now become desperately ill—perhaps but a few hours left to him now. I have spoken a few words to his mother now. She is surprised that there is a 'Christian doctor'. (I wish she knew a better one.)

"I shall always be grateful to you and those others who made it possible for us (USC) to come to your school. I also want you to remember that the life of at least me was thereby changed for good. That may not be saying much perhaps, just now, but it will mean more in the future.

"(Signed) Judith Ahlem."[4]

As the decade of the 1920s began, CME's spiritual influence was already being felt—already bearing fruit. But the 1920s would prove to be years of remarkable progress in many areas.

When Nathan P. Colwell, MD, secretary of the American Medical Association's Council on Medical Education and Hospitals, had first visited Loma Linda in 1912, he afterward recommended that—based on what he had seen—those promoting the idea of a medical school abandon their attempts. The AMA, he noted, was out to crush "one-horse medical schools," and that is all he could conceive of Loma Linda ever establishing.

In its earliest years, the new medi-

cal college could barely merit the AMA's lowest rating—a "C"—which wasn't enough even to ensure that its medical graduates could sit for their various state board examinations.

In 1917, just in time to save its medical students from the World War I draft, CME earned a "B" grade. This rating remained until 1922. By then, CME had reorganized and strengthened many of its vital programs and departments as recommended by the AMA.

Through the years, Dr. Colwell had watched the steady progress of Loma Linda's CME from little more than a threadbare dream backed by a shoestring budget to a medical school of the first rank. At first a thoroughgoing pessimist concerning CME's future, Dr. Colwell had now become one of its greatest admirers.

Invited now to a banquet in Los Angeles, Dr. Colwell shared his journey from skeptic to enthusiastic supporter:

"When the Seventh-day Adventists first started…a number of us felt they were doomed for defeat. I told them over and over again not to make a start. But today I must confess that their faith has triumphed over my unbelief. Some years ago Dr. Magan took me over the place which their hospital now covers. It was then a mass of weeds and cockleburs, and there were two or three sorry-looking animals feeding upon it. Dr. Magan remarked to me

COUNCIL ON MEDICAL EDUCATION
AND HOSPITALS

American Medical Association

**Council on Medical Education
and Hospitals**

ARTHUR D. BEVAN, CHAIRMAN . CHICAGO
WILLIAM PEPPER . . . . PHILADELPHIA
MERRITTE W. IRELAND . WASHINGTON
RAY LYMAN WILBUR . STANFORD UNIV.
SAMUEL W. WELCH . . . MONTGOMERY
N. P. COLWELL, SECRETARY . . CHICAGO

535 North Dearborn Street, CHICAGO,

November 16, 1922.

Dr. P. T. Magan, Dean,
    College of Medical Evangelists,
        White Memorial Hospital,
            Los Angeles, California.

Dear Dr. Magan:

          After watching the efforts you have been
making to develop your medical school during the past
several years, it is my most pleasing duty to inform you
that at its business meeting on November 14th, the
Council on Medical Education and Hospitals voted that
the College of Medical Evangelists be granted a class
A rating.

          Considering the manner in which improve-
ments in the past have been made, the Council voted
this higher rating fully confident that the places which
are still comparatively weak will be strengthened, and
that the institution will continue to improve.

          You are undoubtedly already fully familiar
with the fact that improvements can be made with great
advantage in the following particulars: (a) further
enlargement and improvement of the medical library at
Los Angeles; (b) the making of adequate provision whereby
medical research can be carried on, and (c) that the
best methods of clinical instruction be installed for
seniors at the bed-side of patients in the hospital, in
the establishing of clinical clerkships etc.

          With sincere congratulations for the
favorable action by the Council and with best wishes for
the further development of your medical school, I am

                    Very truly yours,

                    N P Colwell   Secretary.

Council on Medical Education and Hospitals.

that someday we would have a great medical institution there. I thought to myself: You poor soul, you do not know what you are talking about; you will never be able to have a first-class medical school; but today I walk over the block covered with beautiful buildings, and a veritable hive of medical activities. . . . I am almost certain as to the kind of report I will make, and I am sure you will all be satisfied with it."[5]

On November 16, 1922, Dr. Colwell wrote a letter to Dr. Magan with the news CME had waited years to hear:

"After watching the efforts you have been making to develop your medical school during the past several years, it is my most pleasing duty to inform you that at its business meeting on November 14, the Council on Medical Education and Hospitals voted that the College of Medical Evangelists be granted a 'class A' rating."

CME was now the only "class A" medical school in Southern California. Not only did it ensure the continuing deferment of CME students from active military service, but it also qualified CME graduates to take state board examinations anywhere in the United States. Dr. Magan's reply reflected the feelings of everyone connected with the institution:

"To say that your letter brought happiness to the hearts of the little group of men who have struggled to make this Medical School worthy of the honor you have

The long-awaited letter (left) bringing the good news of CME's "class A" rating.

bestowed upon us, is to state our feelings very mildly indeed. I think I can truthfully say that this was the most blessed piece of information which has come to us since we commenced our long, long struggle . . . .

"Every line of your letter reveals the deep pleasure you have experienced in helping us and we thank you from the bottom of our hearts."[6]

In a later letter, Dr. Colwell acknowledged the personal impact of CME on his own life:

"I feel ashamed of myself sitting here rating you people, which is a little bit of a job, while you are doing the really big things of the world. You have done wonders in your school, and I am proud of you; and while you have not converted me to the Seventh-day Sabbath as yet, you have converted me on practically everything else about your medical work."[7]

As Loma Linda celebrated this good news, some twenty miles to the southwest another pioneering educational institution was just struggling to be born—a school that in time would form a significant part of Loma Linda's total educational program.

With the threatened closing of San Fernando Valley Academy near Los Angeles, Adventists in Southern California urgently looked for a rural location on which to build a new boarding academy with acreage enough for both a campus and a farm.

When discussions between the neigh-

boring Southern and Southeastern California conferences as to possibly joining to support one school failed to produce agreement, Southeastern California chose to go it alone.

Scouring the land from Yucaipa east of Loma Linda and southward almost to San Diego, the conference ultimately found a 330-acre tract of land south of Riverside, which they pur-

chased—mostly on credit—for $102,550.

School was scheduled to open on October 3, 1922, but very little was in readiness. James I. Robison, the first president of La Sierra Academy, would later recall:

"We did not have a building. We did not have a book in our library, nor a test tube for the laboratory. We did not have a desk or a chair. We did not even have a faculty. . . . But we did have faith . . .

and so with faith and courage and loyal cooperation and united effort we stepped forward, facing every difficulty."[8]

Well, there was in fact a faculty by opening day—but a very small one indeed. The four faculty included the principal, Professor Robison; the Bible teacher, Pastor Elson H. Emmerson; the preceptress, Mrs. J. J. Koehn; and the farm manager, Mr. A. Logan.

Much like its only moderately older sister institution to the northeast that had been born of dreams and hard work and struggle, La Sierra too began to grow. In 1927, La Sierra Academy became Southern California Junior College; in 1939, La Sierra College. It would achieve full senior college status in 1944 and confer its first bachelor's degrees in 1945. Many years would pass when, in 1967, La Sierra College would become the College of Arts and Sciences of Loma Linda University.

The year 1922 had brought a "Class A" rating for CME from the AMA—and had seen the birth of a sister educational institution at La Sierra. This was also the year when CME would add a new school of dietetics. Headed by Harold M. Walton, MD, this was the first new department since the opening of the nursing school in 1906 and the medical school in 1909. In 1863 Ellen White first wrote on the topic of a healthful diet, and it had become a vital part of the

Church's overall philosophy of healthful living. The new school would immediately begin supplying trained food specialists to staff the Church's growing number of schools, colleges, and sanitariums.

The 1920s moved on with growth and progress and expansion, and as the year 1927 arrived, Dr. Evans decided the time had arrived to step down as president of CME. For one year, Edward H.

Risley, MD, professor of biochemistry, occupied the position; then he too wished to be relieved of it. The Board then elected Dr. Magan as the new president of CME—a position he would occupy with distinction until 1942.

The arrival of 1928 brought a major milestone in Loma Linda's history. Through the years, Loma Linda's on-campus medical institution had transitioned

The year 1928 brought a new Loma Linda Sanitarium and Hospital to the "Hill Beautiful." This Spanish-style facility would provide patient care and medical training until 1967.

ing room and kitchen, office spaces for the entire medical staff, an x-ray room, men's and ladies' hydrotherapy treatment parlors, and rooms for 175 patients.

On the roof were booths for sunbaths and a room for occupational therapy. On the top floor of the octagonal tower above the main lobby was a sunroom that offered a magnificent panoramic view of the surrounding mountains and valley orange groves. Floodlights illuminated the tower at night.

The new Sanitarium and Hospital—which through the years would come to be known simply as "The San"—opened for occupancy on March 20, 1929, after three days of moving patients, staff, and equipment. On March 29, in view of the completion of a new sanitarium, the Board designated the original Sanitarium as the "Sanitarium Annex." The old structure stood until it was razed in 1967.

At a dedication program in the nearby outdoor amphitheater on April 7, President Magan marked this latest advance in Loma Linda's medical ministry:

"It is a wonderful thing of men and women to know that they have been brought into the world for a certain cause. The thought I want to bring before you lies in this, that Loma Linda and all this system of health institutions which encircle the earth are here because of a certain sacred cause, and to this cause

from a sanitarium serving primarily "rest-cure" patients—many of them on extended vacations—to more seriously ill patients who had come for treatment as well as to learn the secrets of better living. This transition, of course, was to the benefit of the medical students

and staff, allowing them to study and serve a greater variety of medical cases.

Groundbreaking and construction on a new Loma Linda Sanitarium and Hospital began on the "Hill Beautiful" on April 22, 1928. The new 200-foot Spanish-style building would contain a huge parlor, din-

and for this cause this place is dedicated, and because of it we are training our young men and women to give their lives to the sacred ministry of health."[9]

In a keynote speech at the dedication, G.H. Curtis, manager of the Loma Linda Sanitarium, acknowledged the generous gifts toward the new facility from the General Conference of Seventh-day Adventists, the Pacific Union Conference, the Southern and Southeastern California Conferences, and Glendale Sanitarium.

In its practical use, the new Loma Linda Sanitarium and Hospital functioned more as a hospital than as an extended-care facility. Surgical and obstetrical patients occupied most of the hospital area, while patients with nonsurgical problems occupied the sanitarium portion.

Repeatedly enlarged, the Loma Linda Sanitarium and Hospital on the hill eventually could accommodate nearly 200 patients. The 1929 building would serve continuously until 1967, when growth and progress forced the need for yet another major expansion of facilities. That year would bring another moving day as patients and staff moved into the new Loma Linda University Medical Center on the campus west of the hill.

In 1976, the old Sanitarium and Hospital building on the hill was extensively remodeled and renamed Nichol Hall, after Francis D. Nichol, an early resident of

With the opening of the School of Dietetics in 1922, students (left) prepared to staff a growing number of institutions across the country.

Loma Linda who served many years as editor of the *Review and Herald*—the official weekly paper of the Seventh-day Adventist Church. Today, Nichol Hall is occupied by the School of Public Health and the School of Allied Health Professions.

The 1920s brought a succession of milestones in Loma Linda's medical ministry: a new "A" rating for the medical school; a new president; a new school; a new hospital building; and to the southwest, a new institution that would in time become Loma Linda's undergraduate division.

Loma Linda might not yet be a mighty redwood; but no longer either was it a fragile seedling. In the 1920s, the young tree grew strong and stretched skyward. So it is when a tree begins with strong roots, rich soil, and the bless-

ings of Heaven's sunlight. For Loma Linda—rooted in dreams of service, rich in prayer and faith, and blessed with bold leaders and a divine Physician's guidance—growth was its natural imperative.

NOTES:

1. CME Board of Trustees, *Minutes,* April 18, 1920, pp. 1, 2.

2. CME constituency meeting, *Minutes,* January 30, 1921, p. 3.

3. CME constituency meeting, *Minutes,* March 22, 1922, p. 8.

4. Ibid., pp. 8, 9.

5. Richard Utt, *From Vision to Reality,* pp. 61, 63.

6. Ibid., p. 63.

7. Ibid.

8. Ibid., p. 65.

9. *The Medical Evangelist,* April 11, 1929, p. 2.

Photo Album

Right: This is the only known photograph of a patient ward inside the first Loma Linda Hospital.

Below right: Hydrotherapy equipment (circa mid-1920s) could not be characterized as elaborate.

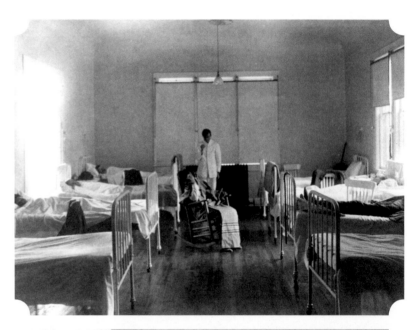

Above: 1920s-era employees of Loma Linda Food Company.

THE IMPOSSIBLE DREAM: RAILWAY TO THE MOON

BELOW: THE ORIGINAL SANITARIUM BUILDING ON THE HILL WAS REPLACED IN 1928 BY A NEW SANITARIUM AND HOSPITAL.

RIGHT: THE NEW HOSPITAL AS BUILDING PROGRESSED.

BOTTOM RIGHT: THE NEW HOSPITAL UPON COMPLETION OF CONSTRUCTION.

Below: La Sierra Academy opened in October of 1922 just south of Riverside, California.

Right top: Labeled "La Sierra Academy Normal," the school bus also served as a farm truck from 1926 to 1931.

Right center: In 1927, La Sierra Academy became Southern California Junior College.

Right bottom: A team pulls a farm trailer in 1932, with the school in the background.

THE IMPOSSIBLE DREAM: RAILWAY TO THE MOON

From three Southern California schools, graduates stepped forward to serve. Below: The La Sierra class of 1923. Right: The White Memorial Hospital nursing class of 1923. Bottom right: The Loma Linda nursing class of 1928.

To Survive, but More— to Thrive

THE DEPRESSION WOULD TEST THE DEDICATION OF EVERYONE ASSOCIATED WITH LOMA LINDA—AND, AS THE NATIONAL FINANCIAL CRISIS DEEPENED, IT WOULD REQUIRE EVER-GREATER SACRIFICES TO RIDE OUT THE LEAN YEARS. THE COLLEGE, SAID PRESIDENT MAGAN, "MUST ELIMINATE EXTRAVAGANCE AND WASTE ... AND MAKE PERSONAL SACRIFICES."

Any student of American history can tell you (as can anyone who lived through the early twentieth century), that the "Roaring Twenties" slammed hard into the Great Depression that began in 1929 and extended through much of the 1930s. What was true for the nation proved true also for Loma Linda. If during the twenties Loma Linda reached for the sky, during the thirties the Depression pulled it quite rudely back to earth.

The First National Bank of Loma Linda opened its doors the same year the stock market crashed but by 1935 simply couldn't survive and—like thousands of banks nationwide—folded forever. Some wondered if Loma Linda's hospital and college would suffer the same fate as had befallen its bank.

But Loma Linda's twin ministries of educating and healing had accumulated hard-won experience at enduring hard times. Men and women of vision early on started a hospital and a college even as many said it couldn't be done. And the combination of divine providence, linked with human vision and effort, helped Loma Linda find a way to survive its earliest years. So Loma Linda's leaders and workers already had not only well-developed survival skills but a will to succeed rooted in the conviction that the mission of Loma Linda was to carry forward God's work of hope and healing from this chosen Southern California valley.

But the Depression would test the dedication of everyone associated with Loma Linda—and, as the national financial crisis deepened, it would require ever-greater sacrifices to ride out the lean years.

As the downward slide continued, the General Conference of Seventh-day Adventists called for a major slashing of the College's budget, with

Left: From its first facilities, dedicated in 1918, the White Memorial Hospital in Los Angeles expanded into a new 180-bed hospital building in 1937.

The steel framework of the new and greatly expanded White Memorial Hospital in Los Angeles (right) took its place against the skyline as construction proceeded during the late 1930s.

worker salaries to be pared between 5 percent and 20 percent.

"It is up to us to make the thing go or turn it over to someone who can," said the president, Percy T. Magan, MD. The College, he added, must "get down to bedrock and put things on a better basis, . . . eliminate extravagance and waste, . . . and make personal sacrifices."

By October of 1932, occupancy rates at White Memorial Hospital in Los Angeles plummeted to only fifty patients—the lowest-ever patient census. In response,

physicians often accepted eggs, flour, chickens, groceries, and other goods as payment for services. A group of nurses from White Memorial Hospital responded with compassion and formed the "Ellen White Nurses" to serve thousands of poor people in the surrounding community. They donated their time. The hospital provided food. And the county of Los Angeles provided transportation. At both Loma Linda and White Memorial Hospital, some nurses took less than full-time work so oth-

ers could have at least a few hours of employment each week.

Even prior to the Depression, maintaining a divided campus at both Loma Linda and in Los Angeles had proven itself an ongoing challenge. But America's financial collapse stressed this arrangement to its limit. "This whole matter of a divided institute is a very expensive one," President Magan noted in highlighting the obvious. Two faculties. Two hospitals. Two nurses' training programs. Two sets of buildings.

As if money weren't already in short supply, new government and professional association requirements called for a stepped-up flow of surveys and reports. This not only further burdened Loma Linda's financial resources, but all the new paperwork created undue demands on time—a limited resource.

Despite the widespread financial failure that now permeated all of American society, the combination of divine blessing, workforce sacrifice, and Church support kept Loma Linda afloat during these bleak years—and not just afloat but actually moving steadily forward.

During the 1930s, Loma Linda continued an aggressive building program. One such significant new addition to the Loma Linda campus came in 1934. The College church had for years met in West Hall, the name given to the first Loma Linda Hospital built in 1913. In 1933, CME's con-

Lacy moved his congregation into the new auditorium following six and a half years of meeting in West Hall. CME named the new auditorium John Burden Hall on October 4, 1934.[4] The naming of this building was an unusual board action in that it occurred almost eight years before John Burden's death on June 10, 1942.

Three new buildings were completed in 1936: an anatomy building, a pathology building, and a physiology building (later renamed Alfred Shryock Hall, Newton Evans Hall, and Edward Risley Hall, respectively)—and an auditorium located in Evans Hall, later named Oran I. Cutler Amphitheater.

Much of this new construction was made possible by generous support of the General Conference of Seventh-day Adventists, which at its annual council

The White Memorial Hospital campus (left), circa 1937.

Graduation ceremony (below) for the 1934 CME School of Nursing class.

troller informed its Board of Trustees that the College Chapel in West Hall—with a seating capacity of about 250 for a membership of 400—was entirely inadequate. The Board voted "to look with favor on building a church at Loma Linda."[1]

On October 25, 1933, the Board voted to ask the General Conference of Seventh-day Adventists to study the possibility of building a new church for the College of Medical Evangelists. After considerable study of financial resources and location, the General Conference committee

approved the construction of the College Church, which was built by Larry C. Havstad in 1934 for $14,995.[2]

To realize economies of use, the new College Church was not designed to be a dedicated building but a multipurpose building. CME and the College Church funded it to be used for scientific lectures, chapel exercises, and community programs, as well as for church services. It also accommodated the college library in the basement.[3]

On September 15, 1934, Pastor H. C.

in 1934 approved an appropriation of $500,000 toward the new buildings.

In 1937, a new Loma Linda Campus Hill Church replaced the old Hill Church built in 1910. But not all the new construction took place at Loma Linda. That same year, White Memorial Hospital in Los Angeles—which since 1918 had occupied a dispensary and some cottage-style buildings—completed and dedicated a new 180-bed, five-story concrete and steel structure at a cost of $330,000. The new building was one of the first earthquake-resistant hospitals in California.

The year 1937 also saw the birth of a new academic department at Loma Linda—the School of Medical Technology, headed by Orlyn B. Pratt, MD. This school would later become a department in the School of Allied Health Professions.

During the decade of the 1930s, even as the College of Medical Evangelists struggled through the Great Depression not only to stay afloat but to expand on a much-reduced budget, it continued to come under fire for its shortcomings: crowded curriculum, excessive class load for the teaching staff, and inadequate administrative organization.

But perhaps the heaviest criticism focused on CME's total lack of research programs. Fred Zapffe, MD, of the Association of American Medical Colleges (AAMC) wrote: "It is the function of every medical school to teach and to do research, and I may add, to care for the sick in its hospitals. A teacher who has not been bitten by the research bug is not a real teacher. He is merely a dispenser of knowledge which can be gotten by reading a textbook or the literature. He merely passes on what he has read, which is not real education at all. Such teaching is being discouraged and even condemned more and more."[5]

The demand that CME become involved in research came not only from outside the school but also from a group of the school's alumni. Forming what they called the Harveian Society (in honor of William Harvey [1578-1657]—an English physician and anatomist who discovered the circulation of the blood), these alumni also insisted that certain other reforms be instituted at CME.

Dr. Magan and his associates were struggling mightily to ensure the very survival of CME during these years of financial depression—years forlorn of any hope for government subsidies or chari-

Present-day photos of three buildings completed in 1936: the pathology building (Newton Evans Hall, above left); the anatomy building (Alfred Shryock Hall, above); and the physiology building (Edward Risley Hall, left). Oran I. Cutler Amphitheater occupies the left portion of Evans Hall.

endowments, and—with the exception of the 1934 capital improvements appropriation—years of diminishing support from the Seventh-day Adventist Church. Understandably, then, Dr. Magan and his colleagues did not especially welcome all the pressure to plunge into research. Yet the combined insistence of the AAMC and the Harveian Society amounted to something close to an ultimatum.

Caught in the middle between financial realities and the voices insisting on change, Dr. Magan expressed his private views on the matter to Pastor Arthur G. Daniells, former president of the General Conference of Seventh-day Adventists:

"There can be no question but that the great medical schools of the world set much store by research work. . . . I am sure that it is a fact that from this angle our school would have a great name in the world if we set ourselves to do a lot of research work. . . . I have never felt that I could conscientiously and fairly, in view of the interest of the school, take a position that we would do no research work, but in a way I have looked upon this much the same . . . as I have looked upon accrediting with these worldly organizations. I have felt that it would undoubtedly be necessary to try to do a little along this line in order to keep the peace and keep our school

from getting into trouble with the men who are at the helm of things medical in the United States. Nevertheless, in my soul I have had very little regard and fondness for this thing. . . .

"First of all, we have everything that we can do to struggle along and keep the school going. We have practically no money to spend except that which we wring from these poor boys in these hard times. To me it has seemed only right that this money should be expended in facilities for them, rather than for highbrow researchers. It should be spent in securing the very best teachers we can find so that these boys and girls can have as good training as it is possible for us in our limited circumstances to give them. Further, it must be recommended that men who make research workers as a rule are wretched schoolteachers. They do not have a sufficient amount of humility or patience to help humble students to understand the elemental things of medicine and its practice. . . . We do not have buildings, money, or equipment to take care of or finance this sort of thing. We are struggling for our very lives."[6]

Having vented clearly enough his personal convictions on the issue of research, Dr. Magan was nonetheless pragmatic enough to accept that the growing demands were not to be wished away. To one of Dr. Zapffe's letters, he replied: "We have already had [the matter] up [for consideration] in our joint faculty meeting and are trying to plan a few good things in the line of research. I think our teachers are getting the idea of what research work is all about and are beginning to get the fact into their noodles that it is something they must initiate themselves."

And to the Harveian Society, Dr. Magan wrote: "I trust that as long as God shall give me breath and strength that I may humbly and in the fear of God labor . . . to better the school scientifically and materially."

Looking back retrospectively, one can perhaps at least understand the views of those on either side of the research debate that occurred at CME in the 1930s. Even then, it was becoming accepted wisdom that a part of the task for medical schools was to do scientific research that would push forward the frontiers of human and medical knowledge—to discover better ways

Early graduation ceremonies took place in the Loma Linda Bowl—an outdoor amphitheater seating about 1,500 people, built in 1924 just east of the Sanitarium. In March of 1935 an acoustic shell and orchestra pit were added. Commencement exercises, such as these in 1938 (left) and 1939 (below) were held at the Bowl until 1950. It was razed in 1964.

Some of the men and women who helped build the College of Medical Evangelists in the decade of the 1930s.

E. H. Risley
Dean, School of Medicine

Martha Borg
Director, School of Nursing

Cyril B. Courville
Neuropsychiatry

Newton G. Evans
Dean, School of Medicine

W. E. Macpherson
Dean, School of Medicine

Oran I. Cutler
Pathology

Marian Bowers
Nursing

Alfred Shryock
Anatomy

Harold Shryock
Anatomy

Taylor G. Bunch
Religion

D. D. Comstock
Medicine

Roger W. Barnes
Urology

Benton N. Colver
Otolaryngology

of improving health, preventing disease, and extending life. And today, Loma Linda's reputation as a leader in original medical-scientific research is secure and known across the nation and around the world.

But when—as was true during the years of the Great Depression—an institution's most urgent priority is survival itself, being pressured to dilute this primary focus and assume the expenses of an additional new enterprise might well have seemed almost one burden too many.

Loma Linda's parent denomination was certainly cool to the idea of allocating funds for research—it struggled to support its work worldwide. And these were not years when either government or private sector sources were eager to underwrite research—especially at a small medical college with limited personnel, equipment, and buildings.

If the research issue posed its challenges to CME's administration, another difficulty was even more serious, as it potentially placed the very existence of the school in jeopardy. In the early thirties, a strong wind of opposition to accreditation blew through the Adventist denomination. At its 1935 annual council, the church's General Conference decided that among its institutions of higher education, only two—Pacific Union College in California and Emmanual Missionary College in Michigan—were to be accredited. Dr. Magan pleaded in vain with the

A sign at the intersection of Anderson Street and Colton Avenue (circa 1932) directed patients and visitors to the Loma Linda Sanitarium and Hospital. Colton Avenue later was renamed Highway 99, and when Interstate 10 opened nearby in 1962, it became Redlands Boulevard.

Council delegates to use "good judgment" and bring "a sound mind" to bear on the question.

Prior to the 1936 annual fall meeting of the American Medical Association's Council on Medical Education—the same entity that had in earlier years steadily improved CME's rating from "C" to "A"—two visitors came to Los Angeles and plied Dr. Magan with questions for four hours, "with all the speed and accuracy of machine-gun fire." After this meeting with Herman Weiskotten, MD, dean of the School of Medicine at Syracuse University, and U.S. Surgeon General M. W.

Ireland, MD. Dr. Magan quipped that he had thought of asking the Lord to do to his two visitors what He had promised to do to the prophet Ezekiel: "And I will make thy tongue cleave to the roof of thy mouth."[7]

Upon inspecting the school, Drs. Weiskotten and Ireland were both congenial and liberal with their praise. Nonetheless, when the Council on Medical Education subsequently met, CME's medical school was placed on probation. If it did not act on certain requirements, it would lose the accreditation it had worked so hard in earlier years to achieve.

Few, however, realized what had happened—the probationary status was confidential and only a few school administrators knew of it. Among the demands in Dr. Weiskotten's report of the inspection were that CME reapportion the work of the two medical deans at Loma Linda and Los Angeles—and that research be undertaken.

The two medical deans at the time were Walter E. Macpherson, MD, a 1924 CME graduate who assumed leadership of the Loma Linda division in 1935—and Edward Risley, MD, who was transferred from Loma Linda to be dean of the Los Angeles division.

The school's administrators made a serious effort to comply with these demands, and four years later in 1940, the probation would be lifted. Again, only the few who

knew of the earlier probationary status for CME realized it had emerged from it. Only they knew the danger through which CME had passed and how close it had come to losing its accreditation altogether.

It would not be until the 1964 publication of Merlin L. Neff's *For God and CME*—the biography of Percy T. Magan—that the story of CME's four-year probation became public.

As the difficult decade of the 1930s closed, CME had not only survived a series of crises just as daunting as any it had encountered in its earliest years, but it had grown in size and strength. At Loma Linda, two parallel rows of new science buildings now faced each other across a wide, grassy campus mall—and in Los Angeles, White Memorial Hospital, which began as a storefront clinic some twenty-five years earlier, was now a fully equipped city hospital of 180 beds.

Each year, CME graduated up to a hundred or more new physicians, forty to fifty new nurses, and five to ten dietitians. Of these, a significant number fanned out across the nation and around the globe to staff various medical missionary outposts. The word *evangelists* in CME's name seemed clearly enough to be both apt and justified.

On the cusp of yet another decade, would that Loma Linda and its institutions

could now dispense with so many struggles to survive—so many threats to existence—and focus fully on growth and service. But as all truly great institutions learn, in the very struggle to overcome threats and challenges lies the secret to strength and success. The combination of unmistakable divine providence and human dedication and commitment had by now brought Loma Linda from little more than a dream and a shoestring to a thriving two-campus center of education and healing.

But the arrival of the 1940s would not bring peace or ease for Loma Linda, the United States, or the world. Soon enough, the entire planet would convulse in the throes of conflict and death. Yet even as human evil seemed to sweep the planet, the light of hope and healing continued to shine brightly from the Hill Beautiful.

NOTES:

1. CME Board of Trustees *Minutes*, September 4, 1933, p. 5.

2. Op cit., May 3, 1934, p. 2.

3. Loma Linda University Heritage Room, DF.190.1.

4. CME Board of Trustees *Minutes*, October 4, 1934, p. 6.

5. Richard Utt, *From Vision to Reality*, Loma Linda University, 1980, p. 89.

6. Ibid., pp. 90, 91.

7. Ezekiel 3:26.

PHOTO ALBUM

RIGHT: SHRYOCK HALL, ONE OF THREE NEW INSTRUCTIONAL BUILDINGS
COMPLETED IN 1936.

BELOW: THE YEAR 1937 BROUGHT THE NEW CAMPUS HILL CHURCH TO THE
CAMPUS.

BELOW RIGHT: UNIT 300 OF LOMA LINDA SANITARIUM AND HOSPITAL, CIRCA
MID-1930S.

THE IMPOSSIBLE DREAM: RAILWAY TO THE MOON

BELOW: THE WOMEN'S RESIDENCE HALL AT WHITE MEMORIAL HOSPITAL.

BELOW RIGHT: PATIENTS IN THE WAITING ROOM AT WHITE MEMORIAL.

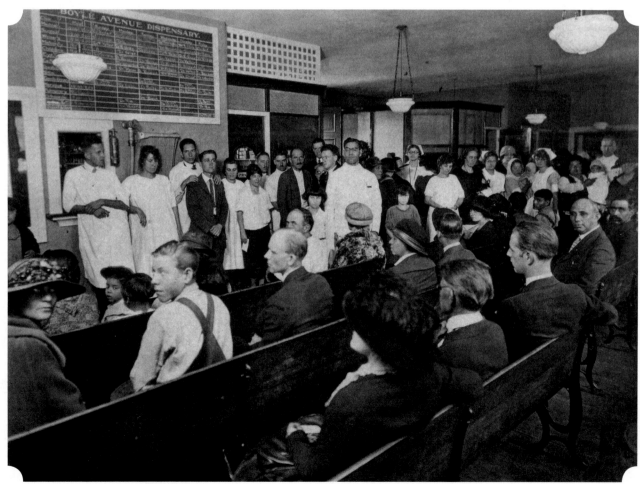

BELOW: SURGERY SUITE AT WHITE MEMORIAL HOSPITAL, CIRCA LATE 1930S.

BELOW RIGHT: WHITE MEMORIAL NURSERY, 1937. BY LOMA LINDA'S CENTENNIAL, ANY OF THESE BABIES STILL LIVING WOULD BE APPROACHING 70 YEARS OF AGE!

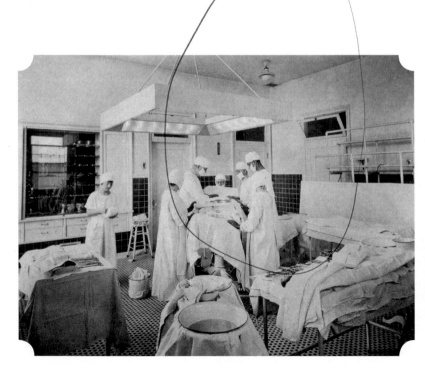

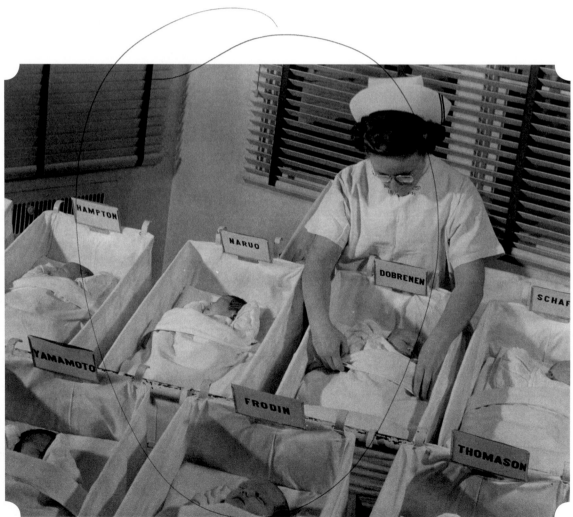

THE IMPOSSIBLE DREAM: RAILWAY TO THE MOON

Below left: White Memorial Hospital admitting area, with the pharmacy in the background.

Below right: As the decade of the 1930s ended, construction began on a new White Memorial Hospital.

The Tides of War

THE IMPACT OF THE WAR ON THE TWO CAMPUSES WAS MOST EMPHATICALLY NOT ONE-WAY. FOR THE TIDES OF WAR THAT REACHED CME WERE ANSWERED BY ITS OWN OUTGOING TIDES OF SERVICE, SACRIFICE, AND PATRIOTISM. THE WAR LEFT ITS MARK ON LOMA LINDA'S TWO CAMPUSES. BUT LOMA LINDA ALSO LEFT ITS MARK ON THE WORLD AT WAR.

In an episode of the 1960s TV series *Star Trek,* Captain James T. Kirk of the starship *Enterprise* and his crew travel back in time to pre–World War II America. Kirk falls in love with a young woman who, as determined by science officer Spock, is destined to directly affect the course of the immediate future. She will either go on to lead a successful pacifist movement in the United States that will delay its entry into the conflict, thus making it possible for Nazi Germany to win the war—or she will die in a traffic accident.

One evening, Kirk, Spock, and Dr. McCoy meet on a town sidewalk. Across the street, the young woman sees them and begins to cross over to meet with them, but she doesn't see the large truck speeding toward her. Dr. McCoy rushes to push her clear of danger, but Kirk—knowing the outcome should she live—restrains Dr. McCoy, and the young woman dies.

A recurring conundrum of time travel stories centers on what happens when a person who travels back in time interferes with an event, thereby setting in motion a "ripple effect" of changes that can amplify till it changes the entire outcome of history.

Whatever the dilemmas posed by science fiction writers, it is no theory that every person alive influences others. Sometimes that influence is only slight or temporary—sometimes it is lasting and profound. Every one of us knows of people whose influence on us has been powerful, perhaps changing the entire course of our lives. No one is an island. We all affect those around us.

What is true of people is also true of institutions. Imagine the countless lives that have been affected throughout the century of Loma Linda's history. At least try to imagine how those lives might have been different had Loma Linda never existed.

Though its full impact on the world around it may never be fully known till seen looking back from the perspective of eternity, Loma Linda's hundred-year existence has incontrovertibly changed its local area, its nation, and its world for the better.

Yet the reverse is also true. For through its first ten decades, the world, the nation, and the local area have also affected Loma Linda. Never was this more true than during the decade of the 1940s, when the incoming tides of a world at

Left: Army trainees line up outside the new men's dormitory, Daniells Hall, circa 1943.

Daniells Hall (right), the new men's residence, was completed in 1941 and named for former Seventh-day Adventist General Conference President A.G. Daniells (above).

war spilled across the Loma Linda campuses—to be answered by outgoing tides of service, sacrifice, and patriotism.

For the second time in its still-young existence, the College of Medical Evangelists was forced to confront and examine its relationship to its nation during a time of war. This time, though, the college was far stronger than it had been a little more than twenty years earlier when it had fought for its very survival, faced with the prospect of losing most of its male students to the World War I draft. Now the school was sufficiently developed to position it to make a significant and highly valued contribution to the new war effort. That contribution, however, it was prepared to make only within the confines of its own principles—chief among them, noncombatancy.

During the first war, various medical schools across the country entered agreements with the Office of the U.S. Surgeon General to form their own military hospital units. Members of the teaching staff at these schools held reserve commissions in the U.S. Army.

Soon after the close of World War I, some of the younger physicians at CME proposed that as a gesture of cooperation and preparedness with the United States government, the college organize a Seventh-day Adventist–staffed, standby military hospital. While this entity would exist during peacetime as little more than a paper organization, it would be ready for immediate activation in the event of another conflict.[1]

Percy T. Magan, MD, at the time dean of the School of Medicine, was so favorably impressed with the idea that he approached officers of the Ninth Corps Area of the U.S. Army in San Francisco and negotiated with them to establish the 47th General Hospital of the U.S. Army Medical Corps. This designation was a carry-over from an army hospital that had existed during World War I and rendered outstanding service in France. After the war, the 47th was demobilized in San Francisco in 1919.[2]

Under auspices of the army, CME officially organized the 47th General Hospital in 1926, with President Newton Evans, MD, as its first commanding officer, with the rank of lieutenant colonel in the Reserves. Not long after, Cyril B. Courville, MD, a member of the class of 1925, succeeded Dr. Evans as commander—a position he would retain until 1943. Dr. Courville's consistent devotion to the hospital helped build it into a highly efficient unit with knowledgeable reserve officers in each department.

The staff of the 47th included physicians, nurses, administrative officers, and physical therapists. The organization was entirely military, with staff carrying ranks from lieutenant to colonel. In its medical and surgical services, it adhered both to accepted hospital practices and U.S. Army regulations. Its reserve officers spent a few days each year in active military training.

With respect to military service, Dr.

Courville and his associates felt a responsibility not only to CME's School of Medicine but also to the Seventh-day Adventist denomination at large. They envisioned some form of training for young Adventist men across the country not otherwise medically oriented so that, in the event of war, their services would be available as noncombatant "medics" rather than as combat soldiers. This led to the organization of the Medical Cadet Corps (MCC)—a paramilitary training program mirroring the active U.S. military in its structure. Officers of CME's 47th General Hospital participated in the training of these young men, and the program quickly attracted favorable attention and support both from Church members and the U.S. Surgeon General's office. At first operating only at CME's Los Angeles campus, in 1939 a new MCC unit was also established on the Loma Linda campus. MCC units for training Adventist young men were thereafter developed in several locations across the country, and through this training, these youth were prepared to offer their country a much-needed military service consistent with the noncombatancy policy of their Church.

On August 11, 1941, leaders of the Seventh-day Adventist Church, with General Conference president J. L. McElhany presiding, met at CME's Los Angeles campus for some concentrated study of the

An aerial view of the basic sciences quadrangle (circa 1942), soon after Daniells Hall (at the top of the photo) was added. Today this space is occupied by the Alumni Hall for Basic Sciences.

War Department

Office of the Surgeon General

Certificate of Appreciation

This Certificate Is Presented To

College of Medical Evangelists

In appreciation of its outstanding contribution to the successful prosecution of World War II. By its patriotic endeavor it unselfishly sponsored, organized and staffed the 47th General Hospital thereby dedicating itself unsparingly to the service of its country. By its experience and skill it reduced the mortality of our troops to a record unequaled by any nation in the annals of war. By its valor it won the admiration and respect of all who were entrusted to its care. The service, cooperation and loyalty of this unit, under circumstances never before encountered in the long history of conflicts is worthy of the highest praise and its achievments are an inspiration to all.

Major General, The Surgeon General

school's relation to the war now spreading across the globe. Some expressed concern over excessive entanglement between the Church and the military. But the 47th General Hospital had existed through seventeen years of peace, and a decision was reached that it would continue. The college could hardly abandon its commitment now that America seemed threatened with early involvement in a second world war.[3]

Another concern focused on whether CME faculty should accept military commissions. Ultimately, this decision was left to each teacher to make in consultation with his own conscience.

In the event of wartime, it was assumed that Dr. Courville would command the activated 47th General Hospital. On June 30, 1943, that time arrived, and the dormant 47th was activated at Hammon General Hospital in Modesto, California. But Dr. Courville was regrettably disqualified from his command for health reasons. Instead, the commandant would be colonel Ben E. Grant, MD, a 1920 CME graduate who had been serving as chief of medical services at Barnes General Hospital in Vancouver, Washington.[4]

All but one of the officers of the 47th General Hospital were Adventists, and about sixty of these were CME graduates. Nurses also participated, led by first lieutenant Wealthy E. Lindsay, a 1935 graduate of CME's nursing program. Thirty of the 47th General's nurses were Seventh-day Adventists. But only a few of the enlisted men and women on the staff were Adventists.[5]

In 1944, the *S.S. West Point* transported the 47th General Hospital to the South Pacific, where CME officers helped construct a military facility at Milne Bay on the southern tip of New Guinea. In May of 1945, the 47th marked its first anniversary of foreign service. But by that time, the unit was already beginning to break up, as the U.S. Army transferred medical officers and enlisted personnel to shifting fronts in other theaters of the war.

Even before the United States entered World War II, the government had already called most medical reserve officers to active duty. Since there were few replacements left from which to draw, many physicians—including younger medical school faculty members—were being drafted.

This threatened to seriously weaken the training of physicians for the future. The American Medical Association worked out an arrangement with the government for screening the names of faculty members considered essential by their schools. These teachers would be exempted from the draft. With few exceptions, medical schools were thus permitted to retain their highest-priority teachers.

During World War II, the United States

This banner reflects CME's sense of patriotism and solidarity with the national war effort.

War Department virtually commandeered America's medical schools. In part, this was to increase the number of physicians available for the war effort. But it was also in part to ensure that young men would not seek to escape induction into military service by taking a professed interest in studying medicine.

To assure itself of a continuous and adequate supply of young physicians to serve as medical officers in the U.S. military, the War Department on July 1, 1943, instituted its "accelerated program" for medical students.

In cooperation with this program, CME eliminated summer vacations and started classes every nine months. It compressed its four-year curriculum into three years. As a result, two classes were graduated in 1944. In addition, medical students would wear military uniforms and would receive military training as part of their medical studies.

But another provision of the military's proactive effort to assure a sufficient ongoing supply of new physicians for the war effort created a looming crisis for CME. The military itself assumed the right to select promising college students for medical training. This took the selection process out of the hands of the schools of medicine. Each school was assigned a quota—an assigned number—of new freshmen medical students.

This provision created consternation for CME's medical school administrators. Founded by the Seventh-day Adventist Church, CME operated in harmony with the unique principles of the denomination, including such Christian ideals as foregoing the use of alcohol and tobacco, advocating vegetarianism, and honoring the seventh-day Sabbath by holding no classes on that day. The prospect that CME could soon become a training center for students, the majority of whom would be ignorant of or unprepared to harmonize with those ideals, was deeply unsettling.

And what of Seventh-day Adventist young men who would normally seek medical training such as CME was ordained to provide? Suppose that under this new provision, some of them should be assigned to other, totally secular schools of medicine? They would find themselves having to forfeit either their religious convictions regarding the Sabbath, or the opportunity of becoming a physician.

Faced with this complication, the CME Board of Trustees sent President Walter E. Macpherson, MD to Washington, D.C. And evidence seems convincing that divine providence had already anticipated this emergency and had been preparing the way to meet it. In Washington, Dr. Macpherson's first stop was to visit with one of his own CME classmates—Walter S. Jensen, MD (class of 1924), who now served as a colonel in the U.S. Air Corps. Dr. Jensen could readily understand CME's plight, but he did not have the authority to mold military policies relating to medical schools. Nonetheless, he could open doors for Dr. Macpherson, and arranged for CME's president to see Colonel F. M. Fitz in the Surgeon General's office. Colonel Fitz was very receptive to Dr. Macpherson's appeal and said, "I will refer you to Colonel White, who is in charge of drafting plans for assignments to medical schools. At last, Dr. Macpherson had reached the man who did have the authority to get things done on CME's behalf.

What happened next, some might see as simple coincidence. Those familiar with the repeated evidences of divine involvement through the years in times of crisis at Loma Linda would see it as yet another such providential intervention.

As Dr. Macpherson presented CME's dilemma to Colonel White, a soldier entered his office, saluted, and delivered a sealed envelope to the colonel. Colonel White returned the soldier's salute, accepted the envelope, and dismissed the courier. Momentarily, he interrupted his conversation with Dr. Macpherson to open the envelope, and discovered to his surprise and delight that he had just been promoted to the rank of brigadier general.

Dr. Macpherson remained convinced after that meeting that the now General White's elation at that moment spilled over into the matter under discussion and prompted from him a spontaneous promise: "I will keep you folks in mind." And that, he did. CME would become the only school of medicine in America allowed to choose its own students, starting with Seventh-day Adventists about to be assigned to other schools.

As yet another part of its program to take a more aggressive stance in order to ensure a steady supply of physicians for the military, the U.S. War Department stationed on each medical school campus across the country a small detachment of Army personnel who would conduct drills and related activities in order to assure that, upon completion of their studies, new physicians would be able at once to function as medical officers in the military.

In the summer of 1943, the CME Board of Trustees approved the installation of Army Specialized Training Program (ASTP) Number 3934 on both CME campuses. On September 15, CME dedicated its Loma Linda unit, complete with a military headquarters in the new men's dormitory. As a symbol of co-authority, the major in charge of the detachment of two lieutenants and four enlisted men requested that he have an office next to Dean Harold Shryock's office in

the pathology building. At the time, Dr. Shryock was acting dean of the Loma Linda division of CME.

The relationship was to be one of "host" and "guest"—CME acting as host, and the army unit as the guest. At times, however, this relationship was less than peaceful, as the "guest" would try to dominate the "host." The first army officer commanding the detachment incorrectly presumed that he also commanded campus facilities. The school did what it could to make

certain compromises in class scheduling and lab sessions in order to accommodate marching drills, gas mask drills, and the like—and this helped ease tensions. Several months later, the military promoted the officer in charge and replaced him with a new commandant who cooperated with CME's administrators and honored the religious convictions he encountered on the campus.

The cooperative effort between the U.S. Army and the noncombatant Church

worked surprisingly well. Army representatives proved understanding and diplomatic, complying personally with CME's prohibitions on smoking and drinking and even honoring its preference for a vegetarian diet. In return, the Adventists took seriously their responsibilities and privileges as Christians and citizens in a time of war. Occasions of disputed authority were few and not disruptive.

The arrangement had its financial benefits to the eligible medical students. The U.S. military issued their uniforms and paid tuition and a financial stipend. Participants in the program enjoyed discounts on merchandise at the "PX" as well as the prospect of future veterans' benefits. Some faculty even observed that the students fared better financially than did their teachers. At the conclusion of their training, the new physicians became commissioned officers. Some administrators—and doubtless not a few students—considered the highly unusual circumstances to be providential.

By the end of World War II in mid-1945, the cadre of military officers at CME had endeared themselves to the school by their cooperation and their sympathetic attitudes. "We missed them once they had departed," Harold Shryock, MD, would later write.[6] CME had matriculated 160 students in four classes spread across three years. Everyone was tired—both students

and faculty—from the accelerated program with no vacations and no letup in the strenuous combination of medical and military training.

During the war, more than 500 CME alumni performed military service for their country, including many physicians who served outside the auspices of the 47th General Hospital. Many received the Silver Star, the Bronze Star, the Legion of Merit, and the Citation for Meritorious Achievement. CME's graduates attracted favorable attention wherever they went because of the quality of the service they rendered. Some became prisoners of war. And some died in service to their country.

Rather than to catalog the many who made the ultimate sacrifice, perhaps one can be cited as representative. A second lieutenant in the Navy's Medical Corps, Edward Curtin, MD (CME class of 1941), was assigned to a squadron of PT boats operating in the vicinity of New Britain. Though not customary that a squadron medical officer accompany boats on patrol, Lieutenant Curtin thought his services might most be needed there. So he voluntarily and repeatedly participated in hazardous missions in areas of intense combat activity.

On the morning of March 27, 1944, Edward Curtin was mortally wounded when his boat became the target of an aerial bombing and strafing attack. Even

E. E. Cossentine (standing at right in photo to left), president of La Sierra College for twelve years, awarded many hundreds of diplomas to graduates.

as he lay dying, however, he directed the care of others who had been injured and insisted that they be given aid first. For his bravery in the line of duty, he was posthumously awarded the Navy and Marine Corps medal. His citation read,

in part: "By his loyal spirit of self sacrifice and courageous devotion to duty, he upheld the highest traditions of the U.S. Naval Service. He gallantly gave his life for his country."[7]

With the end of the war, CME was able

not only to restore its normal four-year curriculum and summer vacations but to focus its attention once again on urgent matters on its own two campuses.

For several years, the schools of nursing on both CME campuses had been upgrading their academic and clinical programs under the direction of Ethel Walder, RN, and Catherine Graf, RN, in Loma Linda—and Mary Monteith, RN, and Maxine Atteberry, RN, MS, in Los Angeles. Now in 1945, CME president Macpherson and the administrators of the two schools of nursing created plans to unify the two programs.

In 1948, the Board of Trustees approved the formation of a single school of nursing to operate on both campuses, to be administered by one dean, and to offer the bachelor of science degree.

The following year, new CME president George T. Harding III announced the launching of the new unified school, with Kathryn Jensen Nelson serving as its first dean.

New paramedical courses were also started during the 1940s. In 1941, with Fred B. Moor, MD, as medical director, a new physical therapy program began. The same year, a radiology program began, directed by Walter L. Stilson, MD. In 1948, the School of Tropical and Preventive Medicine opened under the direction of Harold N. Mozar, MD. Through the years, this School would broaden in scope

and grow in size to become the School of Public Health.

August 1949 saw the completion of a new seventy-bed addition to Loma Linda Sanitarium and Hospital, complete with six operating rooms. This brought the hospital bed capacity on the two campuses to a total of 356.

During most of the decade, the steady hand at the helm of CME was that of Walter E. Macpherson, MD, who served as president from 1942 to 1948. He would return as president for another term in the 1950s.

A 1924 CME graduate, Dr. Macpherson served successively as dean of the Loma Linda and Los Angeles divisons of the School of Medicine between 1935 and 1942—and again of those two divisions from 1954 to 1962. He was universally esteemed as a physician, an administrator, and as a kindly Christian gentleman.[8]

During the 1940s, La Sierra College south of Riverside—later to join its destiny to that of Loma Linda—was writing its own story through the war years. During World War II, the U.S. Navy had for a time shown an interest in possibly purchasing the La Sierra campus for military purposes. Fortunately, that never happened.

La Sierra may have escaped becoming a military installation, but the war did take its toll nonetheless. Enrollment slowed, and even its parent Church—in the midst of the prevailing uncertainty—took actions with the effect of simply maintaining rather than moving forward. After completion of a new cafeteria in 1941, further construction was interrupted for five years.

With the arrival of peacetime, the Church authorized the school to move forward again toward obtaining full college status. Enrollment, too, rebounded. Standing at 480 in 1940, by the beginning of the 1947-1948 school year, it had risen to 919.

Fulton Memorial Library (today the administration building) was completed in 1946—and the College Church in 1947. Before the end of the decade, construction was completed on Ambs Hall (industrial arts), Palmer Hall (biology and chemistry), and additions to the men's and women's residence halls.

In 1944, La Sierra granted its first baccalaureate degree, and in December of that year received accreditation from the Northwest Association of Secondary and High Schools as a full, four-year college.[9]

During the 1940s, the incoming tides of a world at war did indeed race across the planet to flood over even the campuses of CME at Loma Linda and Los Angeles. The college was dramatically affected. The hospital was affected. Every faculty member and student was affected.

But the impact of the world's war on the two campuses in Southern California was most emphatically not one-way. For the tides of war that reached CME were answered by its own outgoing tides of service, sacrifice, and patriotism. The war left its mark on Loma Linda's two campuses. But Loma Linda also left its mark on the world at war.

That would not end when the guns fell silent. The influence of the center for hope and healing that touched the lives of thousands during World War II would expand to circle the earth. During the 1940s, Loma Linda helped prove that evil can indeed be overcome with good. That proof would become even more evident as the new decade of the 1950s dawned.

NOTES:

1. Harold Shryock, MD. in *Diamond Memories*, p. 104.

2. Ibid.

3. Richard Utt, *From Vision to Reality*, p. 112.

4. Op cit., *Diamond Memories*.

5. *From Vision to Reality*, p. 115.

6. *Diamond Memories*, pp. 107, 108.

7. Ibid., p. 105.

8. *From Vision to Reality*, pp. 118-120.

9. Ibid., pp. 120, 121.

PHOTO ALBUM

RIGHT: THE 47TH GENERAL
HOSPITAL, ENTIRELY MILITARY
IN STRUCTURE, ADHERED
BOTH TO ACCEPTED HOSPITAL
PRACTICES AND U.S. ARMY
REGULATIONS.

THE IMPOSSIBLE DREAM: RAILWAY TO THE MOON

THROUGH BOTH THE 47TH GENERAL HOSPITAL AND THE ARMY SPECIALIZED TRAINING PROGRAM, CME STUDENTS ACTIVELY CONTRIBUTED TO THE WAR EFFORT, SERVING WITH VALOR AND DISTINCTION. ALONG WITH SO MANY OTHERS, SOME OF CME'S STUDENTS PAID THE ULTIMATE PRICE IN DEFENSE OF FREEDOM.

RIGHT: CYRIL B. COURVILLE, MD (LEFT FOREGROUND OF PHOTO), A MEMBER OF THE CLASS OF 1925, SERVED UNTIL 1943 AS THE 47TH'S SECOND COMMANDER.

BELOW: DAVID B. HINSHAW, MD, LATER TO BE THE DEAN OF LOMA LINDA'S SCHOOL OF MEDICINE, WAS AMONG THOSE WHO SERVED IN THE 47TH GENERAL HOSPITAL.

BELOW RIGHT: A MEDICAL CADET CORPS CLASS PRACTICES SPLINTING.

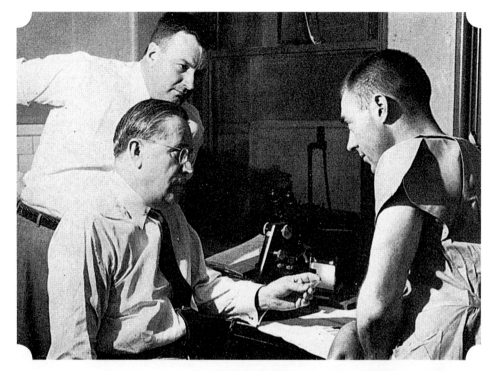

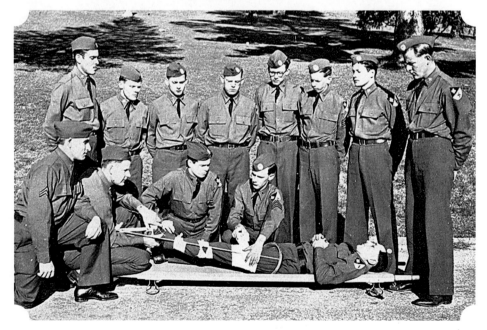

THE IMPOSSIBLE DREAM: RAILWAY TO THE MOON

BELOW: LOMA LINDA SANITARIUM AND HOSPITAL ON THE
HILL AS IT APPEARED IN 1946.

ONE GIANT LEAP

IN 1949, M. WEBSTER PRINCE, DDS, PRESENTED A PAPER STRESSING THE NEED TO FORGE AHEAD AND TAKE IMMEDIATE STEPS TOWARD FOUNDING AN ADVENTIST SCHOOL OF DENTISTRY. A RISING CHORUS OF OTHER VOICES JOINED IN CALLING FOR THE SCHOOL'S ESTABLISHMENT.

Predicting the future—unless you truly possess a divinely bestowed prophetic gift—is risky business. Consider these:

"This 'telephone' has too many shortcomings to be seriously considered as a means of communication. The device is inherently of no value to us"—Western Union internal memo, 1876.

"Everything that can be invented has been invented"—Charles H. Duell, commissioner, U.S. Office of Patents, 1899.

"Louis Pasteur's theory of germs is ridiculous fiction"—Pierre Pachet, professor of physiology at the University of Toulouse, 1872.

"A cookie store is a bad idea. Besides, the market research reports say America likes crispy cookies, not soft and chewy cookies like you make"—Response to Debbi Fields' idea of starting Mrs. Fields' Cookies.

"I think there is a world market for maybe five computers"—Thomas Watson, chair of IBM, 1943.

And let us not forget the prediction of the good Dr. John Harvey Kellogg, who, back in Loma Linda's earliest days, opined that building a medical college there would be *"as impossible as to build a railway to the moon."*

But as the decade of the 1950s dawned, the College of Medical Evangelists stood near the Hill Beautiful—real, alive, and thriving.

And by the end of the next decade, even the "railway to the moon" had been built— albeit without laying a single track. On that amazing July day in 1969, Neil Armstrong would place the first human footprint on the lunar surface and utter those memorable words, "That's one small step for man—one giant leap for mankind."

Loma Linda's history, decade by decade, was composed of both an abundance of small steps and occasional giant leaps. One such giant leap forward occurred in the 1950s with the establishment of the School of Dentistry.

The idea of a Seventh-day Adventist school of dentistry dated back to Loma Linda's earliest years. In fact, the original Articles of Incorporation for the College of Medical Evangelists in 1910 authorized it to grant degrees not only in medicine and nursing but in dentistry as well. But the idea would need till the decade of the 1950s to see reality.

In June of 1914, Wells Ruble, MD, the president of CME, wrote his thoughts on the idea of a dental school in a letter to the man who would later that year succeed him as president—Newton Evans, MD.

Left: Present-day view of Prince Hall—the School of Dentistry building dedicated in 1955.

As construction moved forward on the new School of Dentistry building, hopes and dreams nurtured for decades reached fruition.

"We have been thinking some, Dr. Evans, of starting a course in dentistry. I have investigated this and find that the first two years are almost identical with the first two years of the medical course. The time required for the course is three years. We are in need of a dentist in connection with the Sanitarium [at Loma Linda], then, too, we could largely have the clinical work in connection with the Dispensary in the city [Los Angeles]. What would you think of this plan? We do not want to take on more than we can handle. . ."[1]

Looming ahead unseen on time's horizon in 1914 were struggles to achieve accreditation for CME, two world wars, and a worldwide depression. Taking on the launching of a school of dentistry during those years might well indeed have been more than CME could have handled.

But the possibility provided for in CME's founding documents and the idea nurtured in the vision of its early leaders was not destined to lie endlessly dormant.

In 1932, R. G. Hosking, DDS, an Adventist dentist in San Francisco, believed—along with some other interested dentists and prospective dental students—that the time had arrived when CME should have its own school of dentistry.

But these were the Great Depression years, let us not forget, and in one of his letters, CME president Percy T. Magan, MD—though himself a man of great

On September 1, 1955, the new dental school building opened its doors to faculty and students.

Outdoor dedication ceremonies for the new School of Dentistry building.

CME still did not have a green light to launch its own dental school, but this definitely represented an interim step forward.

Across the nation, dentistry was increasingly gaining prominence as a profession, and many young Adventists aspired to become dentists. But nearly all dental schools of that era routinely scheduled both classes and examinations on Saturdays. Adventist students who attended such schools were obliged to petition for exams on other days, and this led to resentment among the teaching staff, as they had to provide special makeup sessions. For this reason, it became increasingly difficult for Adventist students to be granted admission to dental schools.

So as a follow-through on the 1932 autumn council recommendation, two Adventist dentists, also brothers, carried out this directive. J. Russell and Gerald A. Mitchell successfully persuaded the Atlanta-Southern Dental School in Atlanta, to excuse Seventh-day Adventist students who would attend there from Saturday classes or tests. Atlanta-Southern accepted up to ten Adventist dental students annually. A good number of other Adventist dental students succeeded in having their day of worship honored while attending such schools as the College of Physicians and Surgeons, a proprietary school in San Francisco, California.

The General Conference department

vision—nonetheless voiced his reservations:

"This matter has been up time and time again. The difficulty is that a dental school is an enormously expensive affair to build, equip, and start. . . . We could manage a school all right if we had the money, but the expense is a very great item."[2]

Also in 1932, however, the possibility of starting a dental school was considered by the General Conference committee of the Seventh-day Adventist Church. A smaller committee was appointed to study the question and bring in recommendations. The church's autumn council later that year acted on this committee's work, recommending that for the time being, arrangements be made with one or more existing dental schools for Adventist students to take their professional training there, while being granted the privilege of observing the seventh-day Sabbath.

of education provided a home near the Atlanta school and assigned a couple to be "house parents" for the Adventist students. The first group to graduate under this arrangement was the eight-member class of 1938.

The Mitchells hoped that the new Adventist dentists emerging from Atlanta-Southern would become a nucleus of professionals who would in time prevail on CME and Adventist Church leadership to build and operate a dental school. This hope was well placed, as members of that first graduating class would in 1943 found the National Association of Seventh-day Adventist Dentists (NASDAD) with the expressed aim of establishing a denominational school of dentistry.

Early in the same year that the first Adventists graduated from Atlanta-Southern, CME commissioned Herbert G. Childs Jr., DDS—a Los Angeles dentist who had in 1935 been hired onto the staff of Loma Linda Sanitarium and Hospital—to prepare a proposal advocating a church-operated dental school.[3]

The resulting report of twenty-four pages included addressing what would be needed to establish a preclinical division at Loma Linda and a clinical division in Los Angeles.

Dr. Childs' brief was well received by the CME Board, which even went so far as to approve eight months of postgraduate

In addition to the new dental school, growth was evident as well elsewhere on the CME campus. Percy T. Magan Hall—the new administration building, was completed in 1953. Left: Magan Hall as it appeared during the 1960s. Below left: A present-day view.

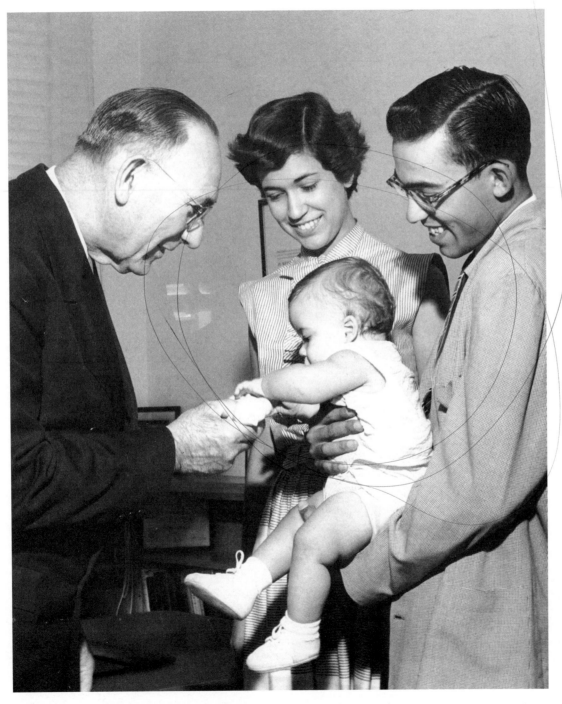

work for Dr. Childs in preparation for his joining the faculty of the proposed school. Nonetheless, they voted in July of 1938 to delay further discussion of the matter until the Church met at its autumn council later that year.

Action wasn't immediately forthcoming. By 1943, CME's administrators still envisioned that, as proposed by Dr. Childs, a dental education program would share basic sciences in Loma Linda with the School of Medicine, while the opening of a dental clinic in Los Angeles would provide the needed clinical experience. Dental patients could be referred from CME's large clinical practice in Los Angeles.

But years of a divided-campus program for the School of Medicine had demonstrated the drawbacks of the two-campus approach. Many, it seemed clear, did not relish the idea of starting yet another divided school. So for yet a while longer, the idea that wouldn't go away languished.

As sometimes happens, though, developments elsewhere would become powerful catalysts for change. After America entered World War II, dental schools in the United States began adopting the policy of accepting only students residing in their geographic regions. In 1943, the American Dental Association took action that all dental schools—many of which had heretofore been operated independently—should be associated with universities. In

THE IMPOSSIBLE DREAM: RAILWAY TO THE MOON

1944, Atlanta-Southern Dental School merged with Emory University. The new administration adopted the growing geographic-region admission policy of other schools and required that its applicants come only from southern states. Again, wherever they applied, Adventist dental students faced Sabbath-keeping difficulties. The need for a Seventh-day Adventist school of dentistry became urgent.

Despite the urgent need, however, for the remainder of the 1940s, progress toward an Adventist dental school resembled the stop-and-go flow of rush-hour traffic that would in later decades become routine on Southern California's freeways.

In 1946, CME's Board appointed a new committee to study the feasibility of a dental school. This committee's report included detailed estimates for start-up costs and annual operating expenses. Loma Linda looked to its parent church to make the necessary capital and operating investments. But in 1947, when the General Conference treasurer's office pointed out the prevailing struggle of the denomination to meet its worldwide financial commitments, further discussion of a dental school was tabled.

By 1949, NASDAD—the Adventist dentists' association—increased the intensity of its efforts toward establishing

a dental school. Twenty-three of its members, in fact, pledged $50,000 as seed money. And that year, M. Webster Prince, DDS, who had helped found NASDAD and now served as its president, presented a paper stressing the need to forge ahead and take immediate steps toward founding an Adventist school of dentistry. A rising chorus of other voices joined in calling for the school's establishment.

In May of 1951, Dr. Prince made yet another powerful appeal for a denominational school of dentistry. In it, he concluded, "No, brethren, we cannot afford to longer delay the decision for this valuable and important help in carrying this Message. We need a dental school! And we need it now! It is your responsibility to decide."[4]

Momentum accelerated, and on October 18, 1951, a committee appointed by General Conference president William H. Branson returned a formal recommendation that the General Conference establish a school of dentistry at Loma Linda. Three days later on October 21, the General Conference unanimously authorized CME to found a school of dentistry and voted $750,000 as its contribution to the project.[5]

The editor of the denomination's official journal applauded the move:

"This means that very shortly our Adventist youth who desire to take up dentistry as a profession can secure their

M. *Webster Prince, DDS, played a leading role in establishing the new School of Dentistry and served as its first dean.*

full training within the walls of an Adventist institution. The reason for creating this school is essentially the same as that for creating our medical college: to keep our young people within the atmosphere and ideals of the Church throughout all their years of training and to provide for the Church professionally trained men and women who can respond to calls from our mission fields and from our medical institutions at home."[6]

Thus was finally approved—after long years of hope and effort and advocacy—the founding of CME's dental school, the forty-third dental school in America, and the sixth west of the Rocky Mountains.

With the road now cleared to move forward, CME's Board met in early 1952 to begin putting together a faculty and curriculum. On January 31 it appointed Dr. Prince to become the first dean of the School of Dentistry.

Dr. M. Webster Prince, so active in the final push toward approval of a new dental school, was a 1910 graduate of the University of Michigan. For forty years, he practiced dentistry in Detroit, distinguishing himself not only as president of the Michigan State Dental Association but as an active leader in various capacities for the American Dental Association (ADA).

At national meetings of the ADA, Dr. Prince met a fellow delegate, Dr. J. Russell Mitchell, who with his brother Gerald had helped in obtaining Sabbath privileges for Adventist students at Atlanta-Southern Dental School in the early 1930s. Not at the time an Adventist, Dr. Prince discovered that Dr. Mitchell was, like himself, an avid fisherman. Dr. Prince accepted Dr. Mitchell's invitations to visit favorite fishing areas, and the two became close friends. As their friendship developed, Dr. Prince learned about Seventh-day Adventists. Dr. Mitchell didn't fish on Sabbath; tists. Dr. Mitchell didn't fish on Sabbath;

he didn't smoke or drink. Because of Dr. Mitchell's positive impression on his life, Dr. Prince eventually became a Seventh-day Adventist himself. Many were convinced that God had providentially chosen Dr. Prince to play a leading and guiding role in the formation of an Adventist dental college.

Sad to say, Dr. J. Russell Mitchell, who with his brother Gerald had done so much on behalf of Adventist students of dentistry and whose influence had led Dr. Prince to become a Seventh-day Adventist, died in 1950 without seeing his dream come true. Upon his death, his brother Gerald picked up his brother's torch, assumed the leadership of NASDAD, and intensified efforts to obtain approval for a new Adventist dental school.

Looking back later on his appointment as dean, Dr. Prince wrote:

"Frankly, in making my decision to accept or refuse, as I looked at the obstacles in the way of success, I was sorely tempted to refuse. But the Lord knows who He had in mind for certain jobs, and He convinced me that this was my job. So here I am, for woe betide the man that refuses the Lord when he is called. Fortunately, I have a faith strong enough to believe that when we do what the Lord wants us to do, we can't fail. So I accepted in faith, and I mean FAITH, with capital letters."[7]

The months ahead were a whirlwind of activity for Dr. Prince as he led in securing a qualified faculty, organizing a curriculum, publishing a bulletin, and preparing admission forms and procedures. In July of 1952, the CME board approved Dr. Prince's choice for assistant dean—W. Ross Stromberg, DDS. Dr. Stromberg led in the process of planning the new building for the School of Dentistry. Two other dentists would join the deans to complete the four-member faculty for the first year: Lloyd Baum, DMD, MSD, and Ralph Steinam, DDS, MS.

On August 26, 1953, forty-three freshman dental students from across the United States—all of them male—enrolled

in the School of Dentistry's first class, and their semester began on August 30. For now, they began their work in the basement of the clinical pathology building behind the Sanitarium on the hill. The dean's office was located a couple of blocks away in the basement of the pathology building on the quadrangle. Until the new building was ready, everyone had to make do with cramped, makeshift quarters.

Members of the first class, after their first meeting with Deans Prince and Stromberg, immediately recognized how these men had ensured that the School's educational program would rest solidly on spiritual values. Charles W. Pettengill, one of the class members, spoke for them in an article published later that year in a Church journal:

"When we walked out, we knew we were glad we had come, and the Christian atmosphere of CME made us realize that

The 1950s also brought construction (above) of a new 200-bed hospital wing to White Memorial Hospital in Los Angeles. Left: Pastor R.R. Figuhr, president of the General Conference of Seventh-day Adventists, wields the spade for groundbreaking. Looking on are W. E. Macpherson, M.D., and A. L. Bietz, PhD.
Above left: E. E. Cossentine, Dr. T. R. Flaiz, Pastor R.R. Figuhr, and Dr. A. L. Bietz.

An aerial view (right) of White Memorial medical complex clustered around the expanded hospital. Then–U.S. vice president Richard M. Nixon (far right) delivered the address at the dedicatory services held March 14, 1955.

we had not erred in waiting for our own dental school."[8]

Assistant Dean Stromberg—now also the new president of NASDAD—proceeded with planning for the new dental building. He presented to the board a full set of architectural plans that envisioned a three-story building, the third floor of which would for the time remain unfinished to allow for future expansion.

But on January 28, 1954—only months after the first dental class had begun—plans for a new School of Dentistry building nearly collapsed. The impact of World War II still rippled through the national economy, and its effects were felt also within the world Adventist Church. Funds for North America were severely limited. Seventh-day Adventist General Conference president and CME Board chair Wil-

liam H. Branson announced to the board that because of this financial stress, construction of the proposed dental building would necessarily have to be delayed—perhaps for as long as five years.

Dean Prince, his faculty, and his students were stunned and dismayed. They had lived for the day when they might occupy proper quarters, with enough elbow room to do their jobs right.

Dr. Prince responded with an eloquent plea, in which he first advised the Board that without the assurance of a permanent building, the American Dental Association would most surely deny accreditation to the new school—rendering worthless the diplomas of the first graduating class.

Discussion continued and various alternate options were proposed. Some on the Board suggested that Quonset huts be provided as temporary quarters for the dental school.

At this point Dr. Prince firmly countered that he had not worked and planned for a full decade, sold his established practice and home in Detroit, and accepted his position as dean only to preside over a Quonset-hut operation.

His words had a profound and immediate impact. Union presidents on the board and Board chair Branson rallied with speeches supporting Dean Prince, and the Board voted to authorize more than $1 million to construct the dental building—some $619,000 for the building itself and almost $428,000 for equipment and furnishings.

Dr. Stromberg's proposed building was scaled back from three stories to two—a reduction of 20,000 square feet of floor space. It was understood that the building would be enlarged later. Architect

The spacious White Memorial Church, part of the medical center complex.

Earl T. Heitschmidt and contractor Larry C. Havstad—a team already known for stretching the CME building dollar—teamed to design and build the new structure.

A little more than a year later, on September 18, 1955, CME dedicated its new School of Dentistry building. The Heitschmidt-Havstad team had brought it to completion under budget. The dedica-tion ceremony was attended by more than a thousand people, and Pastor H. L. Rudy, vice president of the General Conference, delivered the dedicatory address. The dedication became a significant milestone in CME's year-long fiftieth anniversary celebration.

Thus, at the halfway point of Loma Linda's first century, the new dental building was a reality, and shortly after the

dedication, 133 students and twenty faculty members moved into the new facility.

The building, named Prince Hall after Dr. Prince's death in 1969, took its place as an important addition to Loma Linda's campus. Looking back on the day of dedication, Godfrey T. Anderson, PhD, president of CME, wrote in 1961:

"From that day on, the School of Dentistry building, with its active group of faculty and students, has been a campus landmark to which we direct visitors with pride and satisfaction."[9]

A month before the May 23, 1957, ceremonies for the School of Dentistry's first

graduating class, the American Dental Association, after only one visit, took the unusual step of awarding full accreditation to the School. The following year, the CME School of Dentistry became a member of the American Association of Dental Schools.[10]

Before the end of the decade, the Board chose Charles T. Smith, DDS, to succeed Dr. Prince as dean of the dental school. He was given a year—salary and expenses paid—to observe firsthand major United States schools of dentistry and to take classes in educational administration at the University of Michigan in preparation for his new assignment. He assumed his new position in July of 1960.

Soon after its founding, the School of Dentistry leadership matured into a major force in American dental education, and its graduates became widely known as excellent clinicians. Many set up private practices; others answered calls for overseas mission service.

Through the years the School has pioneered and gained recognition for dental procedures now practiced nationwide and around the world. Its outreach has been local, national, and global.

While the story of CME's School of Dentistry might be the defining "giant leap" of the 1950s at Loma Linda, it was by no means the only important development. The decade also saw the completion of

several significant buildings on the campus. In 1951, the Alumni Research Foundation Building was completed. The following year, the Hector Memorial Clinical Laboratory was added to Loma Linda Sanitarium. In 1953, two other new buildings reached completion: the Vernier Radcliffe Memorial Library and Percy T. Magan Hall—housing the offices of academic administration. Meanwhile, in Los Angeles, the north wing of White Memorial Hospital was opened in 1955. In 1960, a new Loma Linda College (now University) Church seating 2,500 opened its doors to worshipers—and the first section of a new

ally be met—bringing Loma Linda to a major milestone in the 1960s.

NOTES:

1. Margaret R. White, "Perseverance for a Profession—Historical Summary of the School of Dentistry," *The Medical Evangelist*, January 1961, p. 14.

2. Percy T. Magan, MD, letter to E. A. Sutherland, M.D., May 29, 1933.

3. Letter from Percy T. Magan, MD, to J. L. McElhaney, April 4, 1938.

4. "Proposal for a Seventh-day Adventist Owned and Operated Dental School," received May 9, 1951.

5. "CME's Dental School Approved," *The Medical Evangelist*, Nov. 1, 1951, p. 1; *CME Alumni Journal*, Oct. 1953, p. 24.

6. Francis D. Nichol, "High Lights of the 1951 Autumn Council," *Review and Herald*, Nov. 15, 1951, p. 1.

7. M. Webster Prince, DDS, *NASDAD Journal*, Summer, 1959, p. 3.

8. Charles W. Pettengill, "School of Dentistry," *The Youth's Instructor*, Nov. 17, 1953.

9. Godfrey T. Anderson, PhD, "Progress Report on Loma Linda University," *Loma Linda University Dentist Magazine*, fall 1962, p. 14.

10. "News Briefs," *The Medical Evangelist*, May 1958, p. 8.

The University Church of Seventh-day Adventists at night.

Kate Lindsay Hall was also occupied by women students.

Three presidents of CME spanned the decade: George T. Harding III from 1948 to 1951; Walter E. Macpherson from 1951 to 1954; and Godfrey T. Anderson from 1954 to 1961.

Along with growth on the Loma Linda campus and in Los Angeles at White Memorial Hospital, the 1950s also brought expanded enrollment, a strengthened faculty, new land acquisition, and a building boom to its nearby sister institution at La Sierra College.

As the decade closed, the College of Medical Evangelists had grown dramatically and become a far more complex organization. An unresolved issue still faced Loma Linda's leaders: the divided campus of the School of Medicine. Frequent reminders from the American Medical Association warned that this arrangement was unsatisfactory and would have to be terminated. Yet after much study by many committees through many years, the issue remained unanswered.

From its earliest days, a hallmark of Loma Linda's growth and success had been its ability to solve problems and overcome obstacles. This challenge too would eventu-

PHOTO ALBUM

LEFT: STUDENT NURSES IN TRAINING, 1954.

BELOW: IN 1958, STUDENT NURSES REFUEL IN THE CAFETERIA.

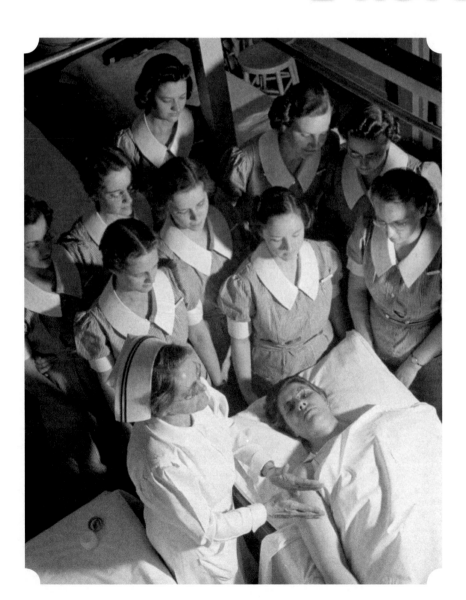

BELOW LEFT: THE NEW LOMA LINDA UNIVERSITY CHURCH DURING CONSTRUCTION.

BELOW RIGHT: THE CONGREGATION AT WORSHIP IN THE NEW SANCTUARY.

BELOW: PEWS FOR THE NEW UNIVERSITY CHURCH ARE PREPARED FOR INSTALLATION.

BELOW RIGHT: UNIVERSITY CHURCH SENIOR PASTOR CHARLES TEEL VISITS A
PATIENT IN THE NEARBY LOMA LINDA UNIVERSITY MEDICAL CENTER.

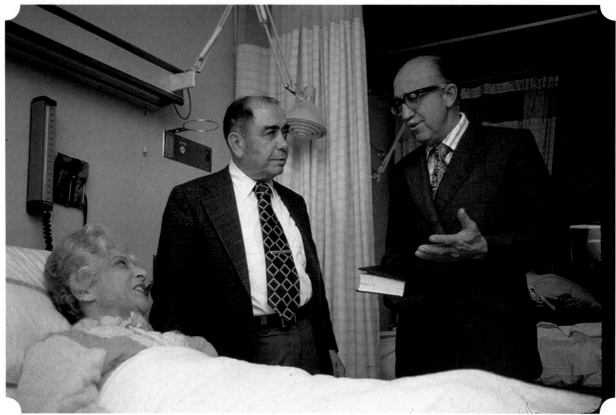

THE IMPOSSIBLE DREAM: RAILWAY TO THE MOON

Right: An aerial view of the Loma Linda campus in the early 1950s. The circular drive—Anderson Street—skirts the western base of the hill on which sat the Sanitarium and Hospital. In the lower center of this photo is the quadrangle. To the right of the quadrangle is the School of Dentistry building.

A New Unity, A New Name, A New Hospital

SEPARATION OF THE TWO CAMPUSES AT LOMA LINDA AND LOS ANGELES—LIKE TWO VINES THAT HAD BECOME TIGHTLY INTERTWINED AS THEY GREW TOGETHER—WAS BOTH DIFFICULT AND PAINFUL. BUT ULTIMATELY, EACH VINE COULD GROW HIGHER AND STRONGER BY FOCUSING ITS GROWTH NEAREST ITS OWN ROOTS.

In the mid-1860s, just before leaving on a trip to revisit his childhood home, Mark Twain wrote: "I shall share the fate of many another longing exile who wanders back to his early home to find gray hairs where he expected youth, graves where he looked for firesides, grief where he had pictured joy—everywhere change! remorseless change where he had heedlessly dreamed that desolating Time had stood still!"

Despite his lamentation about "remorseless change," in 1874 Twain was among the first customers for a brand-new invention produced that year by the Remington Company—a machine that would radically change communication for more than one hundred years—the typewriter.

On December 9, 1874, Mark Twain typed this letter to William Dean Howells (original spelling preserved):

"You needn't answer this; I am only practicing to get three; anothe slip-up there; only practici?ng ti get the hang of the thing. I notice I miss fire & get in a good many unnecessary letters & punctuation marks. I am simply using you for a target to bang at.

Left: Present-day view of the main entrance to Loma Linda University Medical Center, which opened in July of 1967.

Two Loma Linda presidents—Godfrey T. Anderson, PhD (1954–1967, right), and David J. Bieber, EdD (1967–1974, far right)—saw the institution through the many changes of the 1960s.

typewriter, he traded it for a $12 saddle.

Change. Resist it or embrace it—change is inevitable. Once the typewriter revolutionized communication, businesses had a decision to make: stubbornly cling to the old—handwritten documents—and fail, or move forward with the new "technology" and stay current with the times.

Today, typewriters are found primarily in museums or in the hands of nostalgic collectors. New revolutions have overtaken the realm of human communication: the computer, the Internet, satellites, wireless devices.

Loma Linda, like all successful ventures, realized early on that an indispensable key to survival and success was the ability to adapt to the inevitable changes brought by the passing of time. The best solution or arrangement for one time might need—a few years or decades later—to be reevaluated and changed in order to be of maximum benefit and effectiveness.

Such was the case with Loma Linda's two-campus arrangement—one in Loma Linda and the other in Los Angeles. When first instituted, it was a wise and commendable decision to divide the College of Medical Evangelists' education between the two locations.

Early twentieth-century medical education authorities, after all, required both basic science training and clinical experience. In response, from its earli-

Blame my cats, but this thing requires genius in order to work it just right."

This was actually Twain's second letter that day. Earlier he'd written a more friendly one to his brother Orion, but by the time he got to writing Howells, he was apparently growing a little cranky.

In fact, three months later, when the Remington Company contacted him about endorsing the machine he had bought, he confessed he had stopped using it, claiming that it was ruining his morals because it made him want to swear. Though he had originally paid $125 for the

est years, CME acknowledged the need to provide both textbook and hands-on education for its future physicians. In this twin classroom-clinical emphasis, CME was certainly not alone. The majority of medical schools in America at the time, in fact, taught basic sciences on a main campus in a rural setting and clinical education at a larger hospital in a convenient nearby city. In addition to CME, other medical schools that followed this approach in those years included the University of California at Berkeley, Stanford University, and Cornell University.

The sparse population base in the Loma Linda area limited the number of available patients for CME students. Loma Linda's Sanitarium was designed to serve a health retreat and convalescent clientele—not the acute-care patients who could provide clinical experience for the medical students. Attracting a qualified medical teaching staff to a campus in a comparatively remote location without its own associated teaching hospital also stood as an insuperable obstacle.

Thus the decision came early on to provide the bulk of classroom teaching at Loma Linda—and to develop clinical opportunities in Los Angeles. Lacking at first a hospital in Los Angeles, CME arranged for its students to obtain their clinical education at certain existing Los Angeles hospitals—primarily, Los Angeles County General Hospital. But soon, this facet of training could also be carried forward as CME established its own clinic in Los Angeles—a modest beginning that in time grew into White Memorial Hospital.

Even from the beginning, however, the two-campus situation posed challenges. Soon after clinical teaching had moved to Los Angeles, Nathan P. Colwell, MD, representing the American Medical Association (AMA), commented in amazement after inspecting CME, that "this part of the school [the dual campuses] does not represent any semblance

For decades prior to the early 1960s, Loma Linda's clinical education took place primarily in Los Angeles, most of that time at White Memorial Hospital.

to proper organization.... The manner in which this portion of the work has been scattered is beyond comprehension."

Clinical training for CME's earliest medical students was sketchy and primitive at best. "There was practically nothing to our last two years of medical work," Percy Magan, MD, reflected. "The students were sent down to Los Angeles and permitted to browse around the County Hospital and pick up whatever they could. Two or three physicians at that time gave them a little bit of work here, and that was all there was to their junior and senior years."[1]

Improvements came swiftly, however, and only seven years after clinical training began in Los Angeles, CME was well situated not only to provide training for its own junior and senior medical students but to accommodate thirty-four stranded students from the University of Southern California (USC). Stranded, because in 1919, USC's School of Medicine was judged deficient in a number of areas and expelled from the Association of American Medical Colleges.

With the approval of the AMA's Council on Medical Education, CME

For nearly forty years, beginning in 1928, the Loma Linda Sanitarium and Hospital (right), located on the "Hill Beautiful," served the health needs of patients both local and from afar.

agreed to allow the stranded junior and senior USC medical students to complete their training and receive CME diplomas upon graduating.

On receiving its charter in 1910, CME had been one of only five medical schools operating in the Los Angeles area. A decade later, the others had all closed—CME was the lone survivor. As such, it had exclusive access to the clinical facilities of greater Los Angeles. The clinical program based at White Memorial Hospital had not only survived but proved a credit to its founders and its parent denomination.

Nonetheless, after evaluations in 1936 and again in 1939, the Council on Medical Education of the AMA and the Executive Council of the Association of American Medical Colleges (AMC) referred to CME's two-campus setup as a handicap.

Between 1946 and 1951, study and effort were expended to explore the possibility of relocating the clinical division from Los Angeles to a less densely urbanized site on Ramona Boulevard in Alhambra—closer to, but still some distance from, Loma Linda. For a number of reasons, this plan created a

significant amount of controversy, and ultimately the option was abandoned.

After their earlier evaluations in the 1930s, subsequent association reports in 1951 and 1954 each noted the disadvantages of CME's dividing its medical teaching between two locations and again recommended unification of the School of Medicine.

For decades, Loma Linda's administrators wrestled with the problems inherent in maintaining dual campuses: costly duplication of administrative functions, teaching facilities, equipment, libraries, and curriculum—to say nothing of the time and expense involved in travel between the two locations, separated by sixty miles.

In 1946, the CME Board first seriously addressed the idea of moving the clinical division to the Loma Linda campus. Walter Macpherson, MD, at the time the dean of the School of Medicine, indicated his willingness to do so, yet stated his reservation that over the intervening years, one perceived obstacle that had led to the original two-campus solution remained: the Loma Linda area still did not have a large enough population, in Dr. Macpherson's estimation, to assure the number of patients needed for clinical teaching.

Ellen White had reportedly counseled that Seventh-day Adventist medical institutions would be more successful outside of big cities. Mindful of this, yet also of Dr. Macpherson's assessment, the Board appointed a twenty-one-member committee to study the issue.

Early in 1951, the CME Board authorized Dr. Macpherson to conduct another investigation of the dual-campus situation and report back at its April 11 meeting. Dr. Macpherson's conclusion was that the possibility of consolidation was still "questionable" and indicated that further study would be needed to arrive at a solution. By November of 1951, AMA and AMC representatives recommended after one of their periodic inspections of the medical school that the Board seriously consider uniting the two divisions on the Los Angeles campus.

Again in April of 1953, representatives of the AMA council and the AMC association met with a committee composed of CME and General Conference representatives to reiterate and emphasize their earlier recommendation to consolidate in Los Angeles. A few days later the Board acknowledged that this option was theoretically feasible but appointed a fact-finding commission to study the matter further and to consider also the option of consolidating instead at Loma Linda.

Frequent references in the writings of Ellen White to Loma Linda influenced a majority of the commission's members to believe that any consolidation should not be in Los Angeles. Yet after weeks of study,

Once Loma Linda's medical training was consolidated on one campus, the need for a new hospital became urgent. Left: The architect's preview.

the commission concluded that both financial and professional staffing considerations dictated the impracticality of uniting the medical school in Loma Linda. In fact, the commission was convinced that the anticipated deficiencies of attempting unification at Loma Linda carried a high risk that CME could lose its AMA accreditation.

After much discussion, the Board—acting on the commission's findings—voted on September 20, 1953, to continue the medical school on both campuses. But the problem hadn't gone away, and pressure began to

increase on CME to find a solution.

Following the 1958 evaluation of CME, accrediting officials, instead of recommending consolidation of the two campuses as they had so many times before, now required it, in what one Board member described as "a polite ultimatum."[2] While early in the century, most American medical schools divided their training between campuses, by 1959, CME was the only medical school in America still operating on two campuses.

No longer could a decision be deferred. Consolidation was imperative. But

As construction began on the new hospital, at first it was only a large "hole in the ground." Above: Excavation for the new facility as seen from the north. Right: Another view from the south.

where? The debate intensified—with sincere and often passionately adamant voices raised on behalf of each location. Not surprisingly, the basic sciences faculty in Loma Linda favored Loma Linda—the clinical faculty in Los Angeles favored Los Angeles. The Church constituency and a majority of CME's councilors favored Loma Linda. The CME administration and Board were split.

Those supporting the Loma Linda location warned that consolidating in Los Angeles could very well alienate the Church constituency, whose continuing support was vital. Many were convinced that Loma Linda, at some distance from the heart of Los Angeles, had originally been and thus remained a divinely ordained site for Christian education. These supporters voiced concern that the spirituality of medical students, surrounded by all the problems and temptations of a large city, could suffer. With rapid population growth closer to Loma Linda, they argued, the need to look to Los Angeles for clinical opportunities was now less urgent.

Los Angeles supporters had their own arguments and their own warning—that with an inadequate number of patients in Loma Linda, CME risked losing its accreditation. They pointed to Los Angeles County General Hospital as an invaluable asset for clinical experience and education. County General was also paying $800,000 per year to CME for its services rendered to the hospital, along with added subsidies for research. The large and well-equipped White Memorial Church, completed in 1956, provided a strong spiritual center on the Los Angeles campus. White Memorial Hospital itself had recently been enlarged, and CME owned an outstanding adjacent professional office building.

Those promoting consolidation in Los Angeles felt that its advantages were significant and the value of its clinical facilities proven—a lot to simply leave behind, should unification take place at Loma Linda. By comparison, they were convinced that consolidating at Loma Linda could be risky and fraught with problems.

In truth, some of the risks and problems that had long mitigated against the option of consolidating at Loma Linda were substantially answered as the 1960s dawned. Throughout the years, the Los Angeles and Loma Linda divisions of CME had come to be affectionately known as "the city" and "the farm." Yet as the Loma Linda-San Bernardino-Riverside area steadily grew in population, it increasingly transformed from a rural area of farms and orchards into a sprawling urban center in its own right—a bustling area that came to be called the Inland Empire. As the decade of the 1950s closed, the population of Riverside and San Bernardino counties was being projected to reach 1.25 million by

1966. By 1960, the two county hospitals nearest to Loma Linda were on target to complete multimillion-dollar expansion programs that would bring their combined bed capacities to 1,100. Both of these hospitals would be available to provide clinical experience for CME's medical students.

Clearly, some of the factors that had originally led to a dual-campus medical school and later made consolidating at Loma Linda seem an unworkable option were progressively disappearing.

On February 8, 1960, School of Medicine dean, Dr. Walter E. Macpherson, recommended to CME's board that the medical school be consolidated—and construction of necessary facilities begun—at Loma Linda. But CME president Godfrey T. Anderson, PhD, General Conference president Rueben R. Figuhr, and Board chair Maynard V. Campbell felt that a decision should not be voted at this meeting. Convinced that some on the Board who favored Los Angeles might—with additional information and time—eventually vote for Loma Linda, they tabled the motion until a later Board meeting.

The controversy over consolidation seemed destined to go on endlessly, and it fostered both apathy and discouragement,

While the 1928 Sanitarium still dominated the hill, some of the remaining citrus groves would yield to the new hospital, which would occupy a site seen in part to the lower left of this photo.

Step by step, the new triple-towered hospital rose steadily higher into the Southern California sky (this and facing page).

making it difficult to fill faculty vacancies.[3]

On September 12, 1960, a three-day meeting was convened to seek a solution to the two-campus dilemma. The result was something of a compromise: a decision to strengthen the basic science program at Loma Linda and clinical facilities at Los Angeles, to develop a university with Loma Linda serving as the principal campus, and to explore the option of offering the fourth year of premedical studies at Loma Linda rather than as part of the undergraduate programs at various Adventist colleges.

While again no decision was accomplished to consolidate the campuses, the Board did vote a recommendation to be sent to the Church's autumn council that contained clear support in the direction of Loma Linda:

"Move deliberately and plan only minimum facilities in Los Angeles, and in Loma Linda to strengthen clinical facilities and recruit Adventist scientists for the basic sciences, and to go forward with plans for the University."[4]

The fall council approved this recommendation, and plans to reorganize CME's program moved ahead. Since its beginnings, the name "College of Medical Evangelists" had served well. But with plans in place to offer not just medical training but a full liberal arts program, the time had arrived to consider a new name for the institution that would provide an umbrella over not just medical training but other academic disciplines as well. Thus, on July 1, 1961, the College of Medical Evangelists officially became Loma Linda University.

In the summer of the next year, the last issue of *The Medical Evangelist*—the news publication of CME—appeared, an issue covering the first commencement of Loma Linda University. With the expansion of the institution into a university, and to reflect the change of its name, administrators approved enlarging the publication and retitling it *Loma Linda University Magazine*.

September 3, 1963 saw the debut of the University *Scope*, which became Loma Linda University's weekly newspaper, succeeding *The Voice of CME Employees*—an eight-page monthly employee publication that had been launched in September of 1952. In an editorial, *Scope*'s first editor, Jerry L. Pettis, described its relationship to *Loma Linda University Magazine* by noting that *Scope* would provide "hard news . . . while it is still news," whereas the magazine would cover subjects of special interest in greater depth.

Later decades would bring their own changes to the University's publications. On June 17, 1970, *Scope* replaced *Loma Linda University Magazine*—and in September of that year, the *Observer* became the campus newspaper. Later still, in 1988, the *Observer* gave way to *Today*, which served both the Loma Linda and La

After July of 1961, the "College of Medical Evangelists" sign on campus would be no more. CME became Loma Linda University.

Sierra campuses—and *Newsbreak,* which served employees of the Medical Center.

The year after the College of Medical Evangelists became Loma Linda University, David B. Hinshaw, MD, chair of the department of surgery, succeeded Dr. Macpherson as dean of the School of Medicine. Of the new dean, Keld Reynolds, PhD, vice president for academic affairs, would later write: "The young dean generated a sort of infectious courage which led the Board to hope that this David just might have the right stone for felling the Goliath of indecision."[5]

Dr. Hinshaw walked resolutely into the controversy and made known that he would be open to accepting any of three plans: using Los Angeles County General Hospital as the primary clinical teaching facility, using White Memorial Hospital for this purpose, or unifying the School of Medicine on the Loma Linda campus.

Finally, on September 25 and 26, 1962, the Board arrived at a historic decision—voting to unify the campuses at Loma Linda. The decision did include, however, a provision to maintain a connection with White Memorial Hospital, where certain graduate, paramedical, and premedical courses could be offered. Church leaders attending autumn council approved the vote of Loma Linda's Board.

Those on both sides of the long effort to reach this decision had for years invested

energy and time and advocacy in promoting their respective wishes for the location of a unified medical school. In the aftermath of the final decision, supporters of Los Angeles as the campus of choice were understandably disappointed. As Dr. Reynolds described it, "The new design did not go unchallenged. There were faculty members who had given many years of devoted service to the School of Medicine, and who sincerely believed that these decisions would destroy it and who sounded their warnings loud and clear, as they had the right to do. There were some of the older faculty members whose roots were

too deep in the city where they had spent a lifetime in practice for them to consider starting anew in Loma Linda, who felt their loss keenly, and whose separation was equally a loss for the School. For a short time the storm was fierce. The Trustees, the president, and the dean stood firm; and so the great decision was made."[6]

Divided for forty-eight years, the School of Medicine was once again united on one campus. As the decision was carried out, control of White Memorial Hospital and its associated facilities passed over to the Southern California Conference of Seventh-day Adventists.

A NEW HOSPITAL

Once the decision to consolidate had been made, one of the most urgent needs was to develop at Loma Linda a new medical center—capable of fully providing for the clinical education of physicians-in-training—to replace the Sanitarium on the hill.

A general design for the new hospital, approved in May of 1963, included plans for an eleven-story, 2,050-room facility. Little more than a year later on June 7, 1964, groundbreaking ceremonies for the new medical complex took place. The last concrete was poured on January 25, 1966—and the completed Loma Linda University Medical Center was occupied on July 9, 1967.

On that sunny summer day, patients and staff from the old Loma Linda Sanitarium and Hospital were efficiently moved to the impressive new facility. Patient rooms circled the perimeter of three circular towers—each seven stories high—these rooms clustered on each floor around a central nursing station hub. The triple towers of the Medical Center were prominently visible from points all across the Inland valley.

By far the largest building ever constructed by the Seventh-day Adventist Church, the new Medical Center—built as a cooperative venture by the Del Webb and Larry Havstad organizations—was

constructed for what, even in 1967, was an amazingly low cost of $17 million.

Now Loma Linda University's medical school had a state-of-the-art facility to accommodate not only basic science training but clinical education as well. But if Loma Linda was truly to live out its new name as a university, it would need a full four-year undergraduate liberal arts school as part of its academic program.

A NEW LIBERAL ARTS UNDERGRADUATE SCHOOL

In the early 1960s, the Western Association of Schools and Colleges

notified Loma Linda that the Association would soon limit accreditation to only those institutions offering an adequate liberal arts program.

While agreeing with this decision in principle, Loma Linda's leaders puzzled over how to implement it. To quickly establish a full liberal arts college as part of the University at Loma Linda was simply not a realistic possibility. A committee of the General Conference with the assignment of providing guidance and coordinating assistance to those Adventist colleges across the country that offered graduate work was asked to address Loma Linda's pressing need.

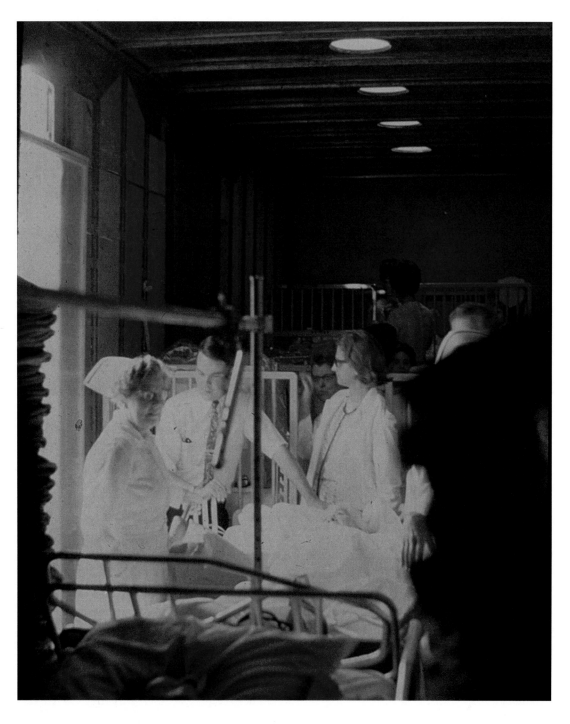

July 9, 1967—moving day from the old Sanitarium on the hill to the new hospital. Right: Surrounded by chrome cribs, babies, and nurses inside a moving van stands Loma Linda University's first pediatrics resident, B. Lyn Behrens, MBBS (just to right of center in photo). Today, of course, Dr. Behrens has new responsibilities— as president/CEO of Loma Linda University Adventist Health Sciences Center. Facing page: Employees assist in moving patients from the old facility into the new.

Surveying the graduate programs of the three existing West Coast colleges—Walla Walla College (WWC) in Washington State, Pacific Union College (PUC) in Northern California, and La Sierra College (LSC) in nearby Riverside—this committee explored the possibility of in some way combining the graduate offerings of WWC, PUC, LSC, and Loma Linda.

Because of distance and other logistical factors, PUC and Walla Walla soon pulled away from the idea of this proposed federation. This left La Sierra and Loma Linda to continue their discussions of some kind of cooperative venture.

As early as the 1930s, the president of La Sierra at that time—E.E. Cossentine—had suggested to his colleague, CME president, Dr. Percy Magan, that they explore the idea of academically combining their two institutions into what might someday develop into a university. At that time, however, Dr. Magan did not favor following through on this option.

As Loma Linda continued its talks with La Sierra in seeking to provide for its University a liberal-arts undergraduate program, the University leadership sought the counsel of three distinguished educators: Charles S. Casassa, SJ, president of Loyola Marymount University of Los Angeles; Earl V. Pullias, professor of higher education at the University of Southern California; and Richard Ham-

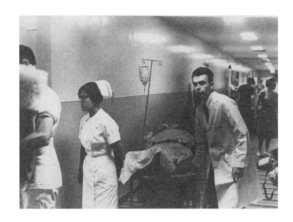

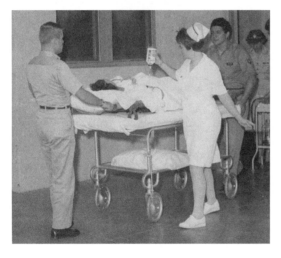

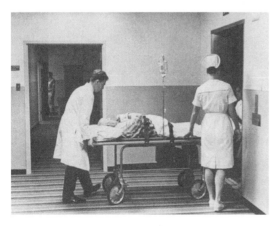

mill, PhD, president of Loma Linda's sister Adventist university—Andrews University, in Berrien Springs, Michigan.

Meanwhile, for approximately a year, an affiliation committee grappled with the logistics and details involved in a possible merger. One issue they addressed was the question of "which institution was to be the bride, and which the groom."[7]

The Loma Linda Board, after studying the committee's report, requested additional study by the committee. But finally, on April 23, 1967, the Loma Linda University constituency approved the merger of La Sierra with Loma Linda. On July 1, 1967, La Sierra officially became the College of Arts and Sciences of Loma Linda University, with Ralph L. Koorenny, PhD, serving as the college's first dean.

NEW CAMPUS CONSTRUCTION AND ACADEMIC GROWTH

As in the previous decade, the 1960s brought forward progress in both new campus construction and academic expansion. While the new medical center was clearly the most ambitious new facility of the decade, the requirements of a growing university brought a steady succession of new buildings to the campus and surrounding community.

Among them: Griggs Hall, the headquarters of the Graduate School, in 1963; a major addition to the library, also in

1963; a biochemistry building—Mortensen Hall—named for Raymond Mortensen, PhD, in 1966; a campus power plant, also in 1966; Dale Gentry Auditorium and Gymnasium in 1968; and a community shopping center at the corner of Barton Road and Mountain View Avenue in 1970.

During the decade of the 1960s, not only did Loma Linda add the liberal arts component to its academic offerings, it greatly expanded its medical curriculum as well, especially in the area of supporting services and paramedical technologies.

In 1963, the University launched a medical records administration program, with E. Faye Brown, MA, as its director. The School of Tropical and Preventive Medicine that had been established in 1958 was succeeded by the School of Public Health, with Mervyn G. Hardinge, MD, PhD, as dean.

Nineteen sixty-six brought the formation of the School of Health Related Professions, with Ivor C. Woodward, PhD, as its dean. The medical records administration program begun three years earlier was incorporated into this new School, along with new departments of medical technology, occupational therapy, physical therapy, and radiologic technology. Other departments were later added, and this School, too, was in time renamed as the School of Allied Health Professions.

Back in the 1920s at La Sierra, a humble

teacher education program was launched—and now, as part of Loma Linda University, this academic program became a flourishing School of Education in 1968, with Willard H. Meier, EdD, serving as dean.

THE LOMA LINDA UNIVERSITY OVERSEAS HEART SURGERY TEAM

In 1963, C. Joan Coggin, MD, and Ellsworth E. Wareham, MD, cofounded the Loma Linda University Overseas Heart Surgery Team. From a small beginning that year, when a group of seven specialists landed in Karachi, Pakistan, the heart team has developed into an

international organization whose influence has been felt around the world. Throughout its more than forty years of service, the team has ministered to patients and also taught local physicians in countries around the world, including Pakistan, Greece, South Vietnam, Saudi Arabia, the People's Republic of China, Zimbabwe, Kenya, North Korea, and Nepal.

The purpose of the heart team program is multifaceted, aiming—as a reflection of Loma Linda's dual mission—to perform both healing and teaching services. In addition, one of the team's primary objectives is to enhance the image of

the Seventh-day Adventist Church in each country where the team works.

"We would not want to go to a place where our presence would not have a positive impact on the work of the Church," explains Dr. Coggin.

CITY OF LOMA LINDA
ESTABLISHED

By the end of the 1960s, Loma Linda had grown from a rural sanitarium and struggling school into a thriving and far-reaching medical and educational center. So, too, the small conclave of staff and employee homes had expanded into a bustling, energetic community of not only residences but all the businesses and services of any prospering town or city. To provide for the oversight and needs of this developing area, the city of Loma Linda was established by a vote of its citizens on September 22, 1970. Douglas F. Welebir, an Adventist attorney, served as the city's first mayor.

A SWEEPING TIDE OF PROGRESS

The 1960s at last brought a solution to the dual-campus problem that had eluded Loma Linda's leadership for decades. If the 1950s saw a giant leap forward with the establishment of the School of Dentistry, the sixties were like a series of great forward strides. Consolidation seemed to open the floodgates to a rapid tide of

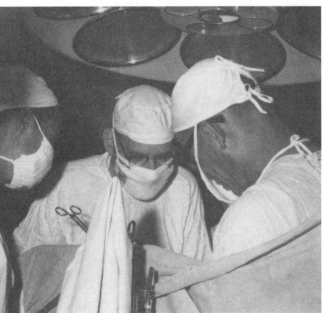

progress. As the decade ended, Loma Linda had a Medical Center of growing influence and service and a full-fledged University. And in Los Angeles, White Memorial Hospital, able now to focus fully on its mission to serve its urban population, entered a new era of dynamic growth. Both institutions today are not only greatly respected by those they serve, but they share a deep and genuine respect for each other, continuing in a number of ways to work together in their shared ministries of teaching and healing.

During the earliest years of the 1900s, the two-campus arrangement made sense and served well. And the link between Loma Linda and Los Angeles grew strong. But the passing of time brought dramatic demographic and academic changes, so that ultimately, neither campus could reach its fullest potential unless freed to pursue individual missions.

Separation of the campuses—like two vines that had become tightly intertwined as they grew together—was both difficult and painful. But ultimately, each vine could grow higher and stronger by focusing its growth nearest its own roots.

What amazing contributions might these two strong, thriving institutions now be positioned to make to their local patients and community, their Church, and the world at large?

Born of vision and divine providence,

both the University and Medical Center in Loma Linda and White Memorial Medical Center in Los Angeles would answer that question in the years just ahead in ways that would cause many to marvel and to feel the deepest gratitude to their Founding Healer.

NOTES:

1. *From Vision to Reality*, p. 154.
2. CME Board of Trustees, *Minutes*, September 11, 1958, p. 5.
3. John E. Peterson, MD, May 8, 1961 letter to Walter E. Macpherson, MD.
4. *From Vision to Reality*, p. 156.
5. Ibid.
6. Ibid., pp. 156, 157.
7. Ibid., p. 158.

Then–vice president Lyndon B. Johnson (left, with heart team cofounders Ellsworth Wareham, MD, and Joan Coggin, MD) recognizes the work of the heart team. Below, left and right: The heart team in action.

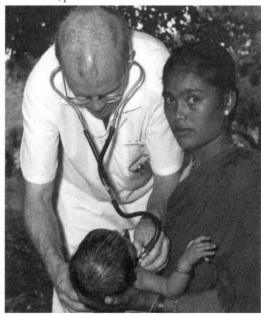

PHOTO ALBUM

BELOW: A VIEW OF THE NEW MEDICAL CENTER'S
TRIPLE TOWERS DURING CONSTRUCTION.

RIGHT: TWO VIEWS OF THE COMPLETED NEW MEDICAL CENTER.

LEFT: ONE OF THE NURSING STATIONS AT THE CENTER OF A CIRCULAR WARD, SURROUNDED BY ROOMS ON THE PERIMETER.

BELOW: LOGISTICAL PLANNING RESULTED IN EFFICIENT TRANSFER OF PATIENTS FROM THE OLD SANITARIUM-HOSPITAL TO THE NEW MEDICAL CENTER ON MOVING DAY.

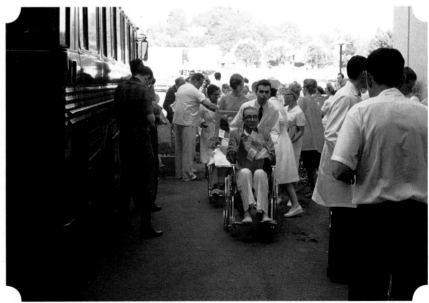

Below: Early 1969 brought the most damaging flood to Loma Linda since 1916. Low-lying areas turned into rivers of rushing water.

Below right: The traditional capping ceremony for nursing students, 1967.

A FEW OF THE MANY OUTSTANDING LEADERS
AT LOMA LINDA DURING THE 1960S:

TOP, LEFT TO RIGHT: MERVYN G. HARDINGE, MD, DRPH,
PHD, DEAN, SCHOOL OF PUBLIC HEALTH; A. GRAHAM
MAXWELL, PHD, DEAN, DIVISION OF RELIGION; JACK
PROVONSHA, MD, PHD, PROFESSOR, RELIGION AND ETHICS.

BOTTOM, FROM LEFT: PAUL C. HEUBACH, MTH, SENIOR
PASTOR, LOMA LINDA UNIVERSITY CHURCH; MAXINE
ATTEBERY, RN, MS, DEAN, SCHOOL OF NURSING.

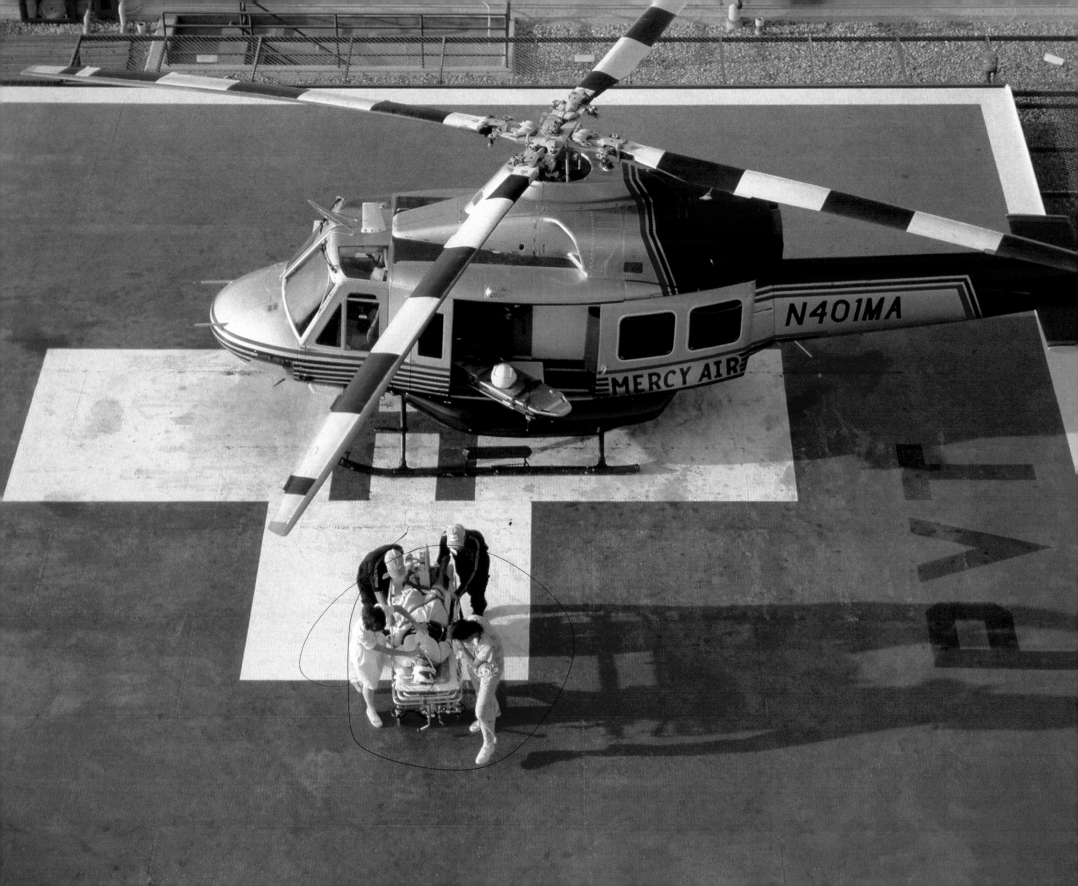

Longer Ropes— Deeper Stakes

COULD JOHN BURDEN, ELLEN WHITE, AND OTHERS WHO HELPED FOUND LOMA LINDA HAVE SEEN THE CAMPUS AS IT STOOD AT THE END OF THE 1970S, THEY UNQUESTIONABLY WOULD HAVE BEEN BOTH ASTONISHED AND FILLED WITH GRATITUDE TO GOD FOR HIS PROVIDENTIAL LEADING.

If you've been camping, you'll readily understand Isaiah 54:2: "Enlarge the place of your tent, and let them stretch out the curtains of your dwellings; do not spare; lengthen your cords, and strengthen your stakes."

Bigger tents—longer ropes—deeper stakes.

What's true of healthy living things is also true of healthy institutions and organizations: time brings growth and strength. Just as a virtually helpless infant—small in size and strength—can grow into a strong, full-sized adult, vital organizations too grow larger and stronger.

Through a century of existence, Loma Linda has continually lengthened its ropes—it has grown and expanded. It has also strengthened its stakes—making sure to become not just larger, but stronger.

In these twin efforts, the decade of the 1970s stands as representative of the entire history of Loma Linda. During the seventies Loma Linda grew both larger and stronger in its enrollment, its buildings and infrastructure, its worldwide outreach, and its healing spiritual mission.

For long years in the late 1800s, speculators tried without success to bring to reality a variety of dreams for the land surrounding a low Southern California hill. But where each of those efforts failed, one dream finally succeeded. Divine guidance, faith and vision, much hard work, and sacrifice combined in the earliest years of the 1900s to create on and around the Hill Beautiful a place of healing and medical education. Small at first—and against intimidating odds—the Schools of Medicine and Nursing grew.

In 1906, CME opened with just thirty-five students. But by 1971, enrollment

Left: Emergency airlift service began with the Air Medical Service in 1972. Today, this service is contracted out, and more than a thousand flights per year land at Loma Linda's two Medical Ceneter heliports.

had grown a hundredfold to 3,500 students. Before the seventies were over, enrollment would pass 5,000.

For many decades, members of the Seventh-day Adventist Church across the United States referred to the College of Medical Evangelists at Loma Linda as "our medical school." Long past now, however, were the years when the term medical school could accurately encompass the curriculum at Loma Linda—for as the 1970s began, a number of other schools had joined the Schools of Medicine and Nursing, including a College of Arts and Sciences on the La Sierra campus. Even the name College of Medical Evangelists was gone, replaced by a more

inclusive name: Loma Linda University.

Looking back on the 1970s from the vantage point of Loma Linda's century mark in the early 2000s, the longer ropes and deeper stakes of its growth during that decade are evident everywhere.

SCHOOLS AND CURRICULUM

In 1971, the School of Health Related Professions became the School of Allied Health Professions. Established within this School that year was a respiratory therapy department. The next year brought departments of anesthesiology and dietetics, and in 1974, a department of health science.

The School of Nursing in February

of 1973 relocated from Loma Linda University Medical Center to new quarters in West Hall. In early June, the School's administration hosted an open house.

Curriculum offerings expanded as well on the undergraduate level, with LLU announcing in May of 1979 a new degree program in geology.

After decades of operating on two campuses—Loma Linda and Los Angeles—the School of Medicine consolidated its program in 1962 at Loma Linda. But in 1975, the medical school reestablished ties with White Memorial Medical Center, allowing students to serve and gain clinical experience there on a rotation

basis. George Kypridakis, MD, served as associate dean of the Los Angeles campus and oversaw the affiliation program.

NEW BUILDINGS AND INFRASTRUCTURE

Both campuses of Loma Linda University—at La Sierra and Loma Linda—saw a variety of needed new buildings and improvements over the decade. Completed at La Sierra in October of 1973 was a new library that included a learning center funded by a $100,000 Kresge Foundation grant. The seventies also brought to La Sierra a new gymnasium and auditorium called the Alumni Pavilion and a consumer sciences building.

At Loma Linda, a $5 million, multi-story expansion of the School of Dentistry building—Prince Hall—reached completion in 1977. Only a few years old, the new LLU Medical Center building—with its fourteen acres of floor space—was already in need of more room. The need for a new faculty practice building became increasingly apparent, and in October of 1977, groundbreaking took place for a new $5.6 million structure. The first outpatients entered the new building in September of 1979.

The preceding month, on August 27, ground was broken—thanks to a $3.85 million grant from the Del E. Webb Foundation and another large donation from

the estate of Harriet Randall-Campbell, MD—for the new 67,500-square-foot Del E. Webb Memorial Library & Randall Visitors Center complex. Opening ceremonies would take place in August of 1981.

Loma Linda's campus infrastructure, strained by years of rapid expansion, led to burgeoning costs for heat, light, and power. So the seventies brought relief as streets were torn up to install an enlarged central plant conducting power to all points of the campus.

THE CITY OF LOMA LINDA GETS ANOTHER HOSPITAL

The lead front-page headline of the January 24, 1964, issue of *Scope* noted,

In 1973, the School of Nursing moved into its new quarters in West Hall (above left, present day). And 1977 brought a multistory expansion to the School of Dentistry building. Above: Prince Hall as it appears today.

Groundbreaking for the Del E. Webb Memorial Library & Randall Visitors Center (right) took place in August of 1979. The 67,500-square-foot complex was made possible by a $3.85 million grant from the Del E. Webb Foundation and another large donation from the estate of Harriet Randall-Campbell, MD.

"Veterans Voice Interest in Federal, State Hospitals Here." Another story on the same page announced that Jerry L. Pettis, Loma Linda's vice president for public relations and development, had resigned to run as a candidate for the U.S. Congress.

According to the lead story, Southern California veteran's organization representatives were strongly recommending Loma Linda as the site for a proposed new Veterans Administration (VA) hospital, convinced that proximity to Loma Linda's Medical Center would be advantageous to both medical facilities.

Since World War II, the VA had developed a policy of building its new hospitals near existing medical schools for the mutual benefit of both entities. In fact, by the mid-1960s, of the eighty-nine schools of medicine in the United States, all but five were affiliated with the VA.

In the 1966 California general election on November 8, Mr. Pettis—by now serving as both assistant professor of legal and cultural medicine in LLU's School of Medicine and as chair of the University Councilors—won a U.S. congressional seat.[1]

On Friday, April 3, 1970, Congressman Pettis conducted a hearing in Burden Hall on the proposed new VA hospital. After the hearing, Mr. Pettis and VA officials toured both Loma Linda's Medical Center and the surrounding Loma Linda-San Bernardino area, where they looked for possible construction sites. "There will be a veterans facility in the vicinity of Loma Linda," he assured a *Scope* reporter. "But I cannot tell you exactly when, because there are too many imponderables."[2]

On August 20, 1971, President Richard M. Nixon visited Loma Linda's campus—accompanied by Congressman Pettis and California governor Ronald Reagan—to announce the government's decision to build a new Veterans Administration hospital in Loma Linda. The facility would replace the VA hospital at Sylmar in California's San Fernando Valley, which was destroyed earlier that year in a major earthquake. In remarks before ten thousand local residents, officials, and the White House Press Corps, the president stated that the new hospital would enable LLU to train even more health care workers in the years ahead. "I can think of nothing that does more to make friends for America abroad," he added, "than that kind of selfless service by people like those from Loma Linda."[3]

The location of the new hospital became a major concern of both the city of Loma Linda and Loma Linda University. The first site chosen was a hill west of the Medical Center. But this site would have

necessitated removal of fifty to seventy-five private homes, thus eroding the city's economic base—and it would also have contributed to campus congestion.

After wrestling with the location issue for many hours, the LLU Board of Trustees reached a decision, communicated on December 22, 1971, in a telegram from LLU president David J. Bieber, EdD, and Board chair R.R. Bietz to the Veterans Administration:

"Loma Linda reaffirms its appeal that the proposed Veterans Administration Hospital be located on the Barton-Benton site [about a half-mile east of Loma Linda's campus]. The University, including the School of Medicine and other health-related schools, and its Board of Trustees remain united in their determination that a viable affiliation can be achieved and that quality health care can be assured if the hospital is located on the proposed site. The University is prepared to make available, as a gift, fifteen

Congressman Jerry L. Pettis and his wife Shirley (above left). On August 20, 1971, President Richard M. Nixon, accompanied by then Governor of California Ronald Reagan (left), visited Loma Linda University to announce the construction of a $28.9 million Veterans Administration hospital in the Loma Linda area.

Jerry L. Pettis Memorial Veterans Medical Center (above and above right) opened on September 25, 1977, about a half-mile east of the Loma Linda campus—on land donated by the University.

acres of university-owned land in the Barton-Benton area for this purpose."[4]

The VA quickly responded: "We accept and are most grateful for your offer to make available to us as a gift fifteen acres of University-owned land in the Barton-Benton area for the purposes indicated. We are proceeding now to finalize this entire matter by seeking appropriate approval of the environmental agency. Again, please accept our appreciation for your understanding attitude and your great generosity. We look forward to a long and close relationship."

On September 25, 1977, the VA opened the new 548-bed, $79 million Jerry L.

Pettis Memorial Veterans Medical Center in Loma Linda. Congressman Pettis, the first Seventh-day Adventist to serve in the U.S. Congress, died in the crash of his private airplane on February 14, 1975, as he traveled on an errand for the hospital that now bears his name. His widow, Congresswoman Shirley N. Pettis—elected to her late husband's vacant congressional seat following his death—delivered the dedication address.

Jerry L. Pettis was a man of extraordinary gifts and achievements. A Seventh-day Adventist minister, he was also a flight instructor, search-and-rescue pilot for the Civil Air Patrol, and during

World War II served as a pilot for the Air Transport Command. He founded the Audio-Digest Foundation (a subsidiary of the California Medical Association). In addition to serving as a vice president for Loma Linda University, he owned a citrus ranch and was an inventor and philanthropist. Veterans considered him—in his capacity as a congressman—to have been the primary influence in motivating the VA to build its new hospital in the Loma Linda area.

Serving nearly 300,000 veterans who live in five surrounding counties, Pettis Memorial Veterans Medical Center has benefited both area veterans and—through affiliation and proximity—LLU Medical Center as well.

THE AIR MEDICAL SERVICE

Addressing the Rialto, California, Rotary Club in the late sixties on the high cost of medical care, LLU Medical Center administrator C. Victor Way noted as an example one machine that, while costing the Medical Center $100,000, would save one life a year.

Afterward, Alec Fergusson, the founder of Western Helicopters, approached Mr. Way with a question: "Have you ever thought of using a helicopter?"

"Yes," Mr. Way responded. "But they're too expensive."

In 1969, the Volunteer Service League of the Medical Center had donated $43,263 toward building a "helistop" on the roof of LLU Medical Center's North Wing. Opened in October of that year, the fifty-four-square-foot landing area received as its first patient an injured workman airlifted from a construction project near Crestline—twenty-four miles away in the San Bernardino Mountains.

Western Helicopters in Rialto responded to the emergency call—and thirty minutes later the patient was in the Medical Center's emergency room.

So Mr. Fergusson already had seen the value of air-transporting patients in need of immediate medical care. He would not be deterred by Mr. Way's concern about

cost. Rather than relying on commercial helicopter services, Mr. Fergusson was convinced Loma Linda needed to have its own helicopter dedicated to responding to urgent medical calls.

"I just heard you tell fifty people that Loma Linda would spend $100,000 for one machine to save one life," he told Mr. Way. "How many lives would a helicopter save?"

"You know," Mr. Way mused, "no one ever approached us on that basis. Give us a proposition."

The proposal that followed included a ten-day trial during the 1970-1971 Christmas-New Year holidays, using a five-passenger, French-built Allouette III

helicopter. Participating in the experiment were the California Highway Patrol, the San Bernardino County Sheriff's Department, and local ambulance companies.

Over the ten-day trial, the helicopter transported to LLUMC ten accident victims—all of them from the San Bernardino Mountains. Though the experiment was considered successful, the need for more interior space for the helicopter was clear.

Assistant LLUMC administrator Norman H. Meyer and director of emergency services Thomas J. Zirkle, MD, who had teamed to lead the trial, acquired two large military surplus Sikorsky H-19s and authorized Western Helicopters to

Attendants remove a patient from an air transport helicopter on the rooftop heliport.

convert one of them into a civilian configuration. Loma Linda would outfit the roomy interior cabin as an air ambulance. The most advanced life support systems available, including a state-of-the-art portable defibrillator, transformed the Sikorsky into a flying intensive care unit. The helicopter could carry four litter patients, one seated ambulatory patient, an air medic, and the pilot. A special emergency radio linked the craft to 150 hospitals throughout Southern California.

On May 22, 1972, the LLUMC Air Medical Service (AMS) was inaugurated, with Dr. Zirkle as its medical director. "We hired only pilots with at least 5,000 hours of flying experience," Dr. Zirkle would later recall. The first helicopter, able to fly between 90 and 100 miles per hour, went into service on June 5, 1972.

Thanks largely to funds contributed by the Medical Center's Volunteer Service League, the second Sikorsky was outfitted with the most advanced medical equipment available and a powerful new turbine engine and pressed into service as well. In January of 1974, the first helicopter assumed a backup role for those few occasions when two emergency calls came in simultaneously.

Western Helicopters fully controlled helicopter maintenance and operation, while LLUMC assumed responsibility for life-saving equip-

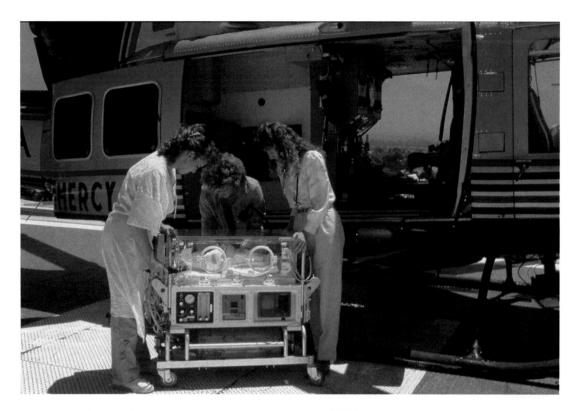

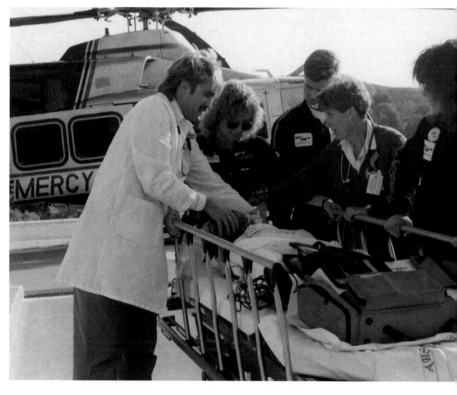

ment, supplies, and air medics.

Physicians in smaller hospitals through-out the four inland counties surrounding Loma Linda requested helicopter transfers for their most critically ill or injured patients who needed the benefits of a larger, more capable medical facility. Over time, inter-hospital transfers accounted for the majority of helicopter calls.

After several years, the Air Medical Service greatly expanded its reach by obtaining a fixed-wing Beechcraft Queen Air capable of interstate and even trans-continental patient transfers. Later still,

the AMS purchased a Beechcraft King Air with twice the power of the Queen Air and capable of flying 270 miles per hour—100 miles per hour faster than the Queen.

Loma Linda's Air Medical Service was the first hospital-owned-and-oper-ated helicopter ambulance service in the nation, and throughout its ten-year history, transported more than 2,000 patients, many of whom survived their illness or injury as a direct result of the air transport.

Today, LLUMC receives in excess of a thousand helicopter landings a year at two heliports—more air traffic than

experienced at many small airports in the United States. At times, when both heliports are busy, a third helicopter can land on the Medical Center lawn.

REACHING OUT WITH HOPE AND HEALING

Perhaps nothing demonstrated Loma Linda's "longer ropes" better in the 1970s than the many ways in which it reached out—both near and far—to those in need.

In January of 1971, the School of Den-tistry inaugurated a mobile dental clinic program to serve nearby communities. And

More than a thousand helicopter flights per year land at Loma Linda University Medical Center's two heliports.

somewhat farther south, in 1977 Loma Linda University provided personnel, equipment, and expertise to help with the launch of a new sister Seventh-day Adventist University in Montemorelos, Mexico. The first Montemorelos class in medicine—twenty-five new physicians—graduated in July of 1979.

But while not overlooking the needs of those close at hand, Loma Linda also looked beyond its nearest neighbors to assist in alleviating suffering and need across the globe.

As an example, in 1975 the University and Loma Linda citizenry joined to help meet a crisis of dire human need, accepting

in May some 400 Vietnamese refugees into the community. Many of these refugees remained in Loma Linda, making valuable contributions both as students and employees. Others moved away to other parts of the country as opportunities for denominational or other employment arose.

Another urgent call came in 1979, to aid in a massive relief effort for Cambodian refugees in Thailand. University alumni, students, and friends responded generously, and on December 2, a first group of physicians, nurses, and public health professionals left for Thailand to provide medical care in cooperation with Seventh-day Adventist World Service.

The Loma Linda University Overseas Heart Surgery Team also continued its worldwide outreach during the seventies. It performed the first-ever open-heart surgery in Vietnam in April of 1974. In January of 1976, the heart team began a six-week mission to Saudi Arabia, where they soon performed the first open-heart surgery ever to take place in that country, mending the heart of a thirteen-year-old girl named Nalwal Abdal Azziz Bakra. Thirty-four additional operations on other patients were also performed during the heart team's stay. Later, the team returned to Saudi Arabia to assist Saudi physicians in developing their heart-surgery capabilities. As a result, in 1977 fourteen Saudi Arabian students enrolled at Loma Linda University—six at La Sierra and eight at Loma Linda.

Loma Linda's world outreach has extended to countries and regions around the globe: Mexico, the Caribbean, Nepal, Africa, the Philippines, and Afghanistan. Beginning in 1974, LLU contracted with the U.S. Department of State's Agency for International Development to provide physicians and nurses to assist the government of Tanzania in East Africa in developing maternal and child health services. Richard H. Hart, MD, DrPH—now Loma Linda University's chancellor—first headed the Tanzanian program, and other such programs have followed. For instance, in June of 1976 the first allied health student missionaries left for Africa.

THE ADVENTIST HEALTH STUDY

In 1973, the National Cancer Institute, a division of the National Institutes of Health (NIH), awarded an $800,000 grant to Roland L. Phillips, MD, DrPH—Loma Linda's first doctorally trained epidemiologist—to begin what would in time become known as the Adventist Health Study-1 (AHS-1). With a special interest in the relationship between cancer and lifestyle, Dr. Phillips launched the study in 1975. Central to the study was a lifestyle questionnaire with a special emphasis on the dietary habits of California Seventh-day

Adventists participating in the research. All subjects completing the questionnaire were followed for at least six years to collect information on the impact of diet on cancer and heart disease.

Unfortunately, Dr. Phillips was killed in a sailplane accident in 1987—the year before the study was completed. One of his colleagues, Gary Fraser, MD, PhD, from New Zealand, took over as the principal investigator of AHS-1 and saw it through to conclusion. By the time Dr. Fraser assumed leadership of the Study, he had received a grant from another entity of the NIH—the National Heart, Lung, and Blood Institute (NHLBI)—to add a major additional heart disease component to AHS-1.

Prior to this, Dr. Fraser had also received one of a small number of NIH five-year Preventive Cardiology Academic Awards in the amount of $305,000. This he used for personal career development, to help teach medical students, and to assist in his writing of *Preventive Cardiology*—a well-used textbook published in 1986 by Oxford University Press.

Among the findings of AHS-1 was that subjects who ate fruit at least twice daily experienced only 25 percent the risk of developing lung cancer when compared with those who ate fruit less than three times per week. The study was also the first to discover that men

The first Adventist Health Study was launched in 1975 by Roland L. Phillips, MD, DrPH (left). After his untimely death, Gary Fraser, MD, PhD (below), assumed leadership of the study.

and women who had a high consumption of tomatoes reduced their risk of prostate cancer in men by 40 percent and ovarian cancer in women by 60 to 70 percent. This finding stimulated other research in the area of phytochemicals, perhaps the most exciting study area in nutrition today. These Loma Linda findings also helped stimulate the current national health education message heard so frequently, "Eat more fruits and vegetables—at least five servings a day."

Another finding from AHS-1 was the first clue that eating nuts reduces the risk of heart disease. People who eat nuts five or more times a week have a 50 percent lower risk of heart attack than those who eat nuts less than once a week. Furthermore, eating whole wheat bread reduces the risk of nonfatal heart attacks by about 45 percent.

California Adventists are perhaps the longest-lived population group yet formally described in lifestyle research. The AHS-1 showed that life expectancy at birth for Adventist women was 82.3 years and for men, 78.5 years.

Not only do Adventist vegetarians in California live substantially longer than other Californians (an extra 9.5 and 6.2 years respectively for males and females), but Adventist vegetarian men live longer than their Adventist nonvegetarian counterparts by 2.1 years—for women the difference is 1.8 years. Lifestyle affects not only quantity of life but probably also quality. Quality of life appears greater for Adventist vegetarians from the fact that at any given age they experience less cardiovascular disease, cancer, diabetes, arthritis, and hypertension; use health services less frequently; and take fewer medications than nonvegetarian Adventists.

In June 2001 the NIH granted $18 million for a new enrollment of Seventh-day Adventists into the Adventist Health Study called AHS-2, which began registration in 2002. Its goal was to enroll 125,000 Adventists above age 35 from across all of North America by 2005. All enrollees have completed 594 questions and will be followed up every two years with a brief questionnaire to ascertain their health status and, in particular, to note any new cancers or heart attacks. Eating habits will be updated every five years.

One thousand people are being randomly selected for follow-up in substudies to validate the questionnaire. About 4,300 Adventist churches are participating in this study. These are very large numbers, and the study requires a staff of more than 50 full- or part-time researchers, programmers, nutritionists, data technicians, scanner operators, and clerks of various types. This large study holds the promise of clarifying the specific effects of many nutrients on the health not only of Adventists but also of all Americans.

THE IMPOSSIBLE DREAM: RAILWAY TO THE MOON

DEEPER STAKES

While lengthening its ropes during the 1970s through campus expansion and service both locally and worldwide, Loma Linda also drove its stakes deeper in a variety of ways: culturally, socially, and especially, spiritually.

In October of 1974, the Adventist church held its annual council on the Loma Linda campus. In January of 1976, the Loma Linda Ellen G. White Estate/Seventh-day Adventist Research Center was dedicated.

The following year, a three-day course in religious witnessing took place at Loma Linda, and also in 1977, a "Creation Weekend" was conducted under the direction of Ariel Roth, PhD. On the La Sierra campus, the first General Conference–sponsored denominational history workshop took place in the summer of 1979.

Cultural activities and opportunities also expanded during the seventies. An annual Fine Arts Festival began in 1974, featuring special programs of music, art exhibits, photography, sculpture, and many other arts and crafts.

Music was the focus of an annual Institute of Orchestral Conducting and Symphonic Performance and an annual workshop in choral rehearsal and performance techniques. Both of these programs drew a wide atten-

dance of students and professionals.

Under LLU auspices, the seventies saw such publishing accomplishments as creation of the *Seventh-day Adventist Periodical Index* and the launching of *Adventist Heritage* magazine.

Could John Burden, Ellen White, and others who helped found Loma Linda have seen the campus as it stood at the end of the 1970s, they unquestionably would have been both astonished and filled with gratitude to the God whose providential leading had been so evident in Loma Linda's founding, survival, and growth.

Loma Linda's "tent" was now large—its ropes long, its stakes deep. Its pioneers could scarcely have dreamed of what

would grow from the seeds they planted. Then again, neither could those observing Loma Linda at the close of the seventies know the amazing things God had yet in mind to take place at this thriving center of healing and education by the time its mission was a century old.

Notes:

1. "Councilor-Faculty Member Wins Seat in US Congress," *University Scope,* November 16, 1966, p. 1.

2. Ibid., pp. 1, 4.

3. "Nixon Reveals Loma Linda as planned VA hospital site," *Scope,* September/October 1971, p. 21.

4. LLU Board of Trustees, *Minutes,* December 23, 1971, p. 2.

January 21, 1976, brought opening ceremonies for the Ellen G. White Research Center at Loma Linda. Left to right: Jim Nix, director of the center (and currently secretary of the Ellen G. White Estate); Arthur White (now deceased grandson of Ellen G. White and then-secretary of the Ellen G. White Estate); Robert H. Pierson, president of the General Conference of Seventh-day Adventists; V. Norskov Olsen, PhD, TheolD, president of Loma Linda University; and George Summers, PhD, director of the Loma Linda University Library. Arthur White holds a letter from Ellen G. White in his hands.

PHOTO ALBUM

BELOW: MEDICAL STUDENTS MAKING ROUNDS, 1977.

BELOW RIGHT: A DENTAL HYGIENE STUDENT WITH A PATIENT, 1975.

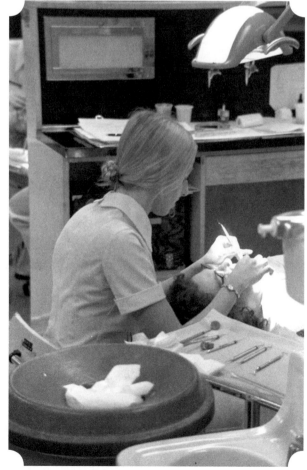

THE IMPOSSIBLE DREAM: RAILWAY TO THE MOON

LEFT: KATHLEEN ZOLBER, PHD. DURING THE 1970S, DR. ZOLBER SERVED AS PROGRAM DIRECTOR FOR THE NUTRITION AND DIETETICS PROGRAM IN THE SCHOOL OF ALLIED HEALTH PROFESSIONS AND AS DIRECTOR OF NUTRITIONAL SERVICES FOR LOMA LINDA UNIVERSITY MEDICAL CENTER.

BELOW LEFT: U. D. REGISTER, PHD. IN 1967, DR. REGISTER BECAME THE CHAIR OF THE DEPARTMENT OF NUTRITION IN THE NEWLY ORGANIZED SCHOOL OF PUBLIC HEALTH. HE SERVED IN THAT CAPACITY UNTIL 1985, WHEN HE WAS NAMED EMERITUS PROFESSOR OF NUTRITION.

BELOW: 1977 DIETETICS STUDENTS AT THEIR PINNING CEREMONY.

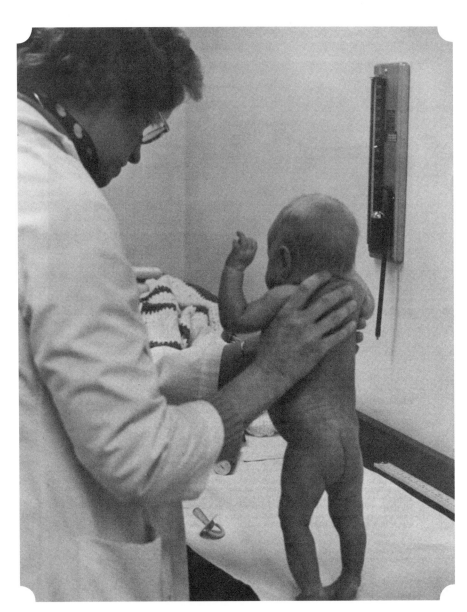

LEFT: ASSISTANT PROFESSOR OF PEDIATRICS B. LYN BEHRENS, MBBS (NOW LLUAHSC PRESIDENT/CEO), IN 1977 EXAMINES ANGELA, A FOUR-MONTH-OLD PATIENT.

BELOW: SCHOOL OF DENTISTRY STUDENTS AND FACULTY ON A MISSION TRIP TO MEXICO.

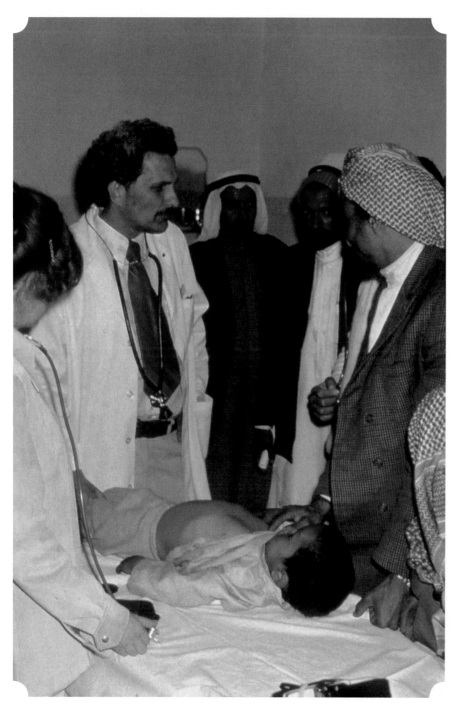

LEFT: DURING THE 1970S, ROY V. JUTZY, MD, WAS CO-DIRECTOR OF THE CARDIOVASCULAR LABORATORY AT LOMA LINDA UNIVERSITY MEDICAL CENTER AND CO-DIRECTOR OF CARDIOVASCULAR RESEARCH. HE BECAME HEAD OF THE SECTION OF CARDIOLOGY IN 1976, A POSITION HE HELD UNTIL 1991. THAT YEAR, DR. JUTZY WAS NAMED CHAIR OF THE DEPARTMENT OF MEDICINE. HERE HE WORKS AS A MEMBER OF THE LOMA LINDA UNIVERSITY OVERSEAS HEART SURGERY TEAM IN SAUDI ARABIA.

BELOW: A DENTAL STUDENT WORKS IN THE MOBILE DENTAL CLINIC, BRINGING CARE TO THE UNDERSERVED POPULATION OF SOUTHERN CALIFORNIA.

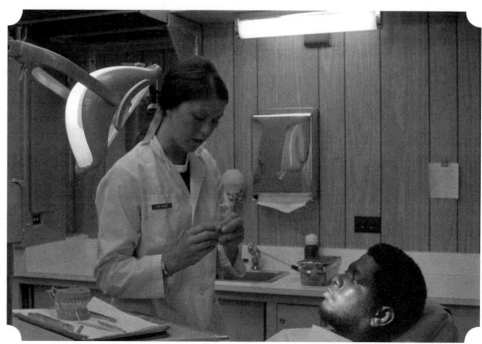

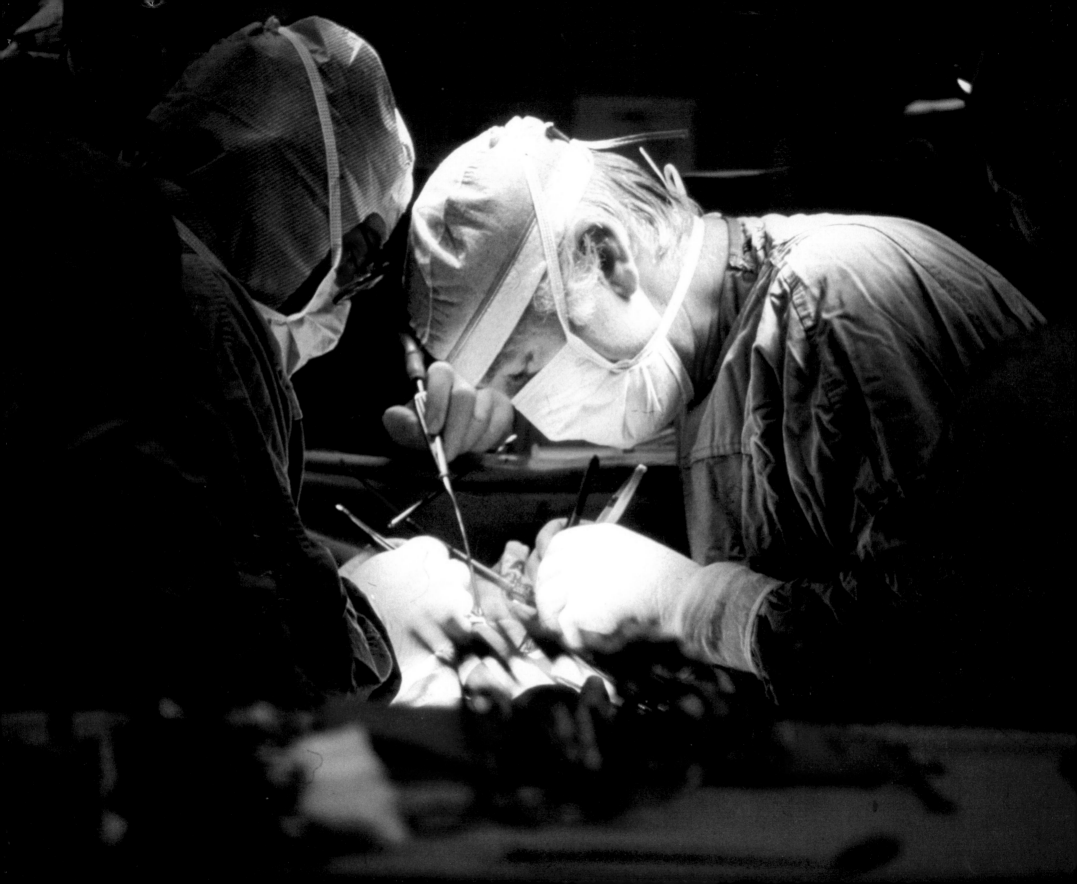

HYACINTHS AND HEADLINES

BABY FAE TRULY CHANGED THE COURSE OF LOMA LINDA'S HISTORY. THE INSTITUTION—
BOTH ITS UNIVERSITY AND ITS MEDICAL CENTER—WERE NOW INTERNATIONALLY
RECOGNIZED. THE MAGNITUDE OF MEDIA ATTENTION WAS DRAMATIC. EVEN IN THE MIDST
OF A PRESIDENTIAL ELECTION, IT BECAME ONE OF THE TOP TEN NEWS STORIES OF 1984.

Not just any news story can shunt aside the political headlines during a United States presidential election year. But during the 1984 election, millions nationwide and around the world followed with hope and rapt attention the ongoing drama of one tiny baby struggling to survive in a Southern California hospital. The media converged there and beamed news of her valiant battle to the nation and the world. Never before had Loma Linda University Medical Center found itself so centered in the national and international spotlight.

But the 1980s at Loma Linda didn't begin with the headlines of 1984. Perhaps it might better be said that the decade began with the hyacinths of 1981.

Eight years earlier, in 1973, Gaines Partridge, EdD, while chairing Loma Linda University president Dr. David Bieber's newly constituted Fine Arts Festival Committee, suggested to its members the idea of commissioning a significant sculpture for the University campus. As an undergraduate at Atlantic Union College, Dr. Partridge had been a sculpture student of

Alan Collins, a distinguished artist and art educator who would later teach at Andrews University in Michigan and at Loma Linda University.

Dr. Partridge suggested that Professor Collins be approached to create a sculpture that would symbolize the mission of Loma Linda University. With the committee's approval, Dr. Partridge asked Alan Collins to submit a clay model for the Board of Trustees to review. This model—a depiction of the Good Samaritan of the biblical parable—Professor Collins submitted to the Board on October 20, 1974.

Left: October 26, 1984. Leonard L. Bailey, MD, and his team perform historic transplant surgery on "Baby Fae."

Dr. Partridge explained that funds were available to complete a full-size sculpture should the Board approve the project.

Some on the Board, however, expressed strong reservations that such a sculpture could engender significant criticism, owing to a perceived "denominational aversion" toward allocating, to the arts, funds that some might believe should better be spent elsewhere.

Almost a year later, Bernard Brandstater, MBBS, a Medical Center physician, addressed the Board on the subject, emphasizing the "need for all of us to turn away from the present urgencies of life and buy 'hyacinths for the soul.'" In voicing these convictions, Dr. Brandstater employed the words of an old Chinese proverb: "If you have but two coins, with one buy bread, but with the other, buy hyacinths for the soul."

In 1927, Marjorie Kinnan Rawlings—who would later author the Pulitzer Prize–winning book titled *The Yearling*—amplified the ancient saying in her poem, "Hyacinths for the Soul."

It is important that human beings feed the body, but both the proverb and the poem underscore that the soul, too, needs to be fed. Deprived of sufficient nourishment, the soul—just as surely as the body—withers. The motto of Loma Linda University—"To Make Man Whole"—recognizes that a human being is not just a body, not just a mind or soul, not just a spiritual being—but an integrated blend of many facets that comprise the whole person.

The figure of hyacinths, which Dr. Brandstater applied to the arts, recognizes the human need for beauty, restfulness, symbolism, creativity, and perceiving the spiritual and sometimes abstract through the tangible and visual.

Alan Collins' sculpture—"The Good Samaritan"—Dr. Brandstater noted to the Board, would serve as a continuing reminder, to all who contemplated it, of the mission and motto of Loma Linda University and of Christ as the supreme example of compassion.

Finally, in 1977, the Board officially commissioned Alan Collins—now on the staff at Andrews University—to create the sculpture, to be located between the Medical Center and the administration building.

Completed in early 1981, the dedication and unveiling of the Good Samaritan sculpture took place on May 3, 1981. Alan Collins, along with a major donor to the project—Reuben Matiko, MD—unveiled the sculpture, and shortly after the unveiling, a wrought-iron enclosure was erected and a bronze

From 1981 to the present, the Good Samaritan sculpture by Alan Collins has given silent voice to the compassion of Christ that inspires the mission of Loma Linda.

plaque and lighting were installed.

In August of 1983, the sculpture was severely vandalized, but Alan Collins was able to restore it to its original condition within only a few weeks. The environmental ravages of time, however, over the succeeding years wrought their own damage to the larger-than-life figures of the sculpture. Working with Professor Collins, the Monterey Sculpture Center of Sand City, California, made plaster casts and from these molds cast the bronze figures now displayed.

Beginning in 1981, the Good Samaritan sculpture spoke silently, to all who passed by, of the compassionate and Christ-inspired mission of the University and Medical Center. Some three years after this silent witness began, Loma Linda's guiding mission would be exemplified in a story that would be heard across the land and around the globe.

In the high-desert Southern California town of Barstow, on October 14, 1984, a premature baby girl was born at Barstow Community Hospital. Soon after her birth, she was transferred to Loma Linda University Medical Center, where, after an examination, doctors found that she had been born with a defective heart condi-

tion—hypoplastic left-heart syndrome (HLHS)—a lethal underdevelopment of the left side of the heart that leaves it unable to pump sufficiently to sustain life for more than a few days. At that time, HLHS occurred once in each 12,000 live births in the United States.

On vacation at the time the baby arrived at LLUMC, Leonard L. Bailey, MD—a 1969 graduate of the Loma Linda University School of Medicine—would shortly return to the Medical Center, where he would become directly involved in the baby's medical treatment.

A pediatric cardiac surgeon, Dr. Bailey

Dr. Bailey shares a moment with one of his young patients.

had studied heart transplantation since his junior year of medical studies. His work in heart transplantation research began shortly after Christiaan Barnard, MD, performed the first successful human-heart transplant in South Africa in 1967. In 1968, Dr. Bailey began a four-month surgery-research rotation as part of his medical curriculum.

Later, Dr. Bailey would complete a residency in pediatric cardiac surgery at the Hospital for Sick Children in Toronto, Canada—the largest children's hospital in the world. He focused his attention on congenital heart deformities in the very young—an area of medical pursuit requiring precise technical expertise.

In the years following, Dr. Bailey dedicated a good part of his career to seeking a successful solution to hypoplastic left-heart syndrome. He deeply lamented that so many parents of HLHS babies had to hear the words: "Your baby isn't going to live."

By the year 1984, two potentially acceptable options were available for treating HLHS—palliative surgery and human-heart transplantation.

Palliative surgery could improve the defect but—because too many vital parts of the heart in HLHS were simply missing—could not cure it. It was necessary to perform palliative surgery in multiple stages—at first two stages, and later, three. While some reports

seemed to indicate a gratifying success rate for the first stage, few babies survived the subsequent surgical stages.

To Dr. Bailey, the solution for HLHS seemed most likely to be found in exchanging the baby's heart. But human-

heart transplantation for infants posed daunting obstacles. Adrian Kantrowitz, MD, a New York surgeon, performed the first such operation in 1967, using the heart of an anencephalic (brain-absent) donor. Today such a donor would not

152

meet more recently developed criteria for brain death. Dr. Kantrowitz's patient died within hours of the procedure—and no infant human-heart transplantation had been attempted since.

As Dr. Bailey considered both palliative surgery and human-heart transplantation, neither option seemed to hold promise for becoming the best longterm solution for HLHS. Yet the only realistic possibility for these babies to live normal, active lives, Dr. Bailey thought, would be some form of complete heart replacement. What, he wondered, might be the potential of using animal hearts?

By 1984, surgeons had already used approximately 50,000 valves made of calf- and pig-heart tissues to replace faulty human-heart valves. But total transplantation had been tried on adults only four times—none of the operations successful. In January of 1964, the first such transplantation had been attempted when—in a last-ditch effort to save the life of a 68-year-old man—James Hardy, MD, had transplanted the heart of a chimpanzee into his patient's chest at the University of Mississippi. But the elderly man was simply too weak to survive the surgery and died almost immediately.

The greatest challenge in heart transplantation had proven to be controlling the efforts of the body's immune system to reject the new organ

just as it would the hostile presence of any invading microbe. Rejection had proven problematic in human-to-human organ transplants, and cross-species transplants posed an even greater risk.

But Dr. Bailey had already devoted thought to the problem of rejection. He theorized that the immune system of a newborn would not yet be fully developed, and if this were true, an infant should be less likely to reject a transplanted organ than would be an older patient. To research this possibility and others, Dr. Bailey set up a laboratory with financial support from forty of his fellow surgeons who contributed monthly to the project for seven years.

The results proved exciting and encouraging. Research from the lab confirmed that newborns—at least animal newborns—indeed had immature immune systems.

Also encouraging was the fact that since the earlier failures in adult human cross-species transplantation, scientific research had made enormous forward strides. Included in this advancing knowledge, medical science now knew far more about the human immune system, about agents to suppress the immune response, and about transplantation surgical techniques.

From 1981 onward, Dr. Bailey and his transplant-research team conducted intensive and ongoing research focused on newborn/infant heart transplantation. Important to this research was the transplanting, under general anesthesia, of sheep hearts into newborn goats. As these goats matured, they could occasionally be seen as they were exercised by their handlers on the north lawn of the Medical Center. More than 250 goats had received transplants—and they each had names and were treated as pets. In time, some of them went to homes in the community.

Meanwhile, six to eight babies every year were dying at Loma Linda University Medical Center from HLHS. After six years of concentrated research, Dr. Bailey began the process to obtain authorization to conduct human clinical trials. Such authorization would not come easily.

Jack W. Provonsha, MD, PhD (left), served as professor of religion and Christian ethics, chair of the department of religion, and director of the Center of Christian Bioethics. He and his colleagues wrestled with many questions of medical ethics, including those relating to transplant surgery.

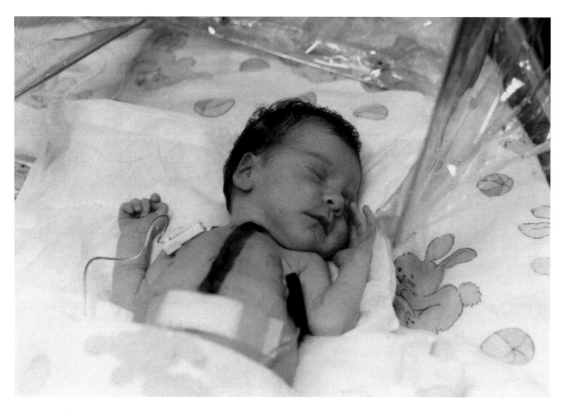

Mandatory in the University setting was that ultimate approval must be granted by the University's Institutional Review Board (IRB). This Board was constituted of local professionals representing a variety of disciplines. Some had no connection with the University or Medical Center other than their proximity. Their task was to evaluate both the ethics and the scientific merits of Dr. Bailey's proposed clinical trials.

Before the IRB could render its final decision, a long list of other entities first had to be convinced that the clinical trials were merited and met various and stringent criteria. Among these entities: the Medical Center administration, the Medical Center's medical ethics committee, the standing transplantation committee, an ad hoc neonatal cardiac transplantation committee, the executive committee of the medical staff, the School of Medicine administration, an advisory committee to the vice president for medical affairs, the department of surgery, the department of pediatrics, the department of anesthesia, the Loma Linda University Center for Christian Bioethics, and ultimately, the Medical Center Board of Trustees.

Through this painstaking and complex process, Dr. Bailey remained both gracious and patient. The varied committees and others reviewing his request considered every possible objection and difficulty. Recommended changes emerged for the protocol to be followed, for the consent form, and for additional external scientific consultants to evaluate the proposed project. Richard Sheldon, MD, chair of the IRB, maintained close communication with the various reviewing entities and with Dr. Bailey.

Supporting the project were scientists from Stanford University, the University of California at Los Angeles, and Albert Einstein College of Medicine in New York.

At long last, after fourteen months of intense discussion, the various groups reached consensus. They agreed that preparation for the clinical trials had been thorough and that human studies should no longer be delayed. A majority vote of the IRB awarded confidential approval to Dr. Bailey to proceed.

Soon after, the premature baby girl from Barstow arrived at the University Medical Center and was diagnosed with HLHS. Doctors presented the available options to the baby's mother, who then chose to take the baby home to die—though she was told she could bring the baby back at any time.

Four days later a pediatrician called the mother to tell her of Dr. Bailey's research.

Having just returned from a family vacation, Dr. Bailey would welcome the opportunity of talking with her about the possibility of an animal-heart transplant.

Accompanied by her own mother and a friend, the mother returned to Loma Linda with her baby. Following the infant's admission to the hospital, Dr. Bailey met with the three adults. For several hours, he reviewed the various options available. After he presented the option of transferring the baby to the eastern United States for palliative surgery, the mother rejected this possibility. Dr. Bailey went on to address the option of a human-heart transplant. But he emphasized that for a number of reasons, it was highly unlikely that a suitable human heart would become available. Dr. Bailey then explained in detail to his visitors the research he had conducted using animal-to-animal heart transplants. At the end of the session, the baby's mother gave Dr. Bailey permission to begin the preliminary testing that would be needed to conduct the proposed surgery. But she also wished to discuss this possibility with the baby's father.

The next day, both parents returned, and Dr. Bailey repeated his proposal in depth. He made sure that they understood that he could not guarantee success, since this kind of surgery had never before been attempted with a newborn human baby. During the next several days, the

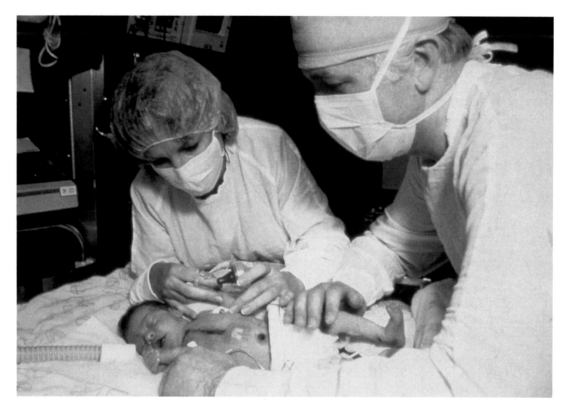

baby's family had several opportunities to ask questions and express concerns. The informed consent form they ultimately signed was the most comprehensive and exhaustive such form ever implemented in the history of the institution.

On Monday, October 22, 1984, the institution's public relations office was apprised of the immediate weekend's developments. The baby girl, they were told—hospitalized on the cardiothoracic surgery intensive care unit on life support—had almost died on her sixth day of life. She was being tested as a pos-

sible candidate for an animal-to-human heart transplant. The potentially historic surgery, unprecedented in its involvement of a newborn, was tentatively scheduled for the following Friday, October 26.

The Medical Center's public relations office staff met with the baby's family to explain their privacy rights. Under California law, only limited and general information can be released about a patient's condition unless the patient or his/her guardian agrees to release additional information.

By the end of this meeting, the family

chose to allow the Medical Center to release the baby's condition and details of the surgery, on the understanding that the family itself would remain anonymous. They further agreed to allow the baby to be known by her given middle name—Fae. This name had great meaning for the family, since it was also the middle name of the baby's mother, grandmother, and great-grandmother.

In preparation for the upcoming surgery, the Medical Center beefed up its security, including its electronic surveillance system, and rekeyed strategic doors. It cancelled all vacations for security personnel and instituted sixteen-hour shifts for the security staff. All police dogs in the service of the institution were on around-the-clock standby.

Few knew what was in the offing—though many had become curious. Why, they wondered, did employees—even physicians—have to show personal identification to enter certain areas of the Medical Center? Rumors spread: a VIP—perhaps even a notorious criminal—was hospitalized. It was indeed a VIP—a five-pound baby girl named Fae, soon to assume a heavyweight's notoriety.

For the next several days, tests proceeded to evaluate the compatibility of potential baboon heart donors to Baby Fae's blood type and immunological profile. The longest of these tests took six days, but the transplant team was determined not to rush into surgery without this vital information.

At 4:00 a.m. on October 26—the scheduled day for Baby Fae's surgery—Sandra Nehlsen-Cannarella, PhD, the project's chief immunologist, received the results of the last test and agreed that the surgery should proceed. Dr. Nehlsen-Cannarella—one of the project's outside scientific consultants—was at the time serving as director of transplant immunology at Montefiore Medical Center and the Hospital of Albert Einstein College of Medicine in New York. She had been invited to join Loma Linda's transplant team for Baby Fae's surgery.

At 6:30 a.m., Baby Fae's support team transported her into a second-floor surgery suite—and into the annals of medical history. Robert D. Martin, MD—the team anesthesiologist—administered her anesthesia with extreme caution because of her weakened condition. Baby Fae's body temperature was gradually lowered to sixty-six degrees Fahrenheit—resulting in a condition resembling animal hibernation called deep hypothermia. Standard practice in infant heart surgery, this process dramatically reduced her metabolic

Dr. Bailey with Hugh Downs, co-host of the ABC newsmagazine 20-20, which in 1994 broadcast a double segment on Loma Linda's infant transplant program.

rate and other bodily functions, allowing the transplant team to stop Baby Fae's circulation for one hour and ten minutes.

Implanting the new heart—about the size of a large walnut and weighing about an ounce—took approximately an hour. At 11:35 a.m., during the warming procedure following the surgery, Baby Fae's new heart began beating on its own—a strong, steady beat of 130 times a minute. A feeling of awe prevailed in the surgery suite. No signs of rejection appeared in those first early minutes, and a brief episode of rapid heartbeat subsided on its own.

Throughout the surgery, Baby Fae's mother—looking anxious but hopeful— waited in the hospital lobby with chaplain Bill Hinton. A few hours after the surgery, the transplant team moved Baby Fae from the surgical suite to an intensive-care room for recovery. With the chaplain, Baby Fae's mother hurried to see her little girl. Her face beamed with hope and with the gratitude of knowing that her baby had been pulled back from the brink of death and given a fighting chance to survive.

Despite all the heartfelt hopes and heroic efforts, Baby Fae died on November 15, 1984. Yet her new heart showed no evidence of the rejection some expected. Instead, she died of kidney failure.

The next day at an emotionally charged press conference, Dr. Bailey said, in part: "Baby Fae's experience of a brief month or so has been a uniquely human one. The courageous decisions made for her by her family and all of us who have loved her have forced us to confront and reexamine our human existence. The discussions and debates should improve all mankind. For her part, I and my colleagues believe Baby Fae has opened new vistas for all, including the as-yet unborn infants with similar lethal heart disease."

Though the effort to save Baby Fae was widely and generally acclaimed and applauded, questions and unfair characterizations inevitably followed Baby Fae's losing battle to survive. Some questioned the parents' informed consent, implying that her parents didn't fully understand their daughter's condition or the options for her treatment. To put minds at ease, the Medical Center invited the National Institutes of Health (NIH) to evaluate the consent process.

The NIH conclusion? That "as a result of the consent process the parents of Baby Fae fully understood the alternatives available as well as the risks and reasonably expected benefits of the transplant. . . . The [NIH] site visitors also believe that the explanation was presented in an atmosphere which allowed the parents an opportunity to carefully consider, without coercion or undue influence, whether to give their permission for the transplant."[1]

Others—particularly some in the media—suggested that Baby Fae's parents were poorly educated as well as insufficiently informed. But a few months later, on April 21, 1985, Arthur Caplan, PhD, then–associate director of the Hastings Center—a bioethics research institute in Hastings-on-Hudson, New York—interviewed Baby Fae's mother at the conclusion of a biomedical ethics workshop in Loma Linda. In a letter to Dr. Bailey, Dr. Caplan expressed his appreciation for the opportunity of chatting with Baby Fae's mother, and said: "I must say the conversation we had was an eye-opening one for me. The press had depicted her

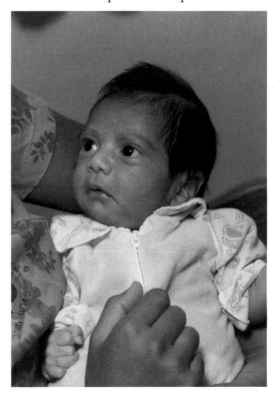

With a donated human infant heart, Dr. Bailey in 1985 performed his second transplant at Loma Linda on "Baby Moses" (left).

as being an ill-informed, undereducated individual. I couldn't help but feel, as a result of my conversation, that the press was not only wrong but insulting to her. She seemed to me to be a very bright, articulate, and thoughtful woman."

Among the most unfair criticism was that focused on Dr. Bailey himself. Those who knew him best saw him as a compassionate, dedicated, and publicity-shy surgeon. Nonetheless, a few critics in both the media and the scientific community accused him of grandstanding and even of child abuse.

Such isolated and unfounded characterizations were virtually lost, however, in the outpouring of admiration and

Several years after his 1985 transplant surgery, "Baby" Moses enjoys a birthday (right). In 2005, he celebrated his twentieth!

support for Dr. Bailey's single-minded determination to hold nothing back in attempting to save just one infant life.

In her brief life, Baby Fae not only brought attention to Loma Linda University Medical Center and its pediatric surgical transplant team—she also focused the nation's attention on the critical need for human infant heart donation. Prior to Baby Fae, as Dr. Bailey himself had recognized, locating a suitable donor had been a virtual impossibility. But Baby Fae's transplant dramatically raised both public and scientific awareness of the possibilities for saving heart-defective infants and of the need for human infant heart donation.

More than a year later—a year during which no other infant heart transplants were attempted anywhere in the nation—Dr. Bailey again performed an infant heart transplant, this time with a donated human infant heart. And again, media attention was immense. On November 20, 1985, "Baby Moses" (a fictitious name), at four days of age, became the youngest person in the world ever to undergo successful heart transplantation. Twenty years now after this second historic surgery, "Baby" Moses is still living!

But had there been no Baby Fae, there could not have been a Baby Moses. Both the donor and recipient were referred to Loma Linda because of the widespread publicity focused on Baby

Fae. And in turn, the public attention surrounding Baby Moses raised even higher the awareness of the public and scientific community to the possibilities for newborn heart transplantation.

In January of 1986, Dr. Bailey again performed a successful transplant on "Baby Eve" (also a fictitious name), who, at seventeen days of age, became the second-youngest person in the world to undergo the procedure.

The California Legislature, in November of 1986, approved Resolution No. 481, honoring Dr. Bailey and his team in recognition of the one-year anniversary of the first successful newborn-heart transplant: Baby Moses.

The year following Baby Fae's death, the legacy of her brief life continued as Dr. Nehlsen-Cannarella—who had served as the chief immunological consultant for Baby Fae's transplant team—joined the faculty of Loma Linda University's School of Medicine. In that capacity, on March 1, 1985, she opened the Loma Linda University Immunology Center, directing both clinical and research laboratories in studying the immunology of transplantation as well as maternal-fetal compatibility.

Baby Fae truly changed the course of Loma Linda's history. The institution—both its University and its Medical Center—were now internationally recognized. The magnitude of media attention

THE IMPOSSIBLE DREAM: RAILWAY TO THE MOON

was dramatic. Whereas, prior to Baby Fae's surgery, Loma Linda's media contacts averaged perhaps a thousand per year, during the days-long drama itself, such contacts skyrocketed to 1,500 per day! Baby Fae so captured public and media attention that even in the midst of a presidential election, it became one of the top ten news stories of 1984.

As of March 2004, Loma Linda's heart transplant team had performed more than 410 infant heart transplants—255 of these on babies under six months of age. Honored by the American Heart Association at a "Stars of the Heart" celebrity gala in June of 2002, Dr. Bailey continues to devote his life and career to saving as many infants as he possibly can. His motivation can be found in his own words:

"It [transplant surgery] is a genuine rebirthing for a baby dying of heart disease, and the process is a very fine moment, indeed, for humanity. It is fundamentally good news, and while it may not necessarily even the score for all the tragedy facing our planet, saving a baby always makes a clear statement for what can and ought to be in the universe. As with the babies and their loved ones, my own life assumes new meaning and affirmation in

Surgeon Bailey (below) with some of the many children whose lives he has helped extend through his dedicated efforts.

the process. I am compelled by the belief that saving babies is the right thing to do."

In a 1989 interview with the editors of *Scope*, Dr. Bailey admitted to being "a real patsy when it comes to looking into a baby's eyes and dreaming about the potential for this little person."[2] And concerning the transplant program's positive results, he added:

"I'm convinced the Almighty has much to do with it. It's almost humanly impossible, given the condition of these babies. These were kids with incurable heart disease, in all states of decomposition.

"From our statistics today, if you're a baby and have a heart transplant, you have an actuarial chance of being alive of about 87 percent at three years—better than you can say for most conventional heart surgery for complex disease."

From Baby Fae's landmark surgery onward, Loma Linda's infant-heart transplant program has captured the attention of the world. The courageous and pioneering efforts of Dr. Bailey and his team—as well as other physicians who subsequently have performed delicate pediatric transplants—have brought life and hope to hundreds of families who would otherwise face the certain loss of their infants to a lethal heart defect.

Unquestionably, the saga of Baby Fae dominated the landscape of the 1980s at Loma Linda. But by no means was it the only noteworthy advance at the University and Medical Center. The forward progress of the institution was not put on hold while so much of the world's attention focused on this one gripping drama. Loma Linda had from the first been a place of life and vitality—of dynamic progress driven by a compelling sense of mission. The 1980s, therefore, witnessed growth and development over a broad range of pursuits.

THE PURCHASE OF LOMA LINDA COMMUNITY HOSPITAL

In April of 1979, Harrison S. Evans, MD, vice president for medical affairs and chair of the department of psychiatry, presented to the Board a preliminary proposal for an affiliation between Loma Linda University Medical Center and the nearby, nonprofit and privately owned Loma Linda Community Hospital (LLCH)—a 120-bed facility. LLCH opened its doors in 1972, accomodating area general practice physicians. Dr. Evans envisioned the potential for developing at LLCH a base for the practice of family medicine. The Loma Linda Board voted to favor the proposal and recommended further study.

In late 1981 the LLCH Board voted to offer LLUMC the opportunity to purchase the community hospital. The university

A view from Anderson Street, looking west down the lower-campus quadrangle toward the Alumni Hall for Basic Sciences at the far end.

voted the purchase on July 15, 1982, and ownership transferred over on August 12. A later decade would bring not just ownership but a complete merger of the two institutions, along with dedication of the former LLCH to a vital component of Loma Linda's medical program.[3]

THE ALUMNI HALL FOR BASIC SCIENCES

Vibrantly alive and thus continuously thriving and growing, Loma Linda accomplished a number of significant additions to its campus throughout the decade.

In 1941, CME built a men's residence hall at the west end of the lower campus quadrangle. On July 2, 1942, the Board named the new dormitory Daniells Hall, in honor of Arthur G. Daniells, who had been president of the General Conference of Seventh-day Adventists for twenty-two years, including the time of Loma Linda's purchase in 1905. He also served as CME Board chair from 1939 to 1950.[4]

Forty years later, in January 1981, the University completed a new fifty-two-apartment housing development on the south side of Sanitarium Hill and razed Daniells Hall to make way for the new 60,600-square-foot Alumni Hall for Basic Sciences. The new apartments were named the A.G. Daniells Residence Complex.

The new Alumni Hall for Basic Sciences now houses the departments of pathology and microbiology. It includes a 276-seat teaching amphitheater, two smaller classrooms, 18 faculty offices, 18 research laboratories, two teaching laboratories, and eight student study rooms. Of the $8.5 million cost, the School of Medicine Alumni Association raised $4.4 million. The University, the General Conference, and others funded the remainder. Loma Linda University dedicated the new building on March 13, 1984.[5]

THE SCHUMAN PAVILION

In the meantime, the Medical Center outgrew its facilities. In September 1986, LLUMC opened the four-story, 54,000-square-foot, $12.5 million, Irwin and Virginia Schuman Pavilion, its first major addition. It houses the Loma Linda International Heart Institute, two magnetic resonance imaging (MRI) scanners, and expansion for diagnostic radiology.

Because Mrs. Virginia Schuman donated $3 million to memorialize her late husband, LLUMC named the building to honor both. The Schuman Pavilion also added much-needed classroom space and conference rooms and a medical library.[6]

The Alumni Hall for Basic Sciences sits at the west end of the lower-campus quadrangle on the site of the old Daniells Hall.

SOUTH WING PHASE I

In the process of doubling its size, in 1989 LLUMC added the $43 million, seven-story, 238,000-square-foot South wing phase I. The new wing provided facilities for computer information services, central service and the operating room linen-processing function, the Medical Center mail service, six new surgical suites, a surgery recovery room, a large preoperative-preparation room, a new fifty-eight-bassinet neonatal intensive care unit (now licensed for seventy-two bassinets), a new cardiac intensive care unit, and a pediatric intensive care unit. The project included

two emergency 900-kilowatt diesel generators, which could provide enough electricity to service forty to fifty homes.[7]

SOUTH WING PHASE II

In 1990 the Medical Center completed its $48 million, 240,000-square-foot South Wing Phase II, encompassing the world's first hospital-based proton treatment center and the final addition to the 250-bed Loma Linda University Children's Hospital. Unique to Children's Hospital is cancer therapy provided by the Proton Treatment Center.[8]

Building these two major additions

brought the total floor space of the Medical Center to more than a million square feet.

THE PROTON TREATMENT CENTER

In 1990, after nearly twenty years of research, Loma Linda University Medical Center, in cooperation with the Fermi National Accelerator Laboratory (Fermilab) in Batavia, Illinois, and the Proton Therapy Cooperative Group, opened the world's first hospital-based proton-beam accelerator dedicated to the treatment of cancer patients. The completed $100 million, three-story facility is truly awe-inspiring. The equipment—which includes the accelerator and the proton guidance system—weighs 400 tons and produces up to 250 million electron volts of radiation. The accelerator portion itself, weighing 50 tons, is a ring of eight electromagnets, sixty feet in circumference and twenty feet in diameter. When activated, the machine accelerates protons up to half the speed of light. Loma Linda's proton accelerator is a giant weapon against the cruel ravages of cancer, as well as certain other diseases.

Before the facility opened, James M. Slater, MD, FACR (School of Medicine class of 1963), co-director of radiation medicine, expressed his high expectations for the accelerator:

"In order for cancer radiation therapy

A present-day view of Loma Linda University Medical Center from the "back" (west) side, showing on the right the Children's Hospital and other south wing construction completed in the 1980s.

to advance, we needed to improve our ability to focus a beam inside the body. The proton accelerator does that. It's a superior tool that's going to produce a major improvement in cancer therapy."[9]

The prevention and curing of cancer has long posed one of medical science's greatest challenges. While decades of research have brought gratifying progress, the arsenal of treatment weapons is at best a mixed blessing. What attacks renegade cancer cells also attacks and brings varying degrees of damage to healthy tissues as well. Surgery, chemotherapy, and conventional radiation can leave in their wake lasting disfigurement, extreme treatment discomfort, loss of function, and damage to a variety of body tissues and systems.

Dr. Slater and his colleagues at Loma Linda had long been convinced that there simply had to be a better way. As early as 1971, Dr. Slater began assembling a team to explore the possibilities for using charged particles, rather than conventional radiation, to treat cancer. Spearheaded in part by the efforts of Dr. Slater, in January of 1985 a group of scientists from around the world convened to study the potential of proton accelerators.

The supreme advantage to proton treatment is that its beams pass through intervening healthy tis-

sue—leaving it largely unaffected—to focus their destructive energy on the underlying tumor itself with almost surgical precision. This high degree of control and selective targeting makes possible the delivery of far higher radiation doses than can be achieved with conventional radiation.

While a limited number of other sites already had proven the benefits of proton therapy for cancer treatment, Loma Linda's proton center was the first-ever to be based at a hospital rather than a research facility. Loma Linda's machine is unique in another respect as well. When installed, it was the first proton unit with sufficient energy to reach even the deepest tumors—being capable of penetrating up to fifteen inches.

Fermilab—owned by the U.S. Department of Energy and operated by Universities Research Association (a consortium of fifty-seven universities spanning the globe)—built and tested Loma Linda's proton accelerator. Its design is based on many hundreds of millions of federally funded and carefully developed technologies. A $19.6 million grant from the United States Congress helped fund Loma Linda's accelerator.

The first patient received treatment at Loma Linda's Proton Treatment Center on October 23, 1990. Full operation

began in the summer of 1994, and the Center now serves up to 160 patients a day, approximately 99 percent of whom are treated on an outpatient basis.

The proton center has become an international resource for the treatment of cancer through the use of charged particles.

REVERSAL OF THE LOMA LINDA-LA SIERRA CONSOLIDATION

When La Sierra College and Loma Linda University merged in 1967, it was expected that this arrangement would last indefinitely. Implemented in part to fulfill a requirement of the Western Association of Schools and Colleges that the University have an undergraduate program, the single

James M. Slater, MD, FACR, played a leading role in establishing Loma Linda's Proton Treatment Center.

university on two campuses had served students for more than twenty years.[10]

But by 1986, the conviction had grown that the University would be more cost effective as well as stronger academically if it were located on one campus. So in August of that year, the Board appointed a committee to study the possibility

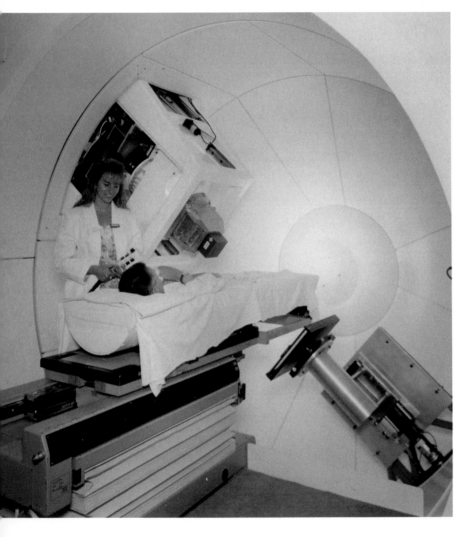

of consolidation in Loma Linda.[11]

For nearly three more years, the issue returned many times to the Board for consideration. Just as nearly thirty years earlier the similar issue of consolidating the two campuses of Loma Linda and Los Angeles had stirred sometimes passionate debate, proponents of both the status quo and of consolidation brought forth their arguments.

Finally, on February 13, 1990, the University Board voted to separate the two campuses, consolidating health sciences education at Loma Linda. The Board also granted the Pacific Union Conference of Seventh-day Adventists authority to name a transition Board of Trustees and an executive committee to operate the Riverside Campus beginning March 1, 1990. The Board was authorized to appoint officers and faculty, and to transact business until the legal transfer had been accomplished. Separate operations were to begin on July 1, 1990.[12]

La Sierra expressed its desire to maintain university status, and the LLU Board—not envisioning any direct competition with La Sierra despite its geographical proximity—made no objection.[13]

The Board also approved a five-year affiliation agreement between the two organizations to provide—to students on the Riverside campus who had been enrolled

or accepted under the 1990-1991 *University Bulletin*—the option of being granted a degree from Loma Linda University.[14]

On August 25 and 26, nearly 200 delegates of the University constituency met in the Campus Chapel to conduct Loma Linda University's quinquennial constituency meeting. With a nearly unanimous decision, they voted to affirm the Board's February 13, 1990, decision to separate the two campuses into distinct corporate institutions.[15]

On September 20, 1990, the Board took formal action to declare Loma Linda University a health sciences university, and on March 7, 1991, the Riverside campus became La Sierra University.[16]

"To make man whole"

Loma Linda's longstanding motto—"To Make Man Whole"—found dramatic, real-life demonstration during the 1980s—in a symbolic sculpture, in heroic efforts to save infant lives, in the war against cancer, and in the thousand daily sacrifices and commitments of its employees, staff, and students.

The struggling little school and sanitarium of the early twentieth century was now a sprawling, complex, yet focused center of education and healing, respected far and wide for its leading role in preventing and alleviating human suffering.

Loma Linda—profoundly committed to serving humanity and lifting up its divine Founder and Healer—strode purposefully past the 1980s and into the 1990s, closing in rapidly on its first amazing century.

What surprises, what miracles, what accomplishments yet lay ahead? For most assuredly, those involved in the mission

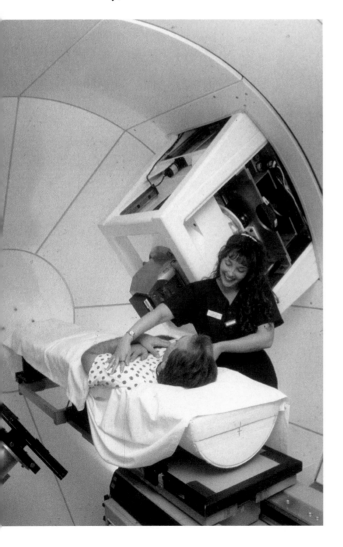

of the Hill Beautiful would have challenging new mountains still to climb.

NOTES:

1. "NIH report released on recent LLU xenograft procedure," *Scope*, April-June,1985, p. 20.

2. Loma Linda *Scope*, July-September 1989.

3. See chapter 11 for later developments involving the Loma Linda Community Hospital facility.

4. Keld J. Reynolds, PhD, "The Brethren," *Diamond Memories*, p. 95.

5. *Scope*, October-December 1981, p. 17; Program: Loma Linda University Alumni Hall for Basic Sciences, Opening Ceremonies, March 13, 1984, p. 3.

6. Rita Waterman, "New wing for LLUMC," *Scope*, July-September 1984, pp. 13-15; Martin Habekost, "Irwin and Virginia Schuman Pavilion dedicated," *Scope*, October-December 1986, p. 19.

7. Richard W. Weismeyer, "LLUMC opens South Wing (phase one)," *Scope*, January-March 1989, pp. 4, 5.

8. Joyce McClintock, "Children's Hospital announced," *Scope*, January-March 1989, pp. 8-10; David B. Hinshaw, MD, "Children's Hospital Update," LLU Board of Trustees, *Minutes*, June 10, 1993, p. 10.

9. Richard A. Schaefer, "Protons: 'A Beam of Hope,'" *Legacy*, p. 48.

10. LLU Board of Trustees, *Minutes*, February 13, 1989, p. 13.

11. LLU Board of Trustees, *Minutes*, August 25, 1986, p. 14.

12. LLU Board of Trustees, *Minutes*, February 13, 1990, p. 23.

13. LLU Board of Trustees, *Minutes*, April 2, 1990, p. 3; "Major changes ahead for LLU," *Scope*, January-June 1990, p. 38.

14. Ibid.

15. "A new beginning," *Scope*, July-September 1990, p. 8.

16. *La Sierra University Alumni Directory*, 1998; pp. iv, v.

Photo Album

Left: Neal C. Wilson, prior to his election as president of the General Conference of Seventh-day Adventists, served as chair of Loma Linda's Board.

Below: During a 1987 visit of Konstantin Kharchev, chair of the Council on Religious Affairs for the Soviet Union, Pastor Wilson explains the Good Samaritan sculpture to Kharchev, Mikhail Kulakov, and W. Augustus Cheatham.

THE IMPOSSIBLE DREAM: RAILWAY TO THE MOON

BELOW: MELVIN P. JUDKINS, MD, WAS CHAIR OF THE DEPARTMENT OF RADIOLOGY AND DIRECTOR OF THE CARDIOVASCULAR LABORATORIES.

BELOW RIGHT: STUDENT NURSES PARTICIPATE IN AN INFORMAL DISCUSSION.

Left: Nursing students at the 1988 dedication ceremony for their class.

Below: A plane sent to retrieve a heart for transplantation at Loma Linda.

THE IMPOSSIBLE DREAM: RAILWAY TO THE MOON

Left: A 1987 view of the north campus, looking past Magan Hall to the snow-dusted San Bernardino Mountains. University Avenue—now a cul-de-sac—was then a through street passing in front of Magan Hall.

Below: A close-up of the Good Samaritan portion of the multi-figured sculpture.

IN FULL FLIGHT

BY THE DAWN OF THE NEW MILLENNIUM, LOMA LINDA WAS A LONG WAY FROM ITS VULNERABLE EARLY YEARS—YEARS WHEN IT STRUGGLED, LIKE THE WRIGHT BROTHERS' FIRST AIRPLANE, TO LIFT OFF AND FLY. AS THE SECOND MILLENNIUM A.D. BEGAN, LOMA LINDA—LIKE A JUMBO JET— HAD ACHIEVED CRUISING ALTITUDE, MOVING SWIFTLY, SURELY, POWERFULLY.

For centuries, men and women watched birds soaring overhead and dreamed of finding a way to join them in the skies.

In 1903, the United States Army was trying hard to develop a flying machine—but they couldn't get it to fly. Skeptical writers at *The New York Times* wrote that perhaps—in somewhere between one and ten million years—the Army might succeed in making a craft that would fly.

But whatever gifts the newspaper's writers possessed, the gift of prophecy was clearly not among them.

Today every high-school student learns the story of the day when the dream of human flight began to come true.

Wilbur and Orville Wright.

Kitty Hawk.

December 17, 1903—the same year the *Times* offered its prediction.

That morning, on a windswept North Carolina beach, Orville Wright clambered aboard a frail-looking contraption he and his brother had designed, fired up its small engine, and launched the human race into the era of flight. For twelve seconds, Orville kept his craft airborne—covering a distance of 120 feet.

One hundred and twenty feet is barely more than half the 212-foot wingspan of a 747-400 jumbo jet. And the difference in complexity between these two aircraft is astonishing. To fly the Kitty Hawk plane, Orville Wright lay prone with his head forward, his left hand operating the sin-

gle manual control—for the elevator. To control lateral movement, Orville shifted his hips from side to side, which flexed a hip cradle from which wires led to the wings and the rudder, warping them in response to the pilot's maneuverings.

In contrast, the cockpit of a 747 is a mind-boggling array of switches, dials, status lights, and computerized controls. The 31 miles per hour achieved by the Wright's first plane is dwarfed by the 567-mph cruising speed of a 747.

About two years after that first flight at Kitty Hawk, a few intrepid pioneers in Southern California gave wings to their own vision: a center for education and healing that would bring glory to the Teacher and Healer they loved and served.

Simple at first, fragile, vulnerable, the

Left: The five-story, 275-bed Loma Linda University Children's Hospital opened in December of 1993.

As a center for mental health care, the Behavioral Medicine Center integrates Christianity and psychiatry in patient treatment.

improbable enterprise started small and progressed slowly as it overcame a succession of intimidating obstacles. But against all odds, it grew. Like a small plane taking off, it gained altitude and speed. Never touching down, it soared higher, grew larger, and gained momentum.

By the 1990s, Loma Linda was in full flight and cruising fast—thriving, growing, moving, dynamically alive. From its simple beginnings, it had grown amazingly complex. From its first small buildings, it had become a place of constant expansion and new construction projects. From a handful of students and staff, it now had thousands enrolled and thousands more employed in its University and Medical Center.

With maturity and growth, organizations often become subject to risks. They can become bogged down in bureaucratic processes that make it difficult to get things done. Communication both within the organization and with those outside can become confused and impersonal. Yet no risk is greater than that an organization may forget its original mission—its reason to exist—the driving vision that led to its founding.

For all its growth in plant and people and programs, Loma Linda has from the first to the present kept a single-minded focus on its unifying mission—"To Make Man Whole." It has remembered that every corner of its far-flung campus, every rung on its organizational flow chart, every activity of every hour of every day exists for the purpose of meeting human need as empowered by the divine.

By the 1990s, Loma Linda's growth and activity was constant. The new was now the norm: new buildings, new services, new alliances, new innovations. What might have filled an earlier decade now fit easily into a year. For that reason, perhaps the most practical way of reviewing the 1990s is to step through it year by year and selectively focus on only some of its developments, marveling at the amazing growth that occurred during just that one decade.

1991: The Behavioral Medicine Center

In 1962, the Loma Linda University School of Medicine opened the department of psychiatry.[1] Five years later the Medical Center opened a new, eighteen-bed psychiatric unit. In addition to providing care for mental health patients, this unit also provided clinical experience for medical students and resident physicians. But limitations of space and services resulted in the necessity of referring many patients to outside facilities.

During a weekly fellowship meeting of the unit's professional staff in 1984, discussion began centered on the dream of establishing a free-standing center for mental health care. In early 1988, the Medical Center Board explored the idea of converting the Loma Linda Manor—a nearby skilled nursing facility—into a seventy- to seventy-five-bed psychiatric hospital.[2] By August, the Medical Center administration scheduled the new hospital to open in the spring of 1989—and in February of that year, the Board voted to merge Loma Linda Manor into LLUMC in preparation for the Manor's transition into a psychiatric hospital.

The process of obtaining necessary permits and approvals moved forward. In anticipation of moving into much larger facilities, the department of p sychiatry doubled the size of its faculty. And then something unexpected happened.

In nearby Redlands, an almost-new and successful psychiatric hospital went on the market. Just after it had been expanded to eighty-nine beds, the parent corporation of Charter Hospital found itself needing cash for debt repayment and decided to sell Charter for its depreciated asset value: approximately $12.6 million.[3]

Addressing his Board, David B. Hinshaw Sr., MD—president of the Medical Center—provided important background for discussion and decision-making. Psychiatry, he noted—along with medicine, surgery, pediatrics, and

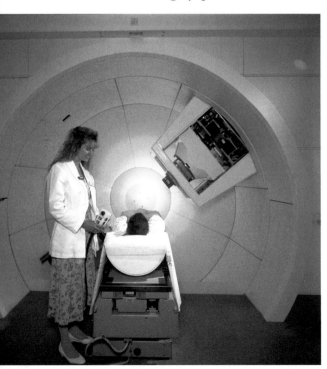

obstetrics/gynecology—is considered one of the five major areas of medical education. He emphasized the desire of Medical Center leadership to strengthen LLUMC's psychiatry program in three areas: inpatient and outpatient services—and research.

Dr. Hinshaw also noted that for many years, there had been no major medical education center in the country incorporating Christianity into psychiatry. Loma Linda University Medical Center, he urged, needed to demonstrate to the nation and the world that psychiatry does not inevitably destroy faith in Christianity—that, in fact, the two can harmonize.[4]

The suddenly available Charter Hospital presented LLUMC with an alternate option to the existing plan of converting Loma Linda Manor into a psychiatric hospital at a cost of $7.5 million. Richard Griffin, MD, compared all aspects of the two options and reported that his faculty highly favored the purchase of Charter Hospital.

In mid-December of 1990, the Medical Center Board voted to purchase Charter Hospital, and on January 18, 1991, LLUMC took over its operations and renamed it Behavioral Medicine Center (BMC).[5]

To the best of LLUMC's knowledge, the BMC is the only Christian academic behavioral medicine center in the world.[6] While integrating

Christianity and psychiatry, the BMC also helps carry out the University's motto: "To Make Man Whole."

Today the BMC offers a wide range of services. It contains units for child and adolescent psychiatry, adult psychiatry, and adult chemical dependency. It has a pastoral care department with a full-time chaplain. And as one of its many services to the community, it hosts twenty-seven self-help groups, such as Alcoholics Anonymous, Narcotics Anonymous, and others.

1991: FIRST-IN-THE-WORLD USE OF ROTATING GANTRY FOR PROTON THERAPY

Between late October 1990 and the end of the year, only three patients were treated at the new Proton Treatment Center—the start-up took time. But engineering adjustments brought greater efficiencies and gave the center greater capacity. In June of 1991, the first gantry was commissioned—marking the first-ever use of a gantry to deliver a proton beam. The gantry made possible the first proton treatments at LLUMC for prostate-cancer patients. In time, such patients would compose nearly 65 percent of all patients seeking proton treatment at the center.

Today the center has three proton gantries, and most visitors to the facility find them to be the most impressive part of the center. Each gantry looks like a

The rotating gantry (left) makes possible precise delivery of a proton beam in treatment of prostate cancer.

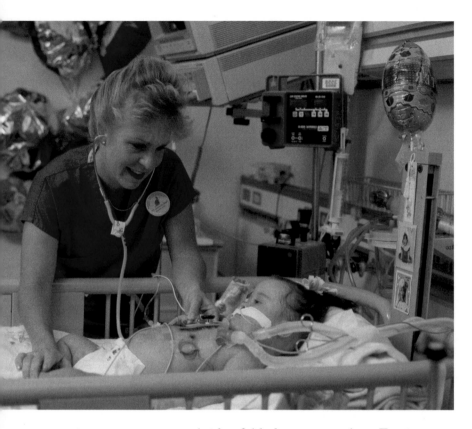

 *A young patient (above) receives care in the Loma Linda University Children's Hospital. The facility opened in December of 1993.*

bridge folded over to make a Ferris wheel and weighs more than ninety tons. Standing three stories tall, each gantry is balanced so delicately that only a small motor is enough to rotate it. The rotating gantries make it possible for physicians to aim the proton beam so it enters the patient from any angle and to potentially treat any localized tumor anywhere in the body.

1992: TotalCare Birth Center

The decade of the 1990s would see the opening of a new, state-of-the-art Children's Hospital adjacent to the main Medical Center. First phases of the hospital to open included a 22,000-square-foot neonatal intensive care unit (NICU) in February of 1989, accommodating seventy-two patients—and a new Total-Care Birth Center in March of 1992.

The NICU includes facilities for newborns who have undergone heart transplantation and is one of the most advanced such facilities in the world. The TotalCare Birth Center contains ten labor-delivery-recovery rooms designed for patient privacy in a homelike atmosphere.

1993: Loma Linda University Children's Hospital

After years of planning, the vision of a major new children's hospital in Southern California came to fruition in 1993. Among the fundraising efforts of early supporters was a December 1991 benefit concert featuring "The Highwaymen"—a country music group led by Johnny Cash and including Willie Nelson, Waylon Jennings, and Kris Kristofferson. The concert brought in $100,000 for craniofacial programs and research at the new hospital.

The Honorable then-congresswoman, Shirley Pettis Roberson (far left) served as the first chair of the LLU Children's Hospital Foundation. California First Lady Gayle Wilson (left), with Loma Linda president/CEO Dr. Lyn Behrens looking on, gave the keynote address at opening ceremonies on November 10, 1993, for Children's Hospital.

On May 20, 1992, the Medical Center Board of Trustees approved formation of the community-based Loma Linda University Children's Hospital Foundation, which devoted itself as a nonprofit agency to raising money for, coordinating, and promoting children's health services and projects. Its first chair was former congresswoman Shirley Pettis Roberson, long known for her active support for service and philanthropic projects in the Inland Empire.

A full week of opening ceremonies culminated on November 10, 1993, with a dedication service. Keynote speaker Gayle Wilson, first lady of the state of California, said in her speech:

"I am one that does believe that we need a special place for children to be treated. And here at this Children's Hospital, from the NICU to the infant heart transplant program to the proton beam cancer treatments, Loma Linda will offer the most advanced services available in this four-county area. The need is great—but it is the people who are here and others who have had the vision to make sure this need is responded to.

I'm here today to congratulate you."[6]

Patients moved into the five-story, 240,000-square-foot facility on December 14. Its 275 beds included the seventy-two in the neonatal intensive care unit.

Today Children's Hospital accommodates more than 11,000 admissions and 100,000 outpatient visits annually and is projected to admit more than 15,000 patients annually by 2010. The American Board of Surgeons has designated the Children's Hospital a level I regional trauma center, providing the highest level of trauma care within the

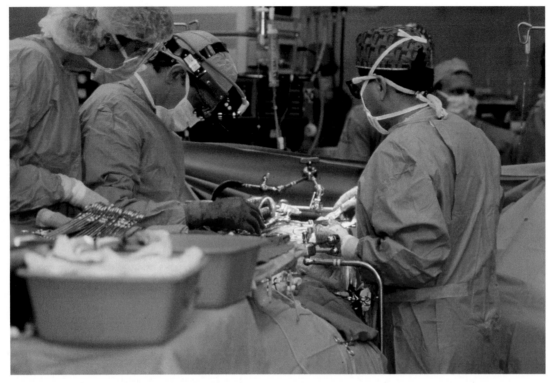

Inland Empire's four-county area, home to more than 1.2 million children.

1992-1993: TRANSPLANT FIRSTS

Throughout a twenty-five-year period, LLUMC had already performed a total of 463 kidney transplants, when, in October of 1992, the United Network for Organ Sharing—the national transplantation regulatory agency—designated the Medical Center as a liver, pancreas, and kidney transplant center. Thus was born the LLUMC Transplantation Institute.

Contributing to this designation

was a decision of the Southern California Transplantation Society—which controls organ distribution in the Los Angeles area—to allow patients needing combined kidney and pancreas transplants to have precedence over patients waiting for a kidney alone.

Another contributing factor was an agreement between all the Los Angeles area transplant centers for LLUMC to become the first institution in the region to perform these combined surgeries.[7]

In January of 1993, the Institute performed its first combined kidney/pancreas transplant. In September of the same year,

the LLUMC Transplantation Institute became the only such facility in the Inland Empire—and the third in all of Southern California—to offer adult liver transplants. Today the Institute performs some twenty-five to thirty liver transplants annually.

As a center for organ transplant surgery, LLUMC has performed kidney transplants since 1967, cornea transplants since 1977, heart transplants since 1984, and bone-marrow and stem-cell transplants since 1998. Pediatric liver transplants began in 2001, and preparations are underway to begin islet-cell transplants in the near future.

LLUMC's liver-transplant program—according to the Scientific Registry of Transplant Recipients—has seen fewer deaths (6 percent) in patients awaiting surgery than any other Southern California transplant center. And according to LegacyOne—a Redlands-based, federally funded nonprofit donor recovery center serving seventeen million residents in seven Southern California counties—only 1.6 percent of the patients undergoing liver transplants at LLUMC died, compared to 8.9 percent nationally.[8]

In August of 1998, the United States Postal Service selected LLUMC—primarily because of its long history of infant heart transplantation—as one of only a handful of sites nationwide to participate

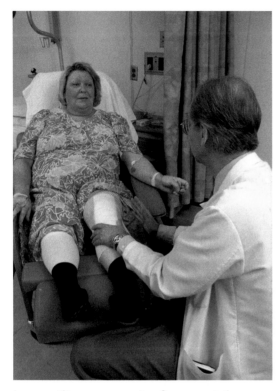

in unveiling ceremonies for a special organ and tissue donation postage stamp.[9]

1994: ORTHOPAEDIC AND REHABILITATION INSTITUTE

In July of 1982, Loma Linda University Medical Center had purchased the nearby Loma Linda Community Hospital. In December 1988, Medical Center President David B. Hinshaw Sr., reported that his administration had explored different possible uses for the Community Hospital, including an orthopedic and rehabilitation facility.

In the meantime, LLUMC com-

pleted its purchase of the nearby Loma Linda Manor. When tentative plans to develop it as a psychiatric hospital were disrupted by the purchase of the Charter Hospital in Redlands, LLUMC administration considered developing it into a rehabilitation hospital or returning it to a skilled nursing facility.

After considerable study, administration determined that the department of physical medicine and rehabilitation needed additional outpatient facilities to address its increasing patient load, and determined that the most feasible solution was to develop the Loma Linda Manor, gradually using more space as needed.

On February 14, 1994, Loma Linda University Medical Center officials broke ground for a $4 million, 34,000-square-foot addition to the outpatient facility that would provide a gymnasium and more than double the size of its Rehabilitation Institute. In so doing, administrators designed the project to bring together all the components of outpatient rehabilitation on one site in order to make the program more efficient and patient friendly.

The facility accommodates orthopaedic, physical therapy, industrial rehabilitation, hand rehabilitation, a special kids intervention program, neurophysical adult program, performing arts program, and rehabilitation physicians clinic.

Meanwhile, in order to create a more

seamless health care delivery system, on May 19, 1993, the Medical Center Board had voted to merge the Community Hospital and the Medical Center, effective July 1. On December 15 it consolidated their two medical staffs, to be known as the medical staff of Loma Linda University Medical Center.

1994: SIR RUN RUN SHAW HOSPITAL

A Hong Kong–based media magnate and philanthropist, Sir Run Run Shaw for years carried the vision of a fully equipped hospital in Hangzhou, the capital city of his native Zhejian Province in the People's Republic of China.

Generously funding the hospital's

The Orthopaedic and Rehabilitation Institute (left) brings together all components of outpatient rehabilitation on one site. Below: Planned and operated by Loma Linda University and Medical Center, the hospital funded and named for Sir Run Run Shaw opened in May of 1994.

construction, Sir Run Run Shaw became acquainted with Seventh-day Adventist health care many years earlier when his mother was treated at an Adventist hospital in the Far East. In bringing to reality the hospital that would bear his name, Shaw requested that it be planned and operated by Loma Linda University and Loma Linda University Medical Center. Loma Linda, it was agreed, would provide key teaching, support, and administrative personnel for the hospital.

On Monday, May 9, 1994, grand- opening ceremonies were held for the new fourteen-story, 400-bed Sir Run Run

Shaw Hospital in Hangzhou. Shortly afterward, former LLU medical school dean G. Gordon Hadley, MD, became chief executive officer of the new hospital—a position he held until 2001.

1994: AGREEMENT BETWEEN LLUMC AND NASA

As early as August, 1980, LLUMC became involved with the National Aeronautics and Space Administration (NASA), when it signed a memorandum of understanding to provide backup emergency medical facilities for Space Shuttle flights.

LLUMC was selected because of its designation as the regional level 1 trauma center serving the area that included Edwards Air Force Base—the landing site for the Space Shuttle's test flight program. In the event of a medical emergency, any astronaut needing urgent medical or surgical attention would be flown to Loma Linda. LLUMC's sister institution—Florida Hospital, in Orlando—has similar agreement with NASA to provide any needed emergency services for Shuttle astronauts landing at nearby Cape Canaveral.

With this background of cooperation between LLUMC and NASA, the two entities in December of 1994 signed a five-year memorandum of agreement to establish formal scientific collaboration between them. This collaboration would involve NASA's Life and Biomedical

Sciences Divisions within its Office of Life and Microgravity Sciences Applications—and most directly, the Loma Linda University Proton Treatment Center.[10]

Of this agreement, NASA administrator Daniel S. Goldin, PhD, said it represented "the ultimate technology transfer," and added that Loma Linda's facility was the only place on Earth where NASA could do everything needed to learn how to protect its astronauts from the dangers of positively charged particles in space. Envisioning a planned future manned mission to Mars, Dr. Goldin even claimed that Loma Linda's proton facility was NASA's "gateway to Mars."[11] Today LLUMC is NASA's West Coast radiation biology laboratory.[12]

One of the biggest problems NASA must solve for such a mission as a manned journey to Mars is the bombardment of high-dose proton radiation that occurs during solar flares. The scientific advances at LLUMC in the area of radiation therapy directly benefit and apply to NASA's research into the action of charged particles on human beings. But the benefits of the LLUMC-NASA agreement are mutual, for the results of NASA's study of life forms in space can lead to important developments in radiation medicine at Loma Linda.

On March 30, 1996, the Space Shuttle Atlantis landed at Edwards Air

Force Base in the Mojave Desert north of Loma Linda. Aboard the craft was a research experiment developed by Gregory A. Nelson, PhD—professor of radiation medicine at Loma Linda University and a member of the LLU/NASA Research Laboratory based at the Proton Treatment Center. Also a researcher at the Pasadena, California, Jet Propulsion Laboratory, Dr. Nelson designed his research to study the effects of galactic and solar radiation on genetic material within microscopic-sized worms called nematodes.[13]

More recently, in January of 2000, researchers from NASA's Johnson Space Center in Houston, Texas, arrived at the Loma Linda University Proton Treatment Center with Russian and American space suits for use in radiation research. This marked the beginning of a research partnership between Loma Linda, NASA, the Lawrence Berkeley National Laboratory, and the University of San Francisco. The Proton Treatment Center can simulate the radiation environment of space to help scientists evaluate the effects and risks of space radiation on human beings.[14]

1995: Drayson Center

The University's motto—"To Make Man Whole"—recognizes that Loma Linda's mission is not alone to heal the body but to minister also to the mind and the spirit. It acknowledges the conviction of Loma Linda's founders and its parent Church that man is an integration of the physical, intellectual, emotional, and spiritual—and that what affects one component affects them all.

So while the obvious goal of the University is to instill knowledge, it would be an unbalanced denial of its motto and mission if intellectual pursuits were emphasized to the detriment or

Drayson Center (above) provides state-of-the-art facilities for the physical development of faculty, students, and staff. The facility was made possible through funding provided by Ronald D. Drayson, PhD, and his wife Grace (above left with their daughter, Darlene Drayson Nemer).

exclusion of the physical and spiritual.

To provide for the physical development of its students and staff, the University and Medical Center committed themselves in the early 1990s to the construction of a comprehensive fitness and wellness center to be named for Ronald D. Drayson, PhD and his wife Grace, who funded an irrevocable trust to underwrite its costs.

Groundbreaking took place on December 8, 1992. During a chapel service at the end of the 1992 school year, University president B. Lyn Behrens, MBBS, paid tribute to her immediate predecessor as president, Norman J. Woods, PhD, and to Gaines R. Partridge, EdD, recently retired as dean of students—both of whom played a vital role in the center's early planning.[15]

At a final cost of $16.7 million, the Drayson Center was dedicated on January 11, 1995 with more than 1,500 in attendance. Calvin B. Rock, DMin, PhD, chair of the University and Medical Center Boards of Trustees, addressed the audience concerning the center's purpose:

"It is a means to an end. Its purpose is to facilitate the larger, overarching reason for your being here—the acquirement of academic knowledge. It is here to stimulate your minds, to energize your bodies, to relieve your tensions,

and to boost your energies—all for the sake of increasing your capacity to learn, to absorb the wisdom that you will acquire, and then, to go forth from here prepared to do a greater good."[16]

Included in Drayson Center are the following:

- A 21,000-square-foot, multipurpose gymnasium with a one-ninth mile, elevated, three-lane, rubberized indoor running track.

- A conference facility with a 210-seat room, ideal for University classes and community programs, and a 40-seat conference room designed for smaller groups.

- Five racquetball courts with a large seating area for observers.

- Fully equipped men's and women's locker rooms, both containing dry saunas and showers.

- A 5,800-square-foot cardiovascular and fitness area with stationary cycles, treadmills, rowers, steppers, and free weights.

- Two aerobic studios with a combined 5,500 square feet of suspended wood floor. Each room holds up to 100 people.

- Outdoor Unlimited—a rental room for camping equipment: backpacks, tents, sleeping bags, stoves, lanterns,

ice chests and coolers, sailboards, and picnic equipment (volleyball sets, tug-of war ropes, and much more).

- Indoor climbing wall with incline and overhang facilities.

- Spiritual life office staffed by a chaplain from the Campus Hill Church of Seventh-day Adventists.

- A wellness office, directed by an exercise physiologist, to provide testing and evaluations.

- A 6,300-square-foot student life facility containing a student lounge and snack bar/restaurant, a game room, an arts and crafts area, a food preparation area, and a child playcare area.

- Lifetime leisure classes, offered quarterly, include: stained glass, brush painting, sculpting, martial arts for children, karate, tai-chi, photography, edible wild plants, and calligraphy.

- Water sports include a ten-lane lap pool with a diving board. It accommodates scuba diving classes. The three-lane recreation pool is wheelchair accessible. A twenty-two-foot high, 150-foot-long water slide ends in this shallow pool. An outdoor Jacuzzi accommodates twelve people.

- An outdoor garden and picnic area, enclosed on four sides, features walkways, trees, benches, and low-voltage lighting for socializing.

- The huge super field is a multiuse, lighted recreation area with four softball fields, surrounded by a half-mile jogging path near six lighted tennis courts and two lighted volleyball courts.

- Intramurals—the largest program in the Adventist higher education system. Drayson Center offers basketball, baseball, softball, flag ball, soccer, ultimate Frisbee, indoor soccer, volleyball, table tennis, weight lifting, tennis, golf tournaments and more.

- A student union for the student association.[17]

- Near the end of 2003, the University added two beach volleyball courts and horseshoe pits to Drayson Center.

1995: GRAND OPENING FOR SAC-NORTON

In 1968, a group of medical students—inspired by Medical Center Social Worker Cynthia Cooley, MSW—founded the Social Action Corps (SAC) to minister to the medical and social needs of underserved families in several communities surrounding Loma Linda.

Funding the outreach program at first were the University Church of Seventh-day Adventists, the Southeastern California Conference of Seventh-day Adventists, and Loma Linda University Medical Center.

Throughout the years as SAC expanded, it became first the Social Action Community Clinics (SACC) and later, the SAC Health System (SACHS). Now a group of primary care medical clinics, SACHS is today an invaluable resource to the San Bernardino County Health Department in providing low-cost medical care to families who otherwise might well go without. Additional funding now comes from foundations, corporations, and individuals, with major grants coming from the Pew and Kellogg foundations.

Richard H. Hart, MD, DrPH (facing page), currently chancellor of Loma Linda University, played a leading role in establishing SACHS and obtaining the old Norton Air Force Base medical/dental facility. Left: The Norton location.

The early SAC program experienced the problems typical of many volunteer organizations. Services and facilities were limited. Students who championed SAC graduated and moved on. But in the mid-1980s the newly reestablished department of preventive medicine in the School of Medicine offered to assume responsibility for the clinics. Three evenings per week, a small group of physicians from the department—including former overseas missionaries—directed clinic activities. Increasingly, the SAC program became built into the School of Medicine curriculum as a valuable opportunity for students to learn the basics of diagnosis and cross-cultural patient care.

In the late 1980s, the nation experienced a deep recession, exacerbated locally by a decline in the area's aerospace and defense industries. This resulted in a significant increase in the number of SAC patients. Lines began forming by mid-afternoon. The need for larger facilities was clear. But without funds to rent or purchase space, the outlook wasn't promising. Program leaders periodically drove through the ghetto areas of San Bernardino looking for abandoned buildings, but nothing materialized.

Then one day at a United Way meeting, someone suggested that SAC leaders might want to talk to personnel at nearby Norton Air Force Base. In one of the recurring rounds of military downsizing, a decision was made to close the base.

"It seemed like a long shot," reported Richard H. Hart, MD, DrPH, then the head of the preventive medicine department practice group and dean of the School of Public Health. "But because Norton was only three miles from Loma Linda and next to a large low-income area in east San Bernardino where many of our patients came from, we decided to investigate."

Dr. Hart then described his visit to the base's clinic with SAC director Janice Cryak:

"Our first visit to the base will always remain in my mind. After obtaining special permission, we were escorted to the clinic and met by the captain in charge. She courteously agreed to show us through the building. Some departments were still in operation, while others were packing and shipping clinic equipment. This fully equipped, 42,300-square-foot facility was so far beyond our dreams that Janice and I refused to get excited. Its forty examination rooms, twenty dental operatories, clinical lab, radiology department, and considerable office equipment simply seemed more than we could hope for. As we completed the tour and were exiting, the captain commented that if we were thinking of applying for the building, she could stop shipping equipment out

as soon as she had written notice of our interest. She had a letter that afternoon!"[18]

Following months of waiting, negotiations, disappointments, uncertainties, and prayers, in 1995 Loma Linda University acquired the medical/dental clinic of the former Norton Air Force Base for one dollar. Dr. Hart negotiated an agreement with the U.S. Department of Education to provide low-cost health care at the $6 million facility to underserved residents of the San Bernardino area.[19]

Located on 6.5 acres, the Norton facility came with a large inventory of medical, dental, and office equipment.

In early 1995, SACHS opened a full-service health care facility at the clinic. It included primary and specialty medical and dental care; behavioral health services; nursing, psychosocial, and allied health services; well-child services; and nutrition and health education.

SACHS offers low-cost medical services to clients of all ages. Many of its services—such as physical examinations and immunizations—are free for children, if their families have limited financial resources. SACHS has become the "court of last resort" for the health care of thousands of local residents.

Community health education offerings include programs focused on lifestyle and nutrition, smoking cessation, alcohol and drug abuse, and domestic violence. In addition to providing clinical and service experience for students, SACHS is an opportunity for Loma Linda to demonstrate to its neighbors the caring ministry Christ Himself exemplified when, on this earth, He "went about doing good" (Acts 10:38).

In addition to the Norton facility, SACHS today operates two other clinics in San Bernardino. Support of the health system has been assumed by LLU and LLUMC. Each of the University's professional schools has committed to developing interdisciplinary primary care training in all of the clinics.

From the lower campus looking south past the Good Samaritan sculpture, Chan Shun Pavilion is on the left and Coleman Pavilion to the right.

1997: THE CENTER FOR SPIRITUAL LIFE & WHOLENESS

Toward a closer integration of the spiritual dimension into the life and ministry of Loma Linda University and Medical Center, in February of 1997, the Center for Spiritual Life & Wholeness was established.

Wil Alexander, PhD, served as the center's founding director and carried forward its mission—to foster the concept of wholeness reflected in Loma Linda's motto, "To Make Man Whole," among the students and health care professionals of the University and Medical Center.

The center provides training in the art of whole-person care; ministers to the spiritual needs of students, staff, and patients; and conducts research exploring the interweaving bio-psycho-social-spiritual dimensions that emerge in the process of restoring broken and ill human beings.

1997: CHAN SHUN AND COLEMAN PAVILIONS; WONG KERLEE INTERNATIONAL CONFERENCE CENTER

Sharing a common lobby, two adjacent structures to the immediate north of Loma Linda University Medical Center were

dedicated and opened in ceremonies spanning March 1 through May 25, 1997. The imposing multi-story centers—Coleman Pavilion (School of Medicine) and Chan Shun Pavilion Cancer Research Institute (Cancer Institute)—represented major additions to the Loma Linda campus.

Chan Shun—a world-renowned businessman and philanthropist based in Hong Kong until his 1974 retirement to Vancouver, British Columbia, Canada—granted a major multimillion-dollar award toward the construction of the Cancer Research Institute. Central to the completion of Chan Shun Pavilion also was the influence and support of U.S. congressman, the Honorable Jerry Lewis—a longtime friend and supporter of Loma Linda

University and Loma Linda University Medical Center. His efforts resulted in the securing of a $10 million government grant for the pavilion. Congressman Lewis earlier had secured a similar $19.6 million grant for the Proton Treatment Center.

Since the first patient was seen at the Proton Treatment Center in 1990, cancer research and treatment have been a continuing major focus at Loma Linda. The Chan Shun Pavilion research center of the Cancer Research Institute has accelerated development of a full-scale, multimodality approach to the treatment of cancer and related diseases.

In remarks at the opening of Coleman Pavilion in early March of 1997, Loma Linda University Adventist Health Sciences Center, Dr. Behrens, chief executive officer, characterized the event as a "landmark in School of Medicine history."

The Pavilion is named for Denver D. Coleman, MD, and his wife Josephine Kent Coleman—whose generosity made the new building possible. A 1925 graduate of the College of Medical Evangelists School of Medicine, Dr. Coleman established a practice and built his own hospital in Alhambra, California, and the Colemans actively supported the mission of the University and Medical School.

The four-level, 139,700-square-foot building contains laboratories, administrative offices, and other departments of the School

of Medicine. From the founding in 1909 of the School of Medicine, its academic departments were located in various buildings on and off campus—some as far as three miles away from the Medical Center.

Coleman Pavilion also contains the 18,190-square-foot Wong Kerlee International Conference Center, designed to host national and international conferences, with a 7,290-square-foot auditorium and eight conference rooms, each seating between twenty and seventy.

Wong Kerlee, whose generosity brought the vision of a conference center to reality, was born in China but later moved his family to Hong Kong, where his business success has been accompanied by philanthropic endeavors that have benefited countless people and institutions worldwide.

Many other individuals contributed to the construction of these two significant pavilions on Loma Linda's campus. Various rooms and floors of the pavilions bear the names of some of these additional contributors.

1997: CREATION OF LOMA LINDA UNIVERSITY ADVENTIST HEALTH SCIENCES CENTER

On March 27, 1997, the constituency of Adventist Health System—Loma Linda, the parent corporation over Loma Linda University Medical Center, voted to change its name to Loma Linda University Adventist Health Sciences

Center (LLUAHSC, pronounced "lew-ask"). They created it to coordinate the academic and health care activities of the health sciences institution, especially the governance relationships between the University and Medical Center.

LLUAHSC now serves as the umbrella organization for its two core organizations—Loma Linda University and Loma Linda University Medical Center—and its affiliate organizations—including Loma Linda University Children's Hospital, the Loma Linda University Medical Center East Campus, and Loma Linda University Proton Treatment Center.

The 1990s: The power of momentum

It would truly require a multivolume, encyclopedic set of books to chronicle all the events—all the progress and change, the developments and activity—that filled this final decade of the past millennium. So much more could be said were the full story to be told. The 1990s also saw in 1995 the launching of the Loma Linda Internet website; the 1996 dedication of the Ricketts Research Library and Learning Center; the 1997 first-ever Seventh-day Adventist International Nursing Conference; and the opening, also in 1997, of the Center for Joint Replacement as well as the Assistive Technology Assessment Center.

Nineteen ninety-eight would bring

groundbreaking for both the Geoscience Research Center and a major expansion to the School of Dentistry. This would also be the year *U.S. News* magazine would recognize LLUMC as one of "America's Best Hospitals." The same year would see the first stem-cell transplant at LLUMC as well as the one-hundredth liver transplant. And the milestone year of 2000 would bring the first autologous stem-cell transplant.

Loma Linda had, by the dawn of the new millennium, come such a long way from its vulnerable early years—the years it struggled, like the Wright brothers' first airplane, to lift off and fly. As the second millennium A.D. began, Loma Linda had—like a jumbo jet—achieved cruising altitude. It moved swiftly, surely, powerfully, carried along by the momentum built of years of vision and sacrifice, of prayer and hard work.

Now even more years have passed since the world crossed the millennial marker—years that have brought Loma Linda not only to its centennial year but propelled it, by its unwavering mission, into a future aglow with the promise of new opportunities for service—for as long as time on Earth continues.

NOTES:

1. LLUMC Board of Trustees, *Minutes*, October 23, 1991, p. 5.
2. Op cit., March 16, 1988, p. 2; June 29, 1988, p. 1.
3. Op cit., November 12, 1990, p. 4.
4. Ibid., pp. 3-5.
5. Op cit., March 20, 1991, p. 1.
6. Op cit., October 23, 1991, p. 5.
7. *University Scope*, spring 1993, pp. 20-23.
8. "LLUMC tops list for liver patients," *San Bernardino County Sun*, July 27, 2003; "LLUMC success a familiar story," Ibid., July 27, 2003.
9. *Scope*, spring 1999, p. 28.
10. Richard A. Schaefer, "NASA to use proton synchrotron," *Legacy*, pp. 54-56.
11. *Scope*, spring 1995, p. 32.
12. Ibid., autumn 1996, pp. 20, 21.
13. Op cit., summer 1996, p. 60.
14. Op cit., summer 2000, p. 70.
15. Op cit., July-September, 1992, p. 28.
16. Op cit., spring 1995, p. 5.
17. Ibid., pp. 5-11.
18. Richard H. Hart, MD, DrPH—grant request prepared by SACHS for the California Endowment, 1996.
19. *Dentalgram*, May 1994, p. 1; *Scope*, summer 1996, pp. 29-31.

Photo Album

Left: A child brings his stuffed animal to the Loma Linda University Children's Hospital Kids' Care Fair "Teddy Bear Clinic" for an examination.

Below: Members of a team led by Leonard R. Brand, PhD, professor of biology and paleontology in the Loma Linda University School of Science and Technology, inspect a fossilized whale skeleton in western Peru during the summer of 1999.

THE IMPOSSIBLE DREAM: RAILWAY TO THE MOON

LEFT: MAY 1, 1996, IDENTICAL TWINS SHAWNA AND JANELLE RODERICK WERE BORN CONJOINED, FACING EACH OTHER—JOINED AT THE LIVER. THEY WERE SEPARATED THIRTY DAYS LATER BY H. GIBBS ANDREWS, MD, CHIEF PEDIATRIC SURGEON AT LOMA LINDA UNIVERSITY CHILDREN'S HOSPITAL, AND HIS TEAM.

BELOW: KENNETH R. JUTZY, MD, ASSOCIATE PROFESSOR OF MEDICINE IN THE SCHOOL OF MEDICINE AND HEAD OF CARDIOLOGY AT LOMA LINDA UNIVERSITY & LOMA LINDA UNIVERSITY MEDICAL CENTER, DISCUSSES TREATMENT WITH A PATIENT.

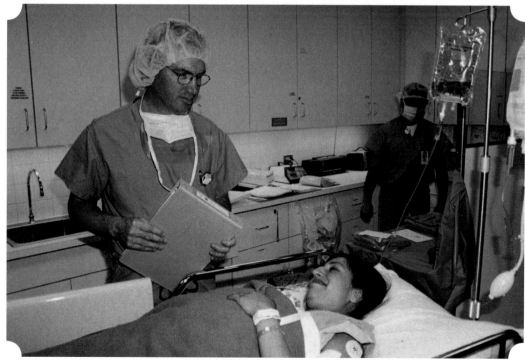

Left: Loma Linda president B. Lyn Behrens, MBBS, meets with Calvin B. Rock, PhD, DMin, chair of Loma Linda's Board for eleven years until his retirement in 2002.

Below: A December 1991 benefit concert featuring "The Highwaymen"—a country music group led by Johnny Cash and including Willie Nelson, Waylon Jennings, and Kris Kristofferson—brought in $100,000 for Loma Linda University Children's Hospital.

THE IMPOSSIBLE DREAM: RAILWAY TO THE MOON

Below: Three of the many physicians whose significant contributions to Loma Linda's mission continued in the 1990s. From left: Lawrence D. Longo, MD, director of the Center for Perinatal Biology; David B. Hinshaw Sr., MD, emeritus professor of surgery, past dean, School of Medicine, and from 1987–1994, president of Loma Linda University Medical Center; Brian S. Bull, MD, chair of the department of pathology and human anatomy at Loma Linda University School of Medicine.

Fulfilling the Vision

New Century, New Millenium

IT IS NO SMALL ACCOMPLISHMENT FOR AN INSTITUTION TO SURVIVE FOR A FULL
ONE HUNDRED YEARS. AND IN ITS CENTENNIAL YEAR OF 2005, LOMA LINDA—
INCLUDING ITS UNIVERSITY, ITS MEDICAL CENTER, AND ITS AFFILIATED
INSTITUTIONS—MARKS THIS MILESTONE WITH GRATITUDE AND VISION.

Loma Linda University Adventist Health Sciences Center—along with the rest of the world—marked entry into a new millennium in the year 2000. And five years later Loma Linda marks its entry as well into a new century—having lived out its mission of teaching and healing for one hundred years since its founding in 1905.

The final years of Loma Linda's centenary—the first of the new millennium—have seen expansion, service, and celebration. Noted here is a sampling of forward progress these most recent years.

EXPANSION

In January of 2002, the Loma Linda branch of savings and loan bank CAL FED donated 1.1 acres of land—valued at $380,000—behind its building to LLUMC for expansion of its East Campus. Specifically, the donation made possible a new entranceway for Loma Linda University Medical Center's Orthopaedic and Rehabilitation Institute.

The East Campus, located a half mile east of the Medical Center, is the site of a twenty-two-acre rehabilitation complex integrating inpatient facilities, an outpatient rehabilitation center, and professional medical offices. The complex provides a total approach toward the goal of preparing patients for a new way of living and maximizing

Left: The centennial banner, with University and Medical Center logos—and buildings as bookends for a century.

renced the metaphor of "longer ropes and deeper stakes." While much of the physical growth on the Loma Linda campus would fall under the heading of "longer ropes" in the form of new construction, on August 28, 2002, the Medical Center demonstrated a new technology that clearly represented "deeper stakes."

A 1994 California law mandated that hospital buildings in the earthquake-prone state had to meet far more stringent seismic and structural requirements by the year 2008. Since this strengthening process necessarily involves drilling, cutting, and even breaking up some existing areas of structures being modified, the noise, vibration, and dust created during this work represented a significant disruption in normal hospital operations.

At the August 28 demonstration, new laser retrofitting technology was shown that was conceived of at LLUMC for cutting and processing concrete without the typical vibration and noise of jackhammers and other conventional equipment. So promising was the concept that Loma Linda succeeded in obtaining a federal grant through the Federal Emergency Management Agency to develop, pilot-test, and demonstrate the technology.

Located on Loma Linda's East Campus, the rehabilitation Institute (above) covers twenty-two acres. Right: A new pediatric emergency department opened in July 2002.

their potential following injury, illness, or surgery.

On July 10, 2002, Loma Linda Children's Hospital held an open house to showcase its new pediatric emergency department. Between the 1993 opening of Children's Hospital and 2001, the seven-bed emergency department had gone from seeing 9,000 children a year to more than 25,000.

The new department has eighteen pediatric treatment spaces, with cardiac monitors at each bed. The much-expanded facility also includes a new, high-speed computed tomography (CT) scanner and an isolation room with negative airflow for treating contagious patients.

A previous chapter of this book refe-

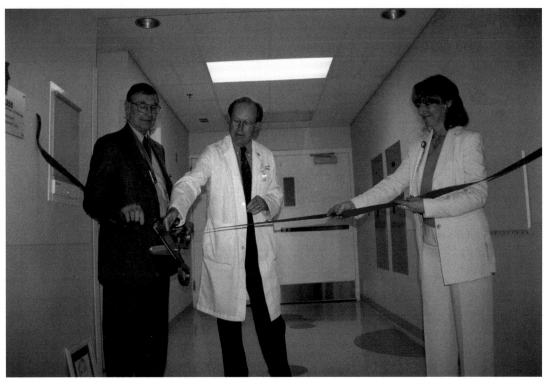

Not all campus expansion is as visible as new buildings; academic expansion is no less important to the life of a university or teaching medical center. Crossing the millennial divide, Loma Linda offered education in the following major schools: Nursing, Medicine, Dentistry, Public Health, and Allied Health Professions.

On September 19, 2002, the School of Pharmacy opened its doors to its inaugural class. Years of planning and development preceded achievement of this milestone. The School of Pharmacy fills an important niche in the offerings of Loma Linda University as a health sciences university.

The four-year program leads to the PharmD degree and is the first offering of the professional doctorate in pharmacy by a Seventh-day Adventist institution of higher learning. The School of Pharmacy faculty and administrative offices are located in West Hall on the LLU campus.

Then, on December 11, 2003, the University opened the School of Science and Technology. The new School houses the behavorial sciences programs (marital and family counseling, social work, and psychology) as well as those focused on the earth and biological sciences (geology and biology).

As of its centennial, Loma Linda is composed of seven major schools. In addition, the Faculty of Graduate Studies and the Faculty of Religion offer curriculum to all schools of the University.

SERVICE

From the beginning, Loma Linda has nurtured the mission of its parent church—a mission that envisions extending a teaching and healing outreach to the entire world.

Every day of the year, Loma Linda ministers to the needs of people in its immediate local area. But it draws no boundaries on its outreach at city limits, state lines, national borders, or continents.

Each decade, Loma Linda's influence and outreach has broadened, so that today it responds to needs anywhere on the planet. In just these most recent years, Loma Linda has shared its expertise and personnel with a variety of faraway nations. Consider, for example, a few such examples from the year 2004.

In early January, Loma Linda University completed five years of offering post-professional physical therapy training at Antillean Adventist University in Mayaguez, Puerto Rico. During that time, approximately eighty students obtained their master's degrees (MPT) through the LLU-operated program.

Now Loma Linda is in the process of establishing the first and only physical

New laser retrofitting technology (left), demonstrated in August 2002 significantly reduces noise and vibration during structural modifications needed to meet new requirements for possible earthquakes.

Loma Linda operated a post-professional physical therapy training program at Antillean Adventist University in Mayaguez, Puerto Rico.

therapy doctoral program in Puerto Rico.

In response to an invitation from the Ministry of Health of the Islamic Republic of Afghanistan, a team of five Loma Linda healthcare professionals spent the week of March 15, 2004, in that country to evaluate a request that Loma Linda operate a major hospital—the Wazir Akbar Khan

Hospital in Kabul, the capital city of 3.5 million residents.

Loma Linda's involvement with Afghanistan goes back to 1962, when under LLU/LLUMC auspices, dean emeritus of the School of Medicine G. Gordon Hadley, MD, began offering teaching and consultation support to Kabul Medical

Institute and other such facilities in the country.

The 2004 team, headed by Richard H. Hart, MD, DrPH, Loma Linda University chancellor, returned from its trip to begin exploring external funding sources for the upgrades that would be needed to fulfill the Afghanistan request.

In late June and early July, Loma Linda provided assistance in the aftermath of devastating floods in Haiti and the Dominican Republic. Following the floods in May that ravaged the island nations, the Loma Linda University International Behavioral Health Trauma Team (IBHTT) teamed with the Adventist Development and Relief Agency (ADRA) to train local health professionals and volunteers in aiding disaster victims.

Since the trauma team was founded in 1997, it has provided service in nearly twenty countries.

IBHTT and ADRA conducted a two-day training workshop in Port-au-Prince, Haiti, from June 28 through July 3, 2004, attended by more than sixty members and workers of the Ministry of Health, the United Nations, and other governmental organizations—as well as volunteers. In addition to offering training, Loma Linda's team assisted with distribution of rice, water, and other needed commodities.

At roughly the same time as Loma Linda's IBHTT team assisted with disaster

His ministry are needed locally, nationally, and internationally. This is our calling at Loma Linda."

The dental team—composed of three dentists, a dental hygienist, five dental students, and four dental hygiene students—offered six days of dental care in Montego Bay, during which they saw about 400 patients.

CELEBRATION

Celebrating accomplishments and marking milestones is a gratifying benefit enjoyed by institutions that have endured and survived to arrive at a place of maturity and strength. In recent years Loma Linda has noted a number of these occasions.

On March 6, 2001, the Loma Linda University Behavioral Medicine Center (BMC) celebrated its first ten years of operation. A decade earlier, the BMC featured an adult psychiatry unit as well as special units for child and adolescent psychiatry and adult chemical dependence. By the ten-year mark, the BMC had expanded to include senior psychiatry, a full range of outpatient services, and a specialized chronic pain and medication dependency program. As part of its service to the community, the BMC also hosts a number of self-help groups, such as Alcoholics Anonymous, Alateen, and Narcotics Anonymous.

A few months later in November, the

In response to an invitation from Afghanistan, a Loma Linda delegation traveled there in March of 2004 to evaluate a request that Loma Linda operate a major hospital in Kabul. Representing Loma Linda, from left: Richard H. Hart, MD, DrPH, Loma Linda University chancellor; Joan Coggin, MD, MPH, co-founder of the International Overseas Heart Team; and G. Gordon Hadley, MD, dean emeritus of the School of Medicine.

relief in Haiti and the Dominican Republic, other Loma Linda representatives were conducting a mission to Jamaica. There, speakers from Loma Linda held an evangelistic series of meetings in Montego Bay, coupled with a dental clinic staffed by the School of Dentistry.

"The mission of healing combined with teaching was overwhelmingly embraced by the Jamaican people," said Leslie Pollard, DMin, special assistant to the chancellor for diversity. "Increasingly," he added, "we at LLU will receive more invitations to do genuinely wholistic outreach around the world. The healing ministry of Jesus minus His teaching is incomplete. The teaching ministry of Jesus minus His healing ministry is also incomplete. Both dimensions of

Social Action Community Health System (SACHS) passed its six-year mark. With the late-nineties acquisition of a flagship clinic—SAC-Norton—the SAC Health System was formed with three additional clinics: SAC-Frazee, SAC-Arrowhead, and SAC-Redlands. Since then, two more clinics—in Riverside and Montclair—have been added.

The year 2003 saw celebrations marking the tenth anniversary of Children's Hospital and the fiftieth anniversary of the School of Dentistry.

INTO A SECOND CENTURY

It is no small accomplishment for an institution to survive for a full one hundred years. And in its centennial year, spanning 2005 and 2006, Loma Linda—including its University, its Medical Center, and its affiliated institutions—marks this milestone with gratitude and vision.

Gratitude…first, to the God by whose providence Loma Linda came into existence—and by whose continuing care and intervention, it survived hardship, threats, and obstacles to fulfill His purpose in its founding.

Gratitude…to Jesus Christ, whose example as Teacher and Healer is the model and inspiration for every phase of Loma Linda's activity—and whose ministry to the whole person is at the center of Loma Linda's mission.

Gratitude…to the dauntless pioneers who sacrificed and dreamed and persevered to build success around the Hill Beautiful—a goal that had eluded the efforts of successive dreamers in the Inland Empire.

Gratitude…to the wise, dedicated, and skilled leaders, teachers, and medical professionals who, throughout Loma Linda's century, made amazing and pivotal contributions to lengthen the ropes and drive deeper the stakes of this place of hope and healing.

Vision…for a continuing expression of its undeviating mission—"To Make Man Whole"—into a new century.

Vision…for accomplishing far greater things than have already occurred, through listening to the divine voice and refusing to settle for anything less than dreaming big dreams.

Vision…for carrying out its mission so faithfully and well that the saving message of the Master Teacher and Healer will reach the last outposts of earth and make possible His return long before a second century can unfold.

Vision…that fervently anticipates a place and a time when illness and injury, suffering and death will no longer exist—where all is unending perfection of health and peace and happiness.

Toward that goal and until that time, Loma Linda's health professionals, its staff, its students, its support personnel, will continue to arrive each new day in classrooms, offices, and patient rooms to carry forward the task of teaching and healing.

May one such day soon be the last one.

196

2001 – 2005

PHOTO ALBUM

BELOW: WOLFF M. KIRSCH, MD (STANDING, CENTER OF PHOTO), PROFESSOR OF NEUROSURGERY AND BIOCHEMISTRY; DIRECTOR OF THE NEUROSURGERY CENTER FOR RESEARCH, TRAINING, AND EDUCATION; AND FORMER DIVISION CHIEF AND PROGRAM DIRECTOR FOR THE NEUROSURGERY RESIDENCY PROGRAM.

RIGHT: HUSBAND-AND-WIFE FACULTY MEMBERS DAISY DE LEON, PhD, AND MARINO DE LEON, PhD, ASSOCIATE PROFESSORS OF PHYSIOLOGY IN THE SCHOOL OF MEDICINE.

LEFT: SEAN P. BUSH, MD, IS ASSOCIATE PROFESSOR OF EMERGENCY MEDICINE AT LOMA LINDA UNIVERSITY SCHOOL OF MEDICINE, AND HE IS ALSO ON STAFF IN THE MEDICAL CENTER EMERGENCY DEPARTMENT AS AN EMERGENCY PHYSICIAN AND ENVENOMATION (VENOMOUS ANIMAL) SPECIALIST.

BELOW: HYVETH WILLIAMS, DMIN, SENIOR PASTOR OF CAMPUS HILL SEVENTH-DAY ADVENTIST CHURCH, AND RANDY ROBERTS, DMIN, SENIOR PASTOR OF LOMA LINDA UNIVERSITY CHURCH OF SEVENTH-DAY ADVENTISTS.

BELOW: ANEES J. RAZZOUK, MD, PROFESSOR OF PEDIATRICS AND
SURGERY IN THE LOMA LINDA UNIVERSITY SCHOOL OF MEDICINE,
AND CHIEF OF CARDIOTHORACIC SURGERY, LOMA LINDA UNIVERSITY
MEDICAL CENTER AND LOMA LINDA UNIVERSITY CHILDREN'S
HOSPITAL.

RIGHT: JERRY D. SLATER, MD, CHAIR OF THE DEPARTMENT OF
RADIATION MEDICINE IN THE SCHOOL OF MEDICINE.

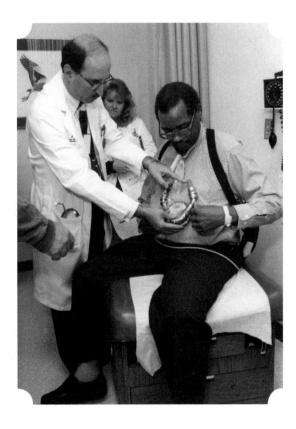

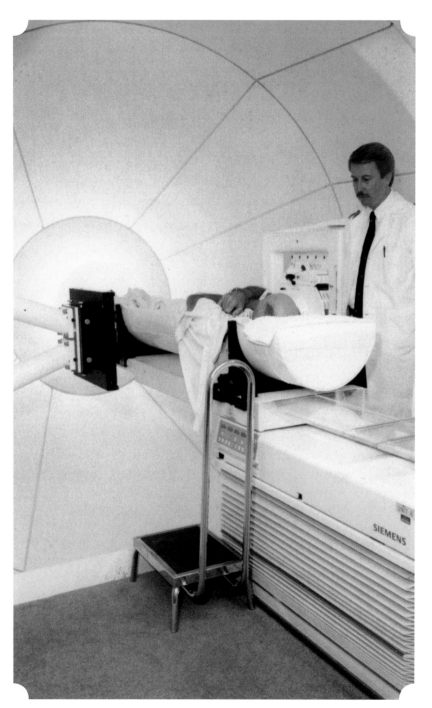

Top right: During weekend alumni centennial celebrations in November 2005, students participating in the Deferred Mission Appointment program are introduced.

Bottom right: A Sunday morning brunch—part of the same centennial weekend observance.

THE IMPOSSIBLE DREAM: RAILWAY TO THE MOON

BELOW LEFT: OKECHUKWU OJOGHO, MD, DIRECTOR OF THE
TRANSPLANTATION INSTITUTE, BEGINNING IN 2005.

BELOW CENTER: WALDO CONCEPCION, MD, DIRECTOR OF THE
TRANSPLANTATION INSTITUTE, 1996–2005.

BELOW RIGHT: JOAN SABATÉ, MD, DRPH, MPH, CHAIR,
DEPARTMENT OF NUTRITION, SCHOOL OF PUBLIC HEALTH,
WITH HIS 2001 BOOK *VEGETARIAN NUTRITION.*

MAKING POSSIBLE "THE IMPOSSIBLE DREAM"

Through the ten decades of Loma Linda's existence, countless men and women have contributed to making possible "The Impossible Dream." Among them: faculty, students, administrators, medical professionals, staff, and friends.

Many of these believers in the impossible dream were mentioned or pictured earlier in this book. In this section, however, we acknowledge others who have also played a significant part in making possible the seemingly impossible. Some in this section committed time or influence. Others gave of their means. But all believed in the greatness and worthiness of Loma Linda's healing and teaching mission to the world.

And that mission is indeed a global one. More than a hundred years ago, Harry W. Miller, MD (the "China Doctor"), left to spend a half century in medical mission service in the Far East. From that time onward, countless graduates from Loma Linda have followed his pioneering example in worldwide healing ministry.

Whether at its home institutions, across America, or around the world, so many have given so much to Loma Linda throughout this past century that this volume can acknowledge the contributions of only a representative few. Hundreds—perhaps thousands—of others are just as worthy of recognition. And Heaven preserves the record of their unselfish and often unheralded giving. May the time come soon when all who have worked to bring Loma Linda's dream to reality are fully honored.

Left: The nameplate gable from the original Loma Linda Sanitarium, now positioned above the entrance inside Del E. Webb Memorial Library.

LEFT: LOMA LINDA PRESIDENT/CEO B. LYN BEHRENS, MBBS, EXPRESSES APPRECIATION ON BEHALF OF LOMA LINDA TO HONG KONG BUSINESSMAN WONG KERLEE, WHO MADE POSSIBLE THE WONG KERLEE INTERNATIONAL CONFERENCE CENTER, HOUSED IN COLEMAN PAVILION OF THE SCHOOL OF MEDICINE.

BELOW: PHILANTRHOPIST CHAN SHUN, WHOSE GENEROSITY MADE POSSIBLE CONSTRUCTION OF THE CHAN SHUN PAVILION CANCER RESEARCH CENTER OF THE CANCER INSTITUTE.

THE IMPOSSIBLE DREAM: RAILWAY TO THE MOON

Left: Violet and Tom Zapara, of Laguna Beach, California. Tom is a business executive and member of the LLUAHSC Board. Together, they have generously contributed to Seventh-day Adventist education and have funded the Thomas and Violet Zapara Distinguished Undergraduate teaching award. In 1981, Loma Linda conferred on Tom its Distinguished Humanitarian Award.

Below: Dr. and Mrs. Frank S. Damazo of Frederick, Maryland, are longtime Loma Linda supporters.

Left: LLUAHSC president/CEO B. Lyn Behrens, MBBS, recognizes the generosity of James Jetton, MD, and his wife, Marge Jetton, RN. The Jettons contributed financially and in volunteer work at Loma Linda into their late 90s. James passed away in 2003 at 96 years of age. Marge reached her 101st birthday in 2005 and near the end of the year was profiled for her longevity in such media as *National Geographic* magazine, CNN, and ABC television.

Below: Claran H. Jesse, MD, and Marjorie Jesse, RN, are both Loma Linda graduates. In 1954, Dr. Jesse started the department of orthopaedic surgery in the School of Medicine. Longtime supporters of Loma Linda, the Jesses have established several charitable trusts with the University. The Marjorie Andersen Jesse Wing in the School of Nursing is named in honor of Mrs. Jesse, and several areas in the Coleman Pavilion School of Medicine building are named after the Jesses.

LEFT: WILLIAM SWATEK, MD, AND HIS WIFE ROSE WERE RECOGNIZED IN 2003 FOR ESTABLISHING THE FIRST FACULTY CHAIR FOR THE SCHOOL OF NURSING, IN HONOR OF THE FOUNDING CHAIR OF THE GRADUATE PROGRAM IN NURSING, R. MAUREEN MAXWELL, EDD, RN. IN APRIL OF 2005, THEY WERE ALSO HONORED AS MAJOR DONORS TO THE CENTENNIAL FELLOWS CAMPAIGN.

BELOW: RALPH THOMPSON, MD, AND HIS WIFE CAROLYN, A BUSINESSWOMAN IN REAL ESTATE DEVELOPMENT AND MANAGEMENT. DR. THOMPSON PRACTICED FOR MANY YEARS AS A SURGEON AT LOMA LINDA UNIVERSITY MEDICAL CENTER. THE THOMPSON SUITE IN COLEMAN PAVILION AND THE CAROLYN AND RALPH THOMPSON LIBRARY OF THE CENTER FOR CHRISTIAN BIOETHICS ARE NAMED IN RECOGNITION OF THEIR GENEROUS SUPPORT THROUGH THE YEARS.

BELOW: CHARLES T. SMITH, DDS (LEFT), DEAN EMERITUS AND SECOND DEAN OF THE SCHOOL OF DENTISTRY. DONALD G. PURSLEY, DBA (RIGHT), WHO RETIRED IN 2004 AS VICE PRESIDENT FOR FINANCE AND CHIEF FINANCIAL OFFICER FOR LLUAHSC.

RIGHT: JOHN RUFFCORN SERVED AS PRESIDENT OF LOMA LINDA UNIVERSITY MEDICAL CENTER FROM 1976–1988. PRIOR TO THAT APPOINTMENT, HE WAS ASSOCIATE ADMINISTRATOR OF GLENDALE ADVENTIST MEDICAL CENTER, AND LATER, PRESIDENT OF WASHINGTON ADVENTIST HOSPITAL.

THE IMPOSSIBLE DREAM: RAILWAY TO THE MOON

BELOW: IVOR C. WOODWARD, PhD, BECAME EMERITUS DEAN OF THE SCHOOL OF ALLIED HEALTH PROFESSIONS IN 2003.

RIGHT: JUDSON KLOOSTER, DDS, DEAN OF THE SCHOOL OF DENTISTRY FROM 1971–1994.

BELOW: IAN M. FRASER, PhD, FORMER LOMA LINDA UNIVERSITY VICE
PRESIDENT FOR ACADEMIC AND RESEARCH AFFAIRS, AND LATER, UNIVERSITY
EXECUTIVE VICE PRESIDENT.

RIGHT: JOYCE W. HOPP, PhD, MPH, FORMER DEAN OF THE SCHOOL OF
ALLIED HEALTH PROFESSIONS.

BELOW: BARRY L. TAYLOR, PhD (LEFT), VICE CHANCELLOR FOR RESEARCH
AFFAIRS AND CHAIR, DEPARTMENT OF MICROBIOLOGY AND MOLECULAR
GENETICS, LOMA LINDA UNIVERSITY. RAYMOND E. RYCKMAN, PhD, FORMER
CHAIR, DEPARTMENT OF MICROBIOLOGY (RIGHT). DR. TAYLOR PRESENTS
TO DR. RYCKMAN A PLAQUE COMMEMORATING THE INAUGURATION OF THE
RAYMOND RYCKMAN LECTURESHIP SERIES, ENDOWED BY DR. RYCKMAN'S
FAMILY.

RIGHT: JAN KUZMA, PhD, CHAIR OF THE BIOSTATISTICS PROGRAM AND
DIRECTOR OF RESEARCH AT THE SCHOOL OF PUBLIC HEALTH.

BELOW LEFT: H.H. HILL, FORMER ADMINISTRATOR, LOMA LINDA UNIVERSITY MEDICAL CENTER.

BELOW RIGHT: W. BART RIPPON, PHD, FORMER DEAN OF THE GRADUATE SCHOOL AND THE SCHOOL OF PHARMACY.

THE IMPOSSIBLE DREAM: RAILWAY TO THE MOON

ELECTED OFFICIALS WHO CONTINUE THEIR LONGTIME SUPPORT OF LOMA LINDA.

FROM LEFT: U.S. REPRESENTATIVE JERRY LEWIS (R-CA); U.S. SENATOR BARBARA BOXER (D-CA); U.S. SENATOR DIANNE FEINSTEIN (D-CA) WITH A YOUNG PEDIATRIC HEART TRANSPLANT PATIENT.

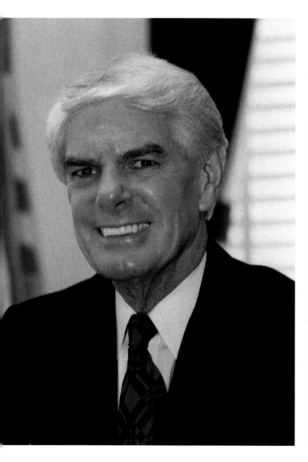

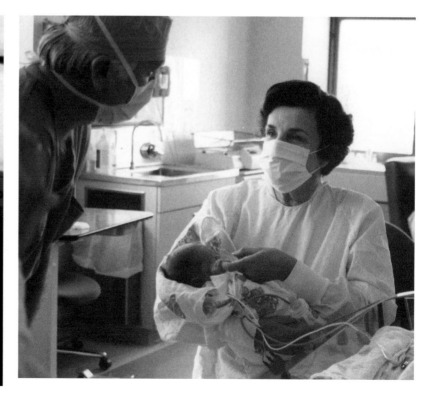

APPENDIX

Loma Linda Timeline

Institutional Profiles

LLUAHSC Board of Trustees and Advisors

LLUAHSC Management Team

LLUAHSC Executive Staff and Leadership

Loma Linda University Mission Statement

Loma Linda University Medical Center Mission Statement

Loma Linda's Presidents

Deans, School of Nursing

LOMA · LINDA · UNIVERSITY

1905

TO MAKE MAN WHOLE

LOMA LINDA TIMELINE

1905	February 4	Ellen G. White's letter says: "A place must be provided to which the sick could be taken, where they could be taught how to live so as to preserve health."
1905	May 5	General Conference telegram to John Burden instructs him not to make deposit on Loma Linda.
1905	May 14	Mrs. White writes, "Dear Brother Burden: …Secure the property by all means."
1905	May 29	John Burden pays $1,000 down to buy Loma Linda.
1905	June 12	Mrs. White visits Loma Linda for first time.
1905	July 26	$5,000 from unexpected sources arrives on deadline of second payment for Loma Linda.
1905	August 22	Mrs. White writes: "This is the most delightful situation for a sanitarium I have ever seen."
1905	August 24	Loma Linda Sanitarium incorporates with John Burden as president.
1905	October 12	Sanitarium admits first patients.
1905	November 1	Loma Linda Sanitarium officially opens.
1905	December	Loma Linda Sanitarium accepts first nursing students.
1906	March 29	Nurses hold dedication service.
1906	April 15	Mrs. White dedicates Loma Linda Sanitarium.
1906	September 20	College of Evangelists declared open.
1906	October 4	College of Evangelists begins instruction with thirty-five students.
1907	July 10	First commencement of nurses is held.
1909	December 13	The state grants charter of incorporation to College of Medical Evangelists.
1910	January 25	Mrs. White writes, "The medical school at Loma Linda is to be of the highest order."
1910	April 4	CME Board decides to offer part of medical training in Los Angeles.
1910	June 15	Loma Linda Sanitarium consolidates with CME Corporation.
1911	February 27	First women's residence hall opens.
1912	April 4	Mrs. White endorses the building of the new hospital and the plan for student physicians to receive some of their clinical education in Los Angeles.
1912	October 28	Dr. Ruble reports that CME opens temporary hospital facilities with eight rooms, accommodating up to ten patients.
1913	September 29	CME launches its Los Angeles dispensary.
1913	October 31	The new Loma Linda hospital, located in the middle of what is now the basic sciences quadrangle, nears completion.
1913	November 24	Board members name the new facility Loma Linda Hospital.
1913	December 1	Loma Linda Hospital opens.
1913	December 1	Patients are moved into the new hospital.
1914	April 11	First physicians graduate from CME.
1914	December 12	The Council on Medical Education secretary visits CME to make a preliminary assessment of its standing with the American Medical Association.
1915	July 16	Mrs. White dies at age 87.
1916	May 28	Board authorizes purchase of Ellen G. White Memorial Hospital site.
1916	October 16-21	National Board holds first examination for CME.
1918	February 3	"B" rating given CME by Council on Medical Education.
1922	November 2	Dietitians Training School begins operation.
1922	November 14	AMA Council on Medical Education votes "A" rating for CME.
1924	February 7	The Board considers an outdoor amphitheater, later named Loma Linda Bowl.

Left: The Loma Linda University seal in the center of the University mace. Right: R. Bruce Wilcox, PhD, professor of biochemistry in the School of Medicine, carries the mace at commencement exercises.

1924	August 24	First unit of second hospital completed.
1928	April 22	Groundbreaking is held for main section of new building, now known as Nichol Hall.
1928	May 17	Board changes the name of the Dietitians Training School to the School of Dietetics.
1929	March 20	Second hospital completed.
1929	April 8, 9	New hospital on hill dedicated after second unit completed.
1937	April 7	CME is accredited by Northwest Association of Secondary & Higher Schools.
1937	April 12	Board approves the School of Laboratory (Medical Technology) Technique.
1937	April 17	CME is accredited by Northwest Association of Secondary & Higher Schools.
1937	August 28	Medical technology program approved by AMA.
1938	May 17	Proposal is made to Seventh-day Adventist Church and CME leaders concerning a School of Dentistry.
1941	February 3	School of Physical Therapy is established.
1941	October 2	Ground is broken for men's residence hall.
1942	June 6	Physical therapy program receives initial approval by American Medical Association.
1942	September	Men's residence is completed, named Arthur G. Daniells Hall.
1943	April 8	Army Specialized Training Program approved.
1943	June 30	47th General Hospital unit activated at Hammond General Hospital in Modesto, California.
1943	July 1	Accelerated program of medical education begins.
1943	August 15	National Association of Seventh-day Adventist Dentists (NASDAD) is organized.
1943	September 15	Army Specialized Training Program is organized in Loma Linda.
1944	April	47th General Hospital unit shipped to New Guinea.
1944	September 28	Oran I. Cutler Auditorium named.
1945	November 19	Radiological technology program receives American Medical Association approval.
1947	February 28	Department of religion is authorized.
1948	April 1	School of Tropical and Preventive Medicine opens.
1948	April 19	Loma Linda and White Memorial nursing courses are combined.
1948	August 30	Baccalaureate degree program in nursing begins.
1949	August 11	New surgical wing opens.
1950	June 11	Last graduation ceremonies are held in Loma Linda Bowl.
1951	October 21	General Conference officers vote to establish CME School of Dentistry.
1951	November 29	AMA completes first inspection of CME since 1936.
1951	December 10	School of Nursing is accredited by National Nursing Accrediting Service.
1952	February 26	School of Dietetics becomes School of Nutrition.
1952	August 31	Hydrotherapy at Sanitarium renamed "Physical Medicine and Rehabilitation."
1952	October 29	Board approves private practice plan for physicians.
1953	April 12	Board recommends CME consolidation; favors Loma Linda campus.
1953	June 14	New library/administration building complex is occupied.
1953	August 30	First classes begin at the School of Dentistry.
1953	September 13	Loma Linda Library dedicated.
1954	January 28	Graduate School is officially organized.
1954	March 9	School of Nursing obtains approval for adoption of quarter unit credit system.
1954	August 25	First CME graduate nursing students are enrolled.
1955	April 26	Founders Day celebrates CME's fiftieth anniversary.
1955	September 1	Faculty and students move into the new dental building.
1955	September 18	School of Dentistry building is dedicated.
1955	November 4	New anatomy building holds first class.
1956	December 27	"To Make Man Whole," first chosen as the theme for the 1955, year-long fiftieth anniversary, adopted as institution's motto.
1957	May 23	Dental program is approved by American Dental Association's Council on Dental Education.
1957	June 9	First dental graduation is held.

1958	October 31	School of Dentistry plans dental hygiene course.
1959	January 28	Board approves a two-year occupational therapy curriculum leading to a BS degree.
1959	May 26	Ground is broken for new women's dormitory.
1959	November 27	Board approves occupational therapy curriculum.
1960	February 24	CME receives WASC accreditation.
1960	June 10	Occupational therapy program is given initial approval by AMA.
1960	June 13	CME's master's program in nursing receives accreditation.
1960	July 22	CME team removes bullet from man's heart—first time heart-lung machine used for this purpose.
1960	September 25	Second Kate Lindsay Hall opens.
1961	July 1	CME becomes Loma Linda University.
1961	September 7	Dental hygiene program approved by ADA.
1962	March 30	OT program approved by AMA's Council on Medical Education.
1962	April 26	Medical records administration curriculum authorized.
1962	April 26	The School of Dietetics becomes the School of Nutrition and Dietetics.
1962	September 26	LLU board votes to unify campus at Loma Linda.
1962	December 4	Ground broken for Graduate School building.
1963	April 29	First open heart surgery team leaves for Pakistan.
1963	June 27	Trustees ratify School of Medicine affiliation with Riverside County General Hospital.
1963	August 9	Vice president Lyndon B. Johnson meets with Loma Linda University Overseas Heart Surgery Team.
1963	September 3	University *Scope* begins publication.
1963	December 1	Medical record administration program begins.
1964	June 7	Ground is broken for LLUMC.
1964	August 25	Clinical pastoral education program is authorized.
1964	September 1	School of Public Health is organized.
1964	November 16	Ground is broken for biochemistry building on LL campus.
1965	February 22	First annual president's convocation is held.
1965	May 25	Trustees vote to expand LLUMC to eleven stories from nine.
1965	June 6	First woman graduates from School of Dentistry.
1965	August 6	HEW awards $129,217 to dentistry to set up and operate oral health service at Monument Valley.
1966	January 25	Completion of the east tower marks structural completion of new hospital.
1966	July 1	School of Health Related Professions is organized.
1966	September 27	Ground is broken for Dale Gentry Gymnasium.
1966	October 1	Monument Valley Dental Clinic begins operation.
1966	October 30	First meeting of Public Health Association of Seventh-day Adventists is held.
1967	February 8	The Division of Public Health becomes the fifteenth school of public health in the nation, and the sixth professional school on the Loma Linda campus.
1967	April 17	First kidney transplant performed at Loma Linda University Hospital.
1967	April 23	Constituency approves LLU/La Sierra College merger.
1967	June 23	School of Public Health receives full accreditation.
1967	July 1	The School of Public Health begins instruction.
1967	July 1	La Sierra College becomes College of Arts and Sciences of LLU.
1967	July 9	LLUH is first occupied.
1967	July 10	The first baby is born in the new University Medical Center.
1967	October 17	Original Loma Linda Sanitarium is razed.
1967	November 1	First open-heart surgery in Greece is performed by LLU team.
1968	February 8	School of Nutrition and Dietetics becomes the department of nutrition and dietetics.
1968	March 7	The Dale Gentry Gymnasium opens.
1968	March 31	LLUH is dedicated.
1968	August 5	School of Dentistry announces new two-year dental assisting program.

1969	January 26	Nichol Hall opens.
1969	January 28	Second hospital is renamed Francis D. Nichol Hall.
1969	February 16	Dedication of LLUH meditation chapel is held.
1969	October 26	Helipad opened at LLUH.
1970	January 27	LLU offers a black history course for credit for the first time.
1970	February 15	LLU mobile dental van begins service among 400 Native Americans living on Morongo Indian Reservation.
1970	February 25	First "School With a Heart" (now called "Clinic With a Heart") is held, providing a day of free dental care for the community.
1970	July 26	School of Dentistry team leaves for Central America.
1970	August 20	Loma Linda University Hospital is renamed Loma Linda University Medical Center.
1970	September 14	School of Public Health is renamed School of Health.
1971	January 15	Mobile dental clinic program is inaugurated.
1971	July 1	School of Health Related Professions becomes School of Allied Health Professions.
1971	August 20	President Richard M. Nixon arrives in Loma Linda to announce VA hospital.
1972	February 23	LLU donates 15 acres for the new VA hospital.
1972	May 22	LLUMC Air Medical Service is inaugurated.
1972	June 5	First helicopter to be operated by a California hospital goes into service at LLU.
1973	February 22	School of Nursing is relocated from LLUMC to West Hall.
1973	June 7	School of Nursing administration hosts open house.
1973	July 6	First LLUMC patient receives pacemaker.
1973	November 11	Councilors Field is dedicated.
1974	April 17	First open heart surgery in Vietnam is done by LLU team.
1974	April 24	First Fine Arts Festival begins at LLU.
1974	June 16	Veterans Hospital groundbreaking held.
1974	August 1	First Seventh-day Adventist Health Study questionnaire is sent to 50,000 Adventists.
1974	October 9	Adventist Church begins annual council session on Loma Linda campus.
1975	May 2	Vietnamese refugees arrive.
1975	October 6	Outpatient Hand Rehabilitation Center opens.
1976	January 20	First open-heart surgery in Saudi Arabia is done by LLU team.
1976	January 21	Loma Linda Ellen G. White Estate/SDA Research Center is dedicated.
1976	March 11	LLU announces accreditation of Hearing, Language & Speech Center.
1976	June 18	First allied health missionaries leave LLU for Africa.
1977	September 25	Grand opening is held for Jerry L. Pettis Memorial Veterans Hospital.
1979	May 10	LLU announces undergraduate degree program in geology.
1979	August 27	Ground is broken for Del E. Webb Memorial Library & Randall Visitors Center.
1979	September 4	Faculty Medical Offices building opens.
1979	December 2	First group of LLU medical personnel flies to Thailand to help Cambodian refugees.
1980	January 3	First recipient of Open Hearts for Children Fund undergoes surgery at LLUMC.
1980	June 2	LLUMC named regional trauma center for Inyo, Mono, Riverside & San Bernardino counties.
1981	March 9	Ground is broken for Alumni Hall for Basic Sciences.
1981	May 3	The first Good Samaritan sculpture is unveiled.
1981	May 30	Six people die in a LLU helicopter crash.
1981	August 24	Opening ceremonies are held for Del E. Webb Memorial Library and Visitors Center.
1982	March	Medical graduates celebrate 50th Annual Alumni Postgraduate Convention.
1982	May 11	Loma Linda Community Hospital purchased by LLUMC.
1982	May 15	LLUMC Hospice begins.
1982	June 3	Adventist Health System/Loma Linda certified by secretary of state.
1984	March 13	Alumni Hall for Basic Sciences opens.
1984	April 23	Ground is broken for Schuman Pavilion.

1984	October 26	"Baby Fae" receives the heart of a baboon.
1985	January 14	Ellen G. White Estate branch office is dedicated.
1985	February	SIMS (Students for International Mission Service) is formed.
1985	August 29	Annual Children's Day begins.
1985	November 20	"Baby Moses" receives a new human heart.
1986	March 28	Ground is broken for new LLUMC wing.
1986	September 16	Irwin and Virginia Schuman Pavilion is dedicated.
1987	February 2	Outpatient Surgery Center is opened.
1987	August 23	School of Religion is organized.
1987	October 16	Paul Holc receives a new heart when 3 hours old.
1988	February 8	Loma Linda International Heart Institute opens.
1988	April 7	Ground is broken for Proton Treatment Center.
1988	December 19	Grand opening ceremonies are held for LLUMC south wing (phase one).
1989	August 26	The first in vitro baby is born at LLU's Center for Fertility and In Vitro Fertilization.
1989	September	The School of Medicine accepts nearly fifty students from the medical school closing at Oral Roberts University, Tulsa, Oklahoma.
1989	October 31	Groundbreaking ceremony is held for Sir Run Run Shaw Hospital in China.
1990	February 12	Board votes to reverse La Sierra College and Loma Linda University twenty-three-year consolidation.
1990	March 7	LLU Riverside Trustees vote to rename the campus "La Sierra University."
1990	May 17	Board of Trustees merges the School of Public Health and the department of preventive medicine.
1990	June 3	Behavioral Medicine Center holds open house.
1990	August 25	Constituency votes to separate Loma Linda and Riverside campuses.
1990	September 20	Board of Trustees votes to formally recognize and designate LLU as a health sciences university.
1990	October 18	Department of pathology and laboratory medicine becomes first academic department of the School of Medicine to be sufficiently endowed to sustain its teaching functions with earnings from endowment assets.
1990	October 23	First patient receives treatment at Proton Treatment Center.
1991	January 18	Behavioral Medicine Center becomes operational.
1991	June 26	First-in-the-world use of rotating gantry for proton therapy.
1991	September 29	"Just For Seniors" program launched.
1992	March 9	Newly remodeled and refurbished TotalCare Birth Center at LLUMC is reopened.
1992	June 3	Groundbreaking services are held for the Ronald McDonald House.
1992	July 9	LLUMC celebrates its twenty-fifth anniversary.
1992	July 20	Children's Hospital Foundation established.
1992	December 8	Drayson Center groundbreaking is held.
1993	January 16	First kidney/pancreas transplant is performed at LLUMC.
1993	August 20	The first local liver transplant is performed at LLUMC.
1993	November 10	Children's Hospital holds grand opening ceremonies.
1994	February 15	Groundbreaking is held for Rehabilitation Institute.
1994	May 9	Grand opening held for Sir Run Run Shaw Hospital.
1994	November 4	First artificial heart is implanted at LLUMC.
1994	December 1	Memorandum of agreement signed between LLUMC and NASA to collaborate on proton research projects.
1995	January 11	Dedication and grand opening held for Drayson Center.
1995	May 15	Center for Molecular Biology and Gene Therapy officially opens.
1995	July 31	Open house is held for LLUMC Adult Day Care Center.
1995	October 14	Unveiling ceremonies for bronze Good Samaritan are held.
1995	October 16	Grand opening ceremonies for SAC-Norton are held.
1995	December 1	LLU & LLUMC launches combined web site.
1996	April 13	Transplantation Institute performs its fiftieth liver transplant.
1996	May 30	Roderick conjoined twins are separated.

1996	June 29	First bone-marrow transplant is performed at LLUMC.
1996	July 16	Ricketts Research Library & Learning Center is dedicated.
1996	September 26	Ribbon-cutting ceremonies are held for the Judefind House.
1996	October 30	Ceremonies are held honoring United States Congressman Jerry Lewis for his longtime support.
1996	November 29	Baby Juan Santiago receives skin transplant, a first at LLUMC.
1997	February 17	Center for Spiritual Life and Wholeness is established.
1997	March 1	Wong Kerlee International Conference Center opens.
1997	March 2	Opening ceremonies are held for LLU Coleman Pavilion.
1997	March 27	Loma Linda University Adventist Health Sciences Center entity is created.
1997	March 30	Chan Shun Pavilion Cancer Institute named.
1997	September 11	Grand opening of Ronald McDonald House is held.
1997	October 20–24	First Seventh-day Adventist International Nursing Conference is held.
1997	November 16	Center for Joint Replacement hosts grand opening.
1997	December 11	Ribbon-cutting ceremonies are held for the Assistive Technology Assessment Center.
1998	February 3	Groundbreaking ceremony is held for Geoscience Research Institute.
1998	February 6	Groundbreaking ceremonies are held for the School of Dentistry expansion.
1998	March 17	Opening ceremonies are held for the A. Gary Anderson Family Foundation Activity Room.
1998	May 20	LLUMC holds open house for children's outpatient program.
1998	July 27	LLUMC is recognized as one of "America's Best Hospitals" by *U.S. News & World Report*.
1998	August 5	Stamp honoring organ donations is unveiled at LLUMC.
1999	February 4	One-hundredth liver transplant is performed at LLUMC.
1999	May 26	First stem-cell transplant is performed at LLUMC.
1999	September 14	"Big Hearts for Little Hearts" is formed.
2000	May 13	First PTA students graduate from Oakwood College.
2000	August 15	First autologous stem-cell transplant is performed at LLUMC.
2000	August 29	Chief of pediatric neurosurgery combines two technologies to remove a tumor in a 13-year-old boy.
2001	March 6	BMC holds open house to celebrate ten years of operation.
2001	May 3	LLUMC implants world's smallest pacemaker into infant.
2001	November 10	SAC Health System celebrates fifth anniversary.
2002	January 8	CAL FED donates deed for East Campus expansion.
2002	July 10	LLUCH celebrates new pediatric emergency department.
2002	August 28	LLUMC demonstrates new technology for non-disruptive retrofits.
2002	September 19	LLU opens its new School of Pharmacy.
2002	December 12	Ritchie Mansion grand opening marks new housing for cancer patients.
2003	February 6–10	School of Dentistry celebrates fifty years of service.
2003	February 28	LLUMC named top company to work for in Inland Empire.
2003	July 17	LLU hosts fifth annual MITHS (Minority Introduction to Health Sciences) program.
2003	October 27	LLUMC named among top one hundred hospitals in cardiovascular care.
2003	October 28	LLUAHSC responds to Southern California fires.
2003	November 4	Walter's Children's Charity Classic raises $260,000 for LLUCH.
2003	December 11	LLU adds School of Science and Technology.
2004	January 7	LLU completes five years of physical therapy education in Puerto Rico; administrators discuss further collaboration.
2004	March 15	LLU/LLUMC medical team travels to Afghanistan to evaluate hospital request.
2004	March 30	*Venom ER* series begins on Animal Planet channel.
2004	April 9	School of Dentistry faculty assist with new residency program in Armenia.
2004	June 28–July 3	Trauma team aids flood victims in Haiti and Dominican Republic.
2005	February 11	LLU & LLUMC centennial celebration begins with Wintley Phipps concert.
2005	March 3	Molina twins, conjoined at head, separated at LLUCH.
2005	September 2	LLUMC employees respond to Hurricane Katrina disaster with Disaster Medical Assistance Team.

INSTITUTIONAL PROFILES

ABOUT LOMA LINDA UNIVERSITY ADVENTIST HEALTH SCIENCES CENTER

Loma Linda University Adventist Health Sciences Center (LLUAHSC), a nonprofit religious corporation in Loma Linda, California, is the umbrella organization for its core and affiliate organizations:

- Loma Linda University
- Loma Linda University Medical Center and its affiliates, such as
- Loma Linda University Children's Hospital
- Loma Linda University Medical Center East Campus, and
- Loma Linda University Proton Treatment Center; and
- Loma Linda University clinical faculty corporations, such as
  - Loma Linda University Health Care
  - Faculty physicians and surgeons of LLUSM, and
  - Faculty Medical Group of LLUSM, and
  - Loma Linda University Behavioral Medicine Center

LLUAHSC directs, sponsors, supports, and harmonizes the activities of these core and affiliate organizations.

Loma Linda University Adventist Health Sciences Center was created on March 27, 1997, when the constituency of Adventist Health System, Loma Linda, met and voted to change its name to Loma Linda University Adventist Health Sciences Center.

The constituency also voted to change the bylaws, making LLUAHSC (pronounced "lew-ask") the corporate member for Loma Linda University, as well as Loma Linda University Medical Center. On March 30, 1997, the Loma Linda University constituency met to change the bylaws of the University to reflect the new corporate membership relationship with LLUAHSC.

ABOUT LOMA LINDA UNIVERSITY

Loma Linda University is a Seventh-day Adventist educational health-sciences institution with 4,000 students located in Southern California. Seven schools and the Faculty of Religion and Faculty of Graduate Studies comprise the University organization. More than fifty-five programs are offered by the schools of Allied Health Professions, Dentistry, Medicine, Nursing, Pharmacy, Public Health, and Science and Technology. Curricula offered range from certificates of completion and associate in science degrees to doctor of philosophy and professional doctoral degrees. Students from more than eighty countries around the world and virtually every state in the nation are represented in Loma Linda University's student body. LLU also offers distance education.

ABOUT LOMA LINDA UNIVERSITY MEDICAL CENTER

An outgrowth of the original Sanitarium on the hill in 1905, the present eleven-story Loma Linda University Medical Center (LLUMC) opened on July 9, 1967. With the completion of Loma Linda University Children's Hospital (LLUCH) in late 1993, nearly 900 beds are available for patient care, including at Loma Linda University Medical Center East Campus and Loma Linda University Behavioral Medicine Center (LLUBMC). Loma Linda University Health Care (LLUHC), a management service organization, supports the many programs and services provided by our 400+ faculty physicians. LLUMC operates some of the largest clinical programs in the United States in areas such as neonatal care and outpatient surgery and is recognized as the international leader in infant heart transplantation and proton treatments for cancer. Each year, the institution admits more than 33,000 inpatients and serves roughly half a million outpatients. As the only tertiary-care hospital in the area, LLUMC is the only level one regional trauma center for Inyo, Mono, Riverside, and San Bernardino counties.

LLUAHSC
BOARD OF TRUSTEES AND ADVISORS

LLUAHSC Management Team

B. Lyn Behrens

B. Lyn Behrens, MBBS
President and Chief Executive Officer

Richard H. Hart

Richard H. Hart, MD, DrPH
Executive vice president, University affairs/Chancellor

Ruthita J. Fike

Ruthita J. Fike, MA
Executive vice president, Hospital affairs

Roger Hadley

H. Roger Hadley, MD
Executive vice president, Medical affairs

Kevin J. Lang

Kevin J. Lang, MBA
Executive vice president, Finance and administration/Chief Financial Officer

LLUAHSC
EXECUTIVE STAFF AND LEADERSHIP

1. Zareh Sarrafian, MBA, senior vice president & administrator, LLUCH

2. David Wren, MHA, senior vice president for faculty practice, LLUAHSC

3. Daniel Fontoura, MPPA, vice president, adult division, LLUMC

4. Orlando Huggins, assistant financial officer/controller, LLUAHSC

5. Robert Frost, director, Foundation, LLU

6. Verlon Strauss, CPA, vice chancellor, financial affairs & compliance officer, LLU

7. Gerald A. Ellis, MBA, senior vice president and administrator, signature programs/institutes, LLUMC

8. Elizabeth Dickenson, MPH, RN, senior vice president, adult division & patient care services, LLUMC

9. Craig Jackson, JD, MSW, dean, School of Allied Health Professions, LLU

10. Lisa M. Beardsley, PhD, MPH, vice chancellor, academic affairs, LLU

11. Anthony Zuccarelli, PhD, interim dean, Faculty of Graduate Studies, LLU

12. Myrna L. Hanna, MA, executive associate, LLUAHSC

13. D. P. Harris, PhD, vice chancellor, information systems, LLU

14. Daniel W. Glang, MD, vice president, medical administration, LLUMC

15. Avis Ericson, PharmD, interim dean, School of Pharmacy, LLU

16. James Kyle, MD, MDiv, dean, School of Public Health, LLU

17. Leslie N. Pollard, DMin, vice president, diversity, LLUAHSC

18. Mark K. Hubbard, senior vice president, human resource management & risk management, LLUAHSC

19. David Taylor, PhD, interim dean, Faculty of Religion, LLU

20. Robert Blades, vice president, health care information services, LLUMC

21. Rick Williams, PhD, assistant vice chancellor, enrollment management, LLU

22. Dulce Pena, associate general counsel, LLUAHSC

23. Helen E. King, PhD, RN, dean, School of Nursing, LLU

24. Steven Mohr, CPA, senior vice president, finance, LLUMC

25. J. Lynn Martell, DMin, vice president, advancement, LLUAHSC

26. Ruthita Fike, MA, CEO/administrator, LLUMC

27. Richard H. Hart, MD, DrPH, chancellor, LLU

28. H. Roger Hadley, MD, dean, School of Medicine, LLU; executive vice president/medical affairs, LLUAHSC

29. B. Lyn Behrens, MBBS, president & chief executive officer, LLUAHSC

30. Kevin Lang, MBA, executive vice president for finance & administration, CFO, LLUAHSC

31. Barry L. Taylor, PhD, vice chancellor, research affairs, LLU

32. W. Augustus Cheatham, MSW, vice president, public affairs, LLUAHSC

Loma Linda University Mission Statement

OUR MISSION

Loma Linda University, a Seventh-day Adventist Christian health sciences institution, seeks to further the healing and teaching ministry of Jesus Christ "to make man whole" by:

- Educating ethical and proficient Christian health professionals and scholars through instruction, example, and the pursuit of truth;

- Expanding knowledge through research in the biological, behavioral, physical, and environmental sciences and applying this knowledge to health and disease; and

- Providing comprehensive, competent, and compassionate health care for the whole person through faculty, students, and alumni.

In harmony with our heritage and global mission:

- We encourage personal and professional growth through integrated development of the intellectual, physical, social, and spiritual dimensions of each member of the University community and those we serve.

- We promote an environment that reflects and builds respect for the diversity of humanity as ordained by God.

- We seek to serve a worldwide community by promoting healthful living, caring for the sick, and sharing the good news of a loving God.

To achieve our mission we are committed to:

Our Students

Our primary responsibility is the education of students, who come from diverse ethnic and cultural backgrounds, enabling them to acquire the foundation of knowledge, skills, values, attitudes, and behaviors appropriate for their chosen academic or health care ministry. We nurture their intellectual curiosity. We facilitate their development into active, independent learners. We provide continuing educational opportunities for our alumni and professional peers. We encourage a personal Christian faith that permeates the lives of those we educate.

Our Faculty, Staff, and Administration

We respect our faculty, staff, and administration who through education, research, and service create a stimulating learning environment for our students. They contribute to the development of new understandings in their chosen fields. They demonstrate both Christian values and competence in their scholarship and professions.

Our Patients and Others We Serve

We provide humanitarian service through people, programs, and facilities. We promote healthful living and respond to the therapeutic and rehabilitative needs of people. We seek to enhance the quality of life for individuals in local, regional, national, and world communities.

Our God and Our Church

We believe all persons are called to friendship with a loving God both now and throughout eternity. We support the global mission of the Seventh-day Adventist Church by responding to the need for skilled Christian health professionals and scholars. We seek to honor God and to uphold the values of the Seventh-day Adventist Church and its commitment to awakening inquiry. We are drawn by love to share the good news of God expressed through the life and gospel of Jesus Christ and to hasten His return.

Loma Linda University Medical Center Mission Statement

OUR MISSION

The mission of Loma Linda University Medical Center is to continue the healing ministry of Jesus Christ, "To Make Man Whole," in a setting of advancing medical science and to provide a stimulating clinical and research environment for the education of physicians, nurses, and other health professionals.

OUR VISION

Innovating excellence in Christ-centered health care.

OUR VALUES

◆ Our Patients

Our first responsibility is to our patients who must receive timely, appropriate medical care with consideration for their privacy, dignity, and informed consent.

◆ Our Employees

We recognize our employees as a valued resource; therefore, we will strive to provide every employee a harmonious and supportive workplace. We will encourage and reward excellence in our employees to achieve their maximum potential.

◆ Our Physicians

We support our physicians, and other professionals, with staff, technology, and facilities within our financial resources. We value and respect the professional skills of our physicians and depend on their loyalty to the mission of the institution.

◆ Our Students

We actively support the training of tomorrow's health care professionals. We will work under the guidance of the School of Medicine of Loma Linda University to provide appropriate educational opportunities to medical students, residents, and fellows. We will work in close cooperation with the other health-related schools of Loma Linda University by making available facilities and expertise.

◆ Our Communities

We will develop and maintain our facilities so as to enhance the quality of life in the local, national, and world communities. We support selected worthy issues and organizations as a corporate civic responsibility.

◆ Our Future

We will secure the future educational, scientific, and financial viability of the Medical Center by maintaining quality programs and supporting selected centers of excellence that will enable the institution to achieve a leading position in health care, education, and research.

◆ Our Church

We uphold the values of the Seventh-day Adventist Church and its rich traditions by caring for the sick, promoting healthful living, awakening inquiry, and spreading the gospel of Jesus Christ.

◆ Our God

We honor our God, the Father, the Son, and the Holy Spirit by demonstrating Divine compassion and kindness through our care of the sick and by respecting and encouraging spiritual values.

LOMA LINDA UNIVERSITY'S PRESIDENTS

Warren E. Howell
1906–1907

George K. Abbott
1907–1909

Wells A. Ruble
1910–1914

Newton G. Evans
1914–1927

Edward H. Risley
1927–1928

Percy T. Magan
1928–1942

Walter Macpherson
1942–1948
1951–1954

George T. Harding III
1948–1951

Godfrey T. Anderson
1954–1967

David J. Bieber
1967–1974

V. Norskov Olsen
1974–1984

Norman J. Woods
1984–1990

B. Lyn Behrens
1990–Present

Richard H. Hart
1995–Present
Chancellor

DEANS, SCHOOL OF NURSING

Kathryn Jensen Nelson
1949–1956

Maxine Atteberry
1956–1969

Marilyn Christian Gearing
1969–1981

Helen Emori King
1981–2005

NOTE: While the nursing program began at Loma Linda's inception in 1905, Kathryn Jensen Nelson was the first dean when, in the late 1940s, a School of Nursing was established.

INDEX

#

47th General Hospital of the U.S. Army 78-81, 85, 88-90, 218

A

A. G. Daniells Residence Complex 161
A. Gary Anderson Family Foundation Activity Room 222
Abbott, George K. 232
ABC newsmagazine *20-20* 156
Adventist Development and Relief Agency 194, 226
Adventist Health Study 141, 142, 220
Adventist Health System – Loma Linda 184
Adventist Heritage magazine 143
Agency for International Development 141
Ahlem, Judith, MD 49, 50
Air Medical Service 131, 137-139, 220
Albert Einstein College of Medicine 154, 156
Alexander, Wil, PhD 182, 183
Alumni Hall for Basic Sciences 79, 160, 161, 165, 220
Alumni Pavilion 133
Alumni Research Foundation Building 104
AMA accreditation 115
Ambs Hall 87
American Association of Dental Schools 104
American Board of Surgeons 175
American Dental Association 98, 100, 103, 104, 218
American Medical Association 34, 35, 37, 41, 50, 53, 70, 81, 105, 113-115, 217-219
Anderson, Godfrey T., PhD 104, 105, 112, 117, 232
Andrews, H. Gibbs, MD 187

Andrews University 123, 149, 150
Annual council of the Seventh-day Adventist Church 63, 69, 70, 143, 220
Antillean Adventist University 193, 194
Army Specialized Training Program 83, 89, 218
Assistive Technology Assessment Center 185, 222
Association of American Medical Colleges 64, 113, 114
Atlanta-Southern Dental School 96, 97, 99, 100
Atteberry, Maxine, RN, MS 86, 129, 233
Autumn council of the Seventh-day Adventist Church 22, 96, 98, 118, 120

B

"Baby Fae" 149, 154, 156-160, 221
"Baby Moses" 157, 158, 221
"Big Hearts for Little Hearts" 222
Bailey, Leonard L., MD 149, 151-160
Banks, Otis 43
Barnard, Christiaan, MD 152
Barnes General Hospital 80
Barnes, Roger W., MD 69
Bates, Joseph 16
Battle Creek Sanitarium 13, 24
Baum, Lloyd, DMD, MSD 101
Behavioral Medicine Center 172, 173, 195, 221, 223
Behrens, B. Lyn, MBBS 4, 6, 122, 146, 150, 175, 180, 188, 204, 206, 225, 227, 229, 233
Bieber, David J., EdD 112, 135, 149, 232
Bietz, A. L., PhD 101
Bietz, R. R. 135
BMC. See Behavioral Medicine Center
Board of Trustees 7, 23, 48, 55, 63, 71, 83, 86, 125, 135, 143, 149, 154, 164, 165, 175, 185,

215, 221, 226
Borg, Martha, RN 68
Bower, Marian, RN 68
Boxer, Barbara, Sen. 213
Brand, Leonard R., PhD 186
Brandstater, Bernard, MBBS 150
Branson, William H. 99, 102
Brown, E. Faye, MA 123
Bull, Brian S., MD 189
Bunch, Taylor G. 69
Burden, Eleanor 24
Burden Hall 63, 64, 104, 134
Burden, John 17, 18, 20-22, 24, 25, 32, 33, 63, 143, 217
Bush, Sean P., MD 198
Butler, George I. 38, 39

C

CAL FED 191, 222
California State Articles of Incorporation and Consolidation 25
Cambodian refugees 140, 220
Campbell, Maynard V. 117
Campus Hill Church 64, 66, 72, 180
Caplan, Arthur, PhD 157
Carolyn and Ralph Thompson Library of the Center for Christian Bioethics 207
Casassa, Charles S., SJ 122
Centennial Fellows Campaign 207
Center for Fertility and In Vitro Fertilization 221
Center for Joint Replacement 185, 222
Center for Molecular Biology and Gene Therapy 221
Center for Spiritual Life & Wholeness 182, 183, 222

Center for Christian Bioethics 153
Chan Shun Pavilion 183, 184, 204, 222
Chan Shun Pavilion Cancer Research Center
    204
Charter Hospital 173, 177
Cheatham, W. Augustus, MSW 1, 166, 229
Childs, Herbert G. Jr., DDS 97
City of Loma Linda 124
Class "A" rating 47, 51, 53, 55, 217
Class "B" rating 41, 50, 217
Class "C" rating 50
CME. See College of Medical Evangelists
Coggin, C. Joan, MD, MPH 124, 195
Coleman, Denver D., MD 184
Coleman, Josephine Kent 184
Coleman Pavilion 183, 184, 204, 206, 207, 222
College Chapel 63, 64
College Church 63, 64, 87
College of Arts and Sciences of Loma Linda
    University 53, 123
College of Evangelists 20, 21, 22, 217
College of Medical Evangelists 22, 23, 25, 26,
    31-38, 41-43, 47, 49-53, 55, 62-65, 67-71,
    77-87, 89, 93, 94, 96, 97-105, 112-120,
    122, 125, 131, 132, 161, 184, 217-219
College of Physicians and Surgeons 96
Collins, Alan 149-151
Colver, Benton N., MD 69
Colwell, Nathan P., MD 36, 37, 50-52, 113
Comstock, D. D., MD 69
Cooley, Cynthia, MSW 181
Cooper, Lowell 4
Cornell University 112
Cossentine, E. E. 85, 101, 122
Council on Medical Education of the American
    Medical Association 34, 37, 47, 50, 51, 70,
    71, 113, 114, 217, 219
Courville, Cyril B., MD 68, 79, 90
Cryak, Janice 182
Curtin, Edward, MD 85
Curtis, G. H. 55
Cutler, Oran I., MD 68

D

Dale Gentry Auditorium and Gymnasium 123,
    124, 219
Damazo, Frank S. 205
Daniells, Arthur G. 22, 39, 40, 66, 78, 161
Daniells Hall 77-79, 86, 161, 218
Deans, School of Nursing 233
Del E. Webb Foundation 133, 134
Del E. Webb Memorial Library 133, 134, 203,
    220
De Leon, Daisy, PhD 197
De Leon, Marino, PhD 197
Dietitians Training School 217, 218
Disaster Medical Assistance Team
    Hurricane Katrina 222
Distinguished Humanitarian Award 205
Downs, Hugh 156
Dr. Ruth Temple Health Center 43
Drayson, Grace 179
Drayson, Ronald D., PhD 179, 180
Drayson Center 179, 180, 181, 221

E

"Ellen White Nurses" 62
Edwards Air Force Base 178
Emmanual Missionary College 69
Emmerson, Elson H. 53
Emory University 99
Evans, Harrison S., MD 160
Evans, I. H. 22
Evans, Newton G., MD 37, 39, 40, 47, 53, 68,
    79, 82, 93, 232
Evans Hall 63, 65

F

Faculty Medical Offices building 220
Faculty of Graduate Studies 193, 223
Faculty of Religion 193, 223, 229
Feinstein, Dianne, Sen. 213
Fergusson, Alec 137
Fermi National Accelerator Laboratory 162

Figuhr, R. R. 101, 117
Fike, Ruthita J., MA 227
Fine Arts Festival 143, 149, 220
First National Bank of Loma Linda 61
First Street Clinic, Los Angeles 35-37
Fitz, F. M., Colonel 83
Flaiz, T. R. 101
Florida Hospital 178
For God and CME 71
Fraser, Gary, MD, PhD 141
Fraser, Ian M., PhD 210
Fulton Memorial Library 87

G

"General Sherman" tree 31
Gearing, Marilyn Christian 233
General Conference of Seventh-day Adventists
    4, 16, 22, 23, 31, 33, 34, 38, 39, 55, 61, 63,
    66, 69, 78, 79, 96, 99, 101-103, 115, 117,
    121, 142, 143, 161, 166, 217, 218, 225, 226
Geoscience Research Institute 184, 185, 222
Glendale Adventist Hospital 4
Glendale Adventist Medical Center 16, 208
Glendale Sanitarium 55
Goldin, Daniel S., PhD 178
Good Samaritan sculpture 149-151, 166, 169,
    183, 220, 221
Gotzian, Josephine 39
Graduate School 123, 212, 218, 219
Graf, Catherine, RN 86
Grant, Ben E., MD 80
Gray, Emma 39
Great Depression 61, 62, 64, 69, 94
Griffin, Richard, MD 173
Griggs Hall 123

H

"Hill Beautiful" 3, 6, 8, 9, 14, 15, 41, 53, 54, 71,
    93, 114, 131, 165, 196
"Hyacinths for the Soul" 150
Hadley, G. Gordon, MD 178, 194, 195
Hadley, H. Roger, MD 227

Hammill, Richard, PhD 122
Hammon General Hospital 80
Harding, George T. III, MD 86, 105, 232
Hardinge, Mervyn G., MD, DrPH, PhD 123, 129
Hardy, James, MD 153
Hart, Richard H., MD, DrPH 141, 181, 182, 185, 194, 195, 225, 227, 229, 233
Harveian Society 65-67
Harvey, William 65
Haskell, Stephen N. 20
Haskell, Stephen N., Mrs. 39, 41
Havstad, Larry C. 63, 64, 103, 121
Hearing, Language & Speech Center 220
Hector Memorial Clinical Laboratory 104
Heitschmidt, Earl T. 103
Heliports 137, 139, 140
Heubach, Paul C., MTh 129
Hill, H. H. 212
Hills, H. E. 14
Hinshaw, David B. Sr., MD 90, 120, 165, 173, 177, 189, 226
Hinton, Bill 157
HLHS. See Hypoplastic left-heart syndrome
Holc, Paul 221
Hopp, Joyce W., PhD, MPH 210
Hosking, R. G., DDS 94
Hospital for Sick Children 152
Howell, Warren E. 20, 232
Hydrotherapy 56, 218
Hypoplastic left-heart syndrome 151, 152

I

Inland Empire 14, 117, 175, 176, 196, 222
Institute of Orchestral Conducting and Symphonic Performance 143
Institutional Profiles 223
Institutional Review Board 154
Ireland, M. W., MD 71
Irwin, George A. 34

J

"Just For Seniors" program 221
Jensen, Walter S., MD 83
Jerry L. Pettis Memorial Veterans Medical Center 136
Jesse, Claran H., MD 206
Jesse, Marjorie, RN 206
Jet Propulsion Laboratory 179
Jetton, James, MD 206
Jetton, Marge, RN 206
Johnson, Lyndon B. 219
Johnson Space Center 179
Judkins, Melvin P, MD 167
Jutzy, Kenneth R., MD 187
Jutzy, Roy V., MD 147

K

Kabul Medical Institute 194
Kantrowitz, Adrian, MD 152, 153
Kate Lindsay Hall 32, 44, 105, 219
Keller, Florence, MD 39
Kellogg Foundation 181
Kellogg, John Harvey, MD 13, 23, 24
Kellogg, W. K. 13
Kelly tract 32
Kerlee, Wong 183, 184, 204, 222
Kharchev, Konstantin 166
King, Helen Emori, PhD, MS, RN 233
Kirsch, Wolff M., MD 197
Klooster, Judson, DDS 209
Koehn, J. J., Mrs. 53
Koorenny, Ralph L., PhD 123
Kresge Foundation grant 133
Kulakov, Mikhail 166
Kuzma, Jan, PhD 211
Kypridakis, George, MD 133

L

"Lonesome Linda" 16
Lacy, H. C. 63
Lang, Kevin J., MBA 227

Laser retrofitting technology 192, 193
La Sierra Academy 52, 53, 58
La Sierra College 52, 53, 84, 85, 87, 105, 122, 163, 219, 221
La Sierra University 164, 165, 221
Lawrence Berkeley National Laboratory 179
Lewis, Jerry, Rep. 184, 213, 222
Lindsay, Kate, MD 23
Lindsay, Wealthy E., RN 80
LLCH. See Loma Linda Community Hospital
LLU. See Loma Linda University
LLUAHSC. See Loma Linda University Adventist Health Sciences Center
LLUAHSC Board 7
LLUAHSC Board of Trustees and Advisors 224
LLUAHSC Executive Staff and Leadership 228
LLUAHSC Management Team 227
LLUCH. See Loma Linda University Children's Hospital
LLUMC. See Loma Linda University Medical Center
Logan, A. 53
Loma Linda Association 15, 17
Loma Linda Bowl 67, 217, 218
Loma Linda Campus Hill Church 64
Loma Linda Community Hospital 160, 165, 177, 220
Loma Linda Ellen G. White Estate/Seventh-day Adventist Research Center 143
Loma Linda flood of 1969 128
Loma Linda Hospital 9, 36, 56, 62, 217
Loma Linda International Heart Institute 161, 221
Loma Linda Internet website 185
Loma Linda Manor 172, 173, 177
Loma Linda Sanitarium 8, 13, 14, 19, 20, 23, 25, 28, 33, 47, 53-55, 70, 72, 87, 91, 97, 104, 114, 121, 132, 203, 217, 219
Loma Linda Sanitarium and Hospital 47, 53-55, 70, 72, 87, 91, 97, 114, 121, 132
Loma Linda University's presidents 232
Loma Linda timeline 217

Loma Linda University 1, 4, 6-8, 14, 53, 55, 71, 105, 107, 108, 111, 119-124, 129, 132-136, 138-141, 143, 145, 147, 149-151, 153, 154, 158, 160-165, 171-175, 177-179, 181-189, 191, 193-195, 198, 199, 207, 208, 210-212, 215, 217, 219-223, 225, 226, 230, 231

Loma Linda University Adventist Health Sciences Center 7, 8, 14, 31, 122

Loma Linda University Children's Hospital 140, 162, 171, 174, 175, 185-188, 199, 223

Loma Linda University Children's Hospital Foundation 175

Loma Linda University International Behavioral Health Trauma Team 194

Loma Linda University Magazine 119

Loma Linda University Medical Center 4, 6, 7, 55, 108, 111, 121, 126, 127, 132, 139, 145, 147, 149, 151, 153, 158, 160, 162, 173, 177, 178, 181, 183-185, 187, 189, 191, 199, 207, 208, 212, 215, 220, 223, 225, 226, 231

Loma Linda University Medical Center Cancer Research Institute 184

Loma Linda University Medical Center East Campus 185, 191, 192, 222, 223

Loma Linda University Medical Center Orthopaedic and Rehabilitation Institute 177, 191

Loma Linda University Medical Center south wing 162

Loma Linda University Medical Center Transplantation Institute 176, 201, 221

Loma Linda University Overseas Heart Surgery Team 124, 140, 147, 219

Loma Linda University Proton Treatment Center 162-164, 173, 178, 179, 184, 185, 221, 223
  Proton-beam accelerator 162, 173
  Rotating gantry 173

Loma Linda Volunteer Fire Department 44

Longo, Lawrence D., MD 189

Los Angeles County General Hospital 49, 113, 116, 120

Los Angeles Public Health Department 43

Lowell Cooper, MDiv, MPH 4

M

"Mendocino Tree" 31

"Methusaleh" tree 31

Macpherson, Walter E., MD 68, 71, 83, 86, 87, 101, 105, 114, 115, 117, 125, 232

Magan Hall 97, 104, 169

Magan, Percy T., MD 23, 37, 39-41, 47, 49-51, 53, 54, 61, 62, 65-67, 70, 71, 78, 82, 94, 97, 104, 105, 113, 122, 232

Marjorie Andersen Jesse Wing in the School of Nursing 206

Martin, Robert D., MD 156

Matiko, Frances 150

Matiko, Reuben, MD 150

Maxwell, A. Graham, PhD 129

Maxwell, R. Maureen, EdD, RN 207

McElhany, J. L. 79

Medical Cadet Corps 79, 90

Medical Evangelist, The 55, 105, 119

Meier, Willard H., EdD 124

Meyer, Norman H. 137

Miller, Harry W., MD 203

Minority Introduction to Health Sciences program 222

Mission statement
  Loma Linda University 230
  Loma Linda University Medical Center 231

Mitchell, Gerald, DDS 100

Mitchell, J. Russell, DDS 100

Molina twins 222

Montefiore Medical Center 156

Monteith, Mary, RN 86

Montemorelos University 140

Monterey Sculpture Center 151

Monument Valley Dental Clinic 219

Moor, Fred B., MD 86

Morongo Indian Reservation 220

Mortensen Hall 123

Mortensen, Raymond, PhD 123

Mound City 8, 14, 15, 32

Mound City Land and Water Company 14

Mound City Land Association 14

Mound City Ranch 14, 15

Mozar, Harold N., MD 86

N

NASA–Loma Linda University Medical Center collaboration 178

NASDAD. See National Association of Seventh-day Adventist Dentists

National Association of Seventh-day Adventist Dentists 97, 218

National Heart, Lung, and Blood Institute 141

National Institutes of Health 141, 157

National Institutes of Health Preventive Cardiology Academic Award 141

Navy and Marine Corps medal 86

Neff, Merlin L. 71

Nehlsen-Cannarella, Sandra, PhD 156

Nelson, Gregory A., PhD 179

Nelson, Kathryn Jensen, RN 86, 233

Nemer, Darlene Drayson 179

Neonatal intensive care unit 162, 174, 175

Neurosurgery Center for Research, Training, and Education 197

Newsbreak 120

Nichol, Francis D. 54, 55, 105, 132, 220

Nichol Hall 54, 55, 132, 218, 220

Ninth Corps Area of the U.S. Army 78

Nixon, Richard M. 102, 134, 135, 220

Northwest Association of Secondary & Higher Schools 87, 218

Norton Air Force Base 181, 182

O

Oakwood College 222, 225, 226

Observer 119

Ojogho, Okechukwu, MD 201

Olsen, V. Norskov, PhD, TheolD 132, 143, 233

Oran I. Cutler Amphitheater 63, 65, 218

Outpatient Hand Rehabilitation Center 220

P

Pacific Union College 69, 122
Pacific Union Conference of Seventh-day
    Adventists 20, 34, 55, 164, 225
Palmer Hall 87
Paradise Valley Hospital 4, 16
Partridge, Gaines R., EdD 149, 150, 180
Pettis, Jerry L., Rep. 119, 134-136, 220
Pettis, Shirley N., Rep. 135
Pew Foundation 181
Phillips, Roland L., MD, DrPH 141
Phipps, Wintley 4
Pierson, Robert H. 142, 143
Pollard, Leslie, DMin 195
Postage stamp, organ and tissue donation 177
Pratt, Orlyn B., MD 64
Prince Hall 93, 104, 133, 184
Prince, M. Webster, DDS 93, 98-100, 105
Proton Therapy Cooperative Group 162
Provonsha, Jack W., MD, PhD 129, 153
Public Health Association of Seventh-day
    Adventists 219
Pullias, Earl V. 122
Pursley, Donald G., DBA 208

R

Randall-Campbell, Harriet, MD 134
Randall Visitors Center 133, 134, 220
Rawlings, Marjorie Kinnan 150
Raymond Ryckman Lectureship Series 211
Razzouk, Anees J., MD 199
Reagan, Ronald 135
Reaser, G. W. 17
Register, U. D., PhD 145
Reynolds, Keld, PhD 120
Ricketts Research Library and Learning Center
    185, 222
Rippon, W. Bart, PhD 212
Risley, Edward H., MD 53, 68, 71, 232
Risley Hall 63, 65

Ritchie Mansion 222
Riverside County General Hospital 219
Roberson, Shirley Pettis 175. See also Pettis,
    Shirley N., Rep.
Roberts, Randy, DMin 198
Robison, James I. 52, 53
Rock, Calvin B., PhD, DMin 180, 188, 226
Roderick, Shawna and Janelle 187
Ronald McDonald House 221
Roth, Ariel, PhD 143
Ruble, Wells A., MD 23, 32, 33, 35-37, 93, 217,
    232
Rudy, H. L. 103
Ruffcorn, John 208
Run Run Shaw, Sir 177, 178, 221
Ryckman, Raymond E., PhD 211

S

S.S. West Point 81
Sabbath 52, 83, 96, 99, 100, 104. See also
    Seventh-day Sabbath
SAC-Arrowhead 196
SAC-Frazee 196
SAC-Norton 181, 196, 221
SAC-Redlands 196
SACHS. See SAC Health System
SAC Health System 181, 196, 222
San Bernardino Mountains 8, 19, 137, 169
San Fernando Valley Academy 52
Sanitarium Annex 54
Santiago, Juan 222
School of Allied Health Professions 54, 55, 64,
    123, 132, 145, 209, 210, 220, 229
School of Dentistry 93, 94, 96, 97, 99-105, 109,
    124, 133, 139, 146, 184, 185, 195, 196, 208,
    209, 218-220, 222
School of Dietetics 55, 218, 219
School of Health Related Professions 123, 132,
    219, 220
School of Medical Technology 64
School of Medicine 13, 34, 37, 41, 50, 68, 70, 78,
    79, 87, 90, 98, 105, 113, 114, 117, 120, 132,

134, 135, 151, 154, 158, 161, 162, 172, 182,
    184, 187, 189, 194, 195, 197-199, 204, 206,
    217, 219, 221, 225, 229, 231
School of Medicine Alumni Association 161
School of Medicine at Syracuse University 70
School of Nursing 5, 63, 68, 129, 132, 133, 206,
    207, 215, 218, 220, 229, 233
School of Nutrition and Dietetics 219
School of Pharmacy 193, 212, 222, 229
School of Physical Therapy 218
School of Public Health 54, 55, 87, 123, 129,
    132, 145, 182, 201, 211, 219-221, 229
School of Science and Technology 186, 193, 222
School of Tropical and Preventive Medicine 86,
    123, 218
Schuman, Irwin 161
Schuman, Virginia, Mrs. 161
Schuman Pavilion 161, 165, 220, 221
Seventh-day Adventist Church 4, 5, 7, 16, 55, 66,
    79, 83, 96, 121, 124, 132, 198, 218, 226,
    230, 231
Seventh-day Adventist International Nursing
    Conference 185, 222
Seventh-day Adventist Periodical Index 143
Seventh-day Adventist World Service 140
Seventh-day Sabbath 83, 96
Sheldon, Richard, MD 154
Shryock, Alfred, MD 63, 65, 69
Shryock Hall 63, 65, 72
Shryock, Harold, MD 69, 83, 84
Shun, Chan 183, 184, 204, 222
SIMS. See Students for International Mission
    Service
Sir Run Run Shaw Hospital 177
Slater, James M., MD 162, 163
Slater, Jerry D., MD 199
Smith, Charles T., DDS 208
Social Action Community Clinics 181
Social Action Corps 181
Southeastern California Conference of Seventh-
    day Adventists 52, 55, 181
Southern California Conference of Seventh-day
    Adventists 16-18, 20, 34, 52, 55, 120

Southern California Junior College 53, 58
Southern California Transplantation Society 176
Southern Pacific and Santa Fe Railroad 14
Space Shuttle Atlantis 178
Stanford University 112, 154
Steinam, Ralph, DDS, MS 101
Stilson, Walter L., MD 86
Stromberg, W. Ross, DDS 101-103
Students for International Mission Service 221
Swatek, Rose 207
Swatek, William, MD 207

T

"The Highwaymen" 174, 188
"To Make Man Whole" 150, 164, 172, 173, 179, 183, 196, 218, 231
Taylor, Barry L., PhD 211
Teel, Charles 104, 108
Temple Health Institute 43
Temple, Ruth J., MD 43
Thomas and Violet Zapara Distinguished Undergraduate teaching award 205
Thomason, George, MD 82
Thompson, Carolyn, RN 207
Thompson, Ralph, MD 207
Thompson Suite in Coleman Pavilion 207
Today 119
TotalCare Birth Center 174, 221

U

U.S. Air Corps 83
U.S. Army 78, 79, 81, 84, 88
U.S. Department of Education 182
U.S. Naval Service 86
U.S. Navy 87
U.S. Surgeon General 71, 78, 79
United Network for Organ Sharing 176
Universities Research Association 163
University Church of Seventh-day Adventists 4, 104, 105, 107, 108, 129, 181, 198
University of California 112, 154
University of San Francisco 179

University of Southern California 47-50, 113, 114, 122
University *Scope* 119, 143, 185, 219

V

Venom ER 222
Vernier Radcliffe Memorial Library 104
Vietnamese refugees 140, 220
Voice of CME Employees, The 119
Volunteer Service League of Loma Linda University Medical Center 137

W

Walder, Ethel, RN 86
Walla Walla College 122
Walter's Children's Charity Classic 222
Walton, Harold M., MD 53
War Department 80, 82, 83
Wareham, Ellsworth E., MD 124
Washington Adventist Hospital 208
Way, C. Victor 137
Wazir Akbar Khan Hospital 194
Webb, Del E. 121
Weiskotten, Herman, MD 70
Welebir, Douglas F. 124
Western Association of Schools and Colleges 121, 163
Western Helicopters 137, 138
West Hall 62-64, 132, 133, 193, 220
White, Ellen G. 7, 16-22, 24, 25, 32, 37, 39, 53, 114, 115, 143, 217
White, Julia, MD 19
White, W. C. 17
White Memorial Church 103, 117
White Memorial Hospital 36, 40, 41, 43, 50, 59, 61-64, 71, 73-75, 101, 104, 105, 113, 114, 117, 120, 125, 217
White Memorial Medical Center 125, 132
Wilcox, R. Bruce, PhD 217
Williams, Hyveth, DMin 198
Wilson, Gayle 175
Wilson, Neal C. 166, 226

Wong Kerlee International Conference Center 183, 184, 204, 222
Woods, Norman J., PhD 180, 233
Woodward, Ivor C., PhD 123, 209
World War I 41, 50, 78
World War II 77, 81, 84, 87, 98, 102, 134

Z

Zapara, Tom 205
Zapara, Violet 205
Zapffe, Fred, MD 64, 67
Zirkle, Thomas J., MD 137
Zolber, Kathleen, PhD 145

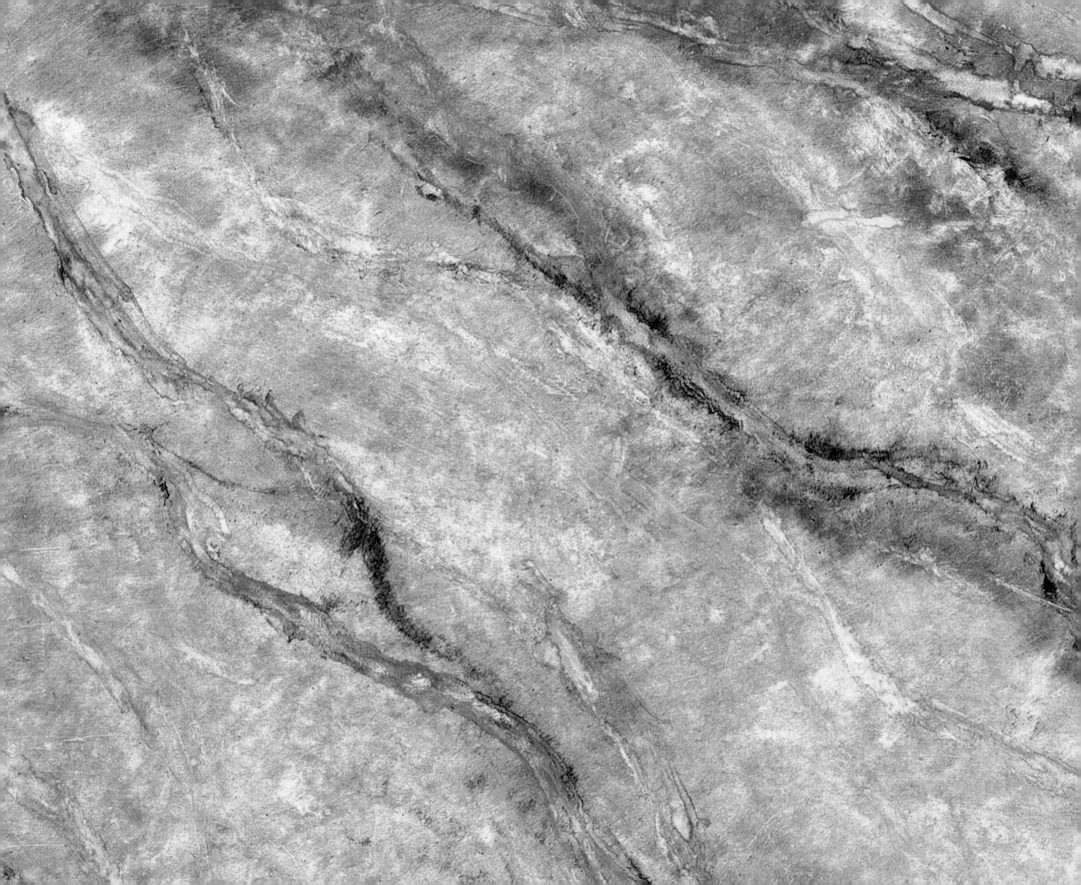